The Book of

HOW

Answers to Life's Most Important Question

RAVEN DANA & SHERRY MARTS PhD

Bird and Beverage Press

Bird and Beverage Press, LLC
Washington, DC

Although the authors and publisher have made every effort to ensure that the information in this book was correct at press time, the authors and publisher do not assume and hereby disclaim any liability to any party for any loss, damage, or disruption caused by errors or omissions, whether such errors or omissions result from negligence, accident, or any other cause.

This book is not intended as a substitute for the advice of physicians or licensed therapists and counselors.

Except for the friends and family who have given permission to appear in this book, all names and all identifying characteristics of individuals mentioned have been changed to protect their privacy. Some examples are composites of more than one client's experiences, so that no one person's experiences are reflected in any single account, and any similarities to persons or narratives is coincidental.

ISBN: 978-0-9893117-2-4

Cover and Book Design by Victoria Valentine Design

Contents

Acknowledgements

Raven:

I am deeply grateful to all those who helped make this book a reality. I appreciate my clients for sharing their stories; my friends, especially Clara Griffin for her love, friendship and insights; and Brad Blanton for everything I learned from him and what I learned about myself because of him.

I appreciate each person who read, commented on, and edited this material, and Vicki Valentine for her wonderful cover and invaluable help without which this book would surely not exist. I appreciate my children for who they are and how often our conversations have been a contribution to this work.

And of course, I am particularly grateful for my partner in crime, Sherry, the delightful beverage, friend, and science gal who has checked the facts, added her meaningful insights, and her life story, co-authored several chapters, and also rearranged some of my rambling words. She also took charge of the all-important details, including the bibliography and endnotes. We had plenty of conversations to make sure this book became the best we could make it. Sherry's "smart girl" style balanced my "smart-ass" style nicely.

Lastly, I also appreciate all those, dead and alive, who visited me in my dreams guiding me, and assisting me to remember that these most important ideas—that we are all connected, and that who we are and how we live—matter.

Sherry:

This book is the product of a friendship rooted in authenticity, honesty, shared values, and a shared determination to create a world in which all of those things are celebrated and rewarded. I am grateful to Raven for her experience, wisdom, and determination to share what she does so well with the world. I am humbled her collaborator in this work.

Clara Griffin introduced me to Brad Blanton and Radical Honesty, and Brad introduced me to Raven, so if you don't like this book blame them, because without them it would not be here in your hands. If you love it (and I'm sure you do), add your gratitude to mine. The Tuesday Night Group gave me a place to grow in this work, and much of what I added to this book came from my work with them. Vicki Valentine, artiste extraordinaire, provided a delightful cover and book design and guided our venture into self-publishing.

I am grateful to my husband, Larry Haller, for his love, support and encouragement, his proofreading skills, and his belief in this work. My family of birth, and my extended family of choice all contributed to this book in some way, and I thank them for their love and steadfastness.

What This Book Is (and What It Is Not)

This book is the owner's manual for your mind. It is about discovering that you are already unimaginably powerful. It is about being the person that in your gut and heart you know you can be, the person who relates, loves, laughs, and makes good, solid, successful decisions most of the time. *The Book of How* is the toolbox and the instruction manual that shows you how to identify and get beyond whatever stops you.

The Book of How will show you how you end up on dead end roads that take you away from what you want in life. You will learn how to uncover and revise the hidden patterns that sabotage your efforts to have success and ease in all parts of your life—including the places where you may have resigned yourself to settle for what you've got. You will find out how to access overlooked knowledge present in your body and in your surroundings, and how to read the road signs that point you in the direction you desire. Ultimately you will learn how to engineer and build new roads that take you where you want to go.

You may have asked, Why do I make that same bad choice over and over? Why do the people in my life act as they do? You will have all of your "Why?" questions answered once and for all time, but more importantly, you will discover *how* your life unfolds and continues to unfold.

If you know HOW you have ended up where you don't want to be, and if you know HOW to get off that path, you have real information that will lead you to a new road. If you know how to get from where you are to where you want to be, emotionally, mentally, and physically, then you can get off that dead end road. You have access to far more information and power than you are consciously aware of. This book is about learning how to access the intelligence and interpret the signals that are now available but hidden in plain sight.

If your life isn't what you want it to be, it's not because of fate, bad luck, or karma. It's not because you are flawed, stupid, or a bad person. It's not because that's just the way things are, and it's not because that's just the way you are.

You may have shelves full of films like *The Secret* and books like Eckhart Tolle's *The Power of Now* that tell you that your problems would evaporate if you could just change your thinking, let go of your attachment to "ego," develop the same habits as highly effective people, follow the right spiritual laws, raise your EQ, find the right guru, and become one with the universe. You may have pored over books about how your brain works, where your mental blind spots come from, and how your intentions get derailed. And you have closed those books asking yourself, "But HOW do I do that?? HOW

2

can I quiet my mind, feel more at ease, relate with confidence, have a truly enjoyable job, a satisfying marriage, recover from a hurt, forgive someone, see things differently, live in the present, and listen to my inner voice?"

This book answers that crucial question. You will discover HOW.

What if you knew *how* you sabotage your efforts to have the money, relationship, home, great job, friendships, satisfying sex life, relaxed nature, self confidence, appreciation, easy decisions, ability to handle anger, freedom from the past, feeling of security, (*insert your desire here*), that you say you want?

What if you knew *how* to interact with your own mind and revise patterns that make unwanted results repeat in your life like a bad rerun?

What if you knew *how* to uncover what was in the gap between what you say you want and what you actually get?

There is no quick fix, silver bullet, or secret mystical teaching that can rewire the programs that drive your ideas, habits, and perceptions. Your full participation is required.

The *Book of How* will give you clear, specific instructions that combine common sense with brain science. It will provide you with useful answers to the questions you've asked yourself in moments of frustration, longing, and optimistic reverie. We're going to dispel the myths, open your eyes, and wake you up to what's really going on in and around you. You will discover how to identify and change the hidden thoughts, beliefs, and habits that sabotage your efforts. You will make friends with your mind. You will even learn how to "read" your own mind and decode some of the clues that minds (yours and others) provide.

As you do this, you will develop more clarity and compassion for yourself and others. You will be able to see through the reality blindness that clouds your judgment. You will then be able to make more intelligent and more honest decisions in every area of your life.

Your mind has plenty of roads that were once adequate and useful, roads that are now full of potholes and lined with misleading signs. Sometimes, when heading for something you desire, you may become so exhausted, bewildered, and lost that you turn back, only to take the same confusing route the next time. The years pass and you are still driving in circles. Regardless of the strength of your intention and your "willpower," it's the only road you've got, so it's the one you've always taken. Until now.

With the tools you'll find in this book, you will be able to build new roads within your mind—to create new patterns of thoughts, emotions and actions in your life that will deliver new results. Getting from *wanting* something to *having* it is like getting from Cleveland to DC: you need to find the roads that will take you there—directly and with ease—and not get on the road that takes you to Kennebunkport, Maine. You can build as many or as few new roads as you like, as your conscious mind learns to partner with, rather than ignore, your subconscious mind. When you read the signs and heed the messages present in your body and your surroundings you can reliably get where you want to go.

Whatever you want, it's already out there. Somebody has it, and you can have it too. There is a road that will take you there, and you will have to build it.

A Note On Pronouns

Throughout this book, the primary voice is Raven speaking, and the first-person pronouns refer to her. When Sherry is speaking it is indicated in the paragraph heading or text.

PART ONE

The User's Manual for Your Mind

CHAPTER 1

The Most Useful Question Is: How?

*"We shall not cease from exploration. And the end of all our exploring will be to arrive where we started and know the place for the first time." —*T.S. Eliot

The power of HOW is life changing. How does your mind work? How can you uncover hidden filters, habits, and repeated behaviors that limit your life? How does your subconscious mind influence your choices? How can you reinforce the patterns that ARE useful? How can you get over feeling angry, attracting conflict, reliving your childhood, or limiting your income? How can you create happy relationships that last? How can you feel at ease, express yourself honestly, stop putting up with crap, get a new career, find a mate, like your body, decrease your stress, and really love yourself by making choices that make you healthy, happy, and satisfied more often than not?

We usually ask the wrong question. We ask "Why?" Why does this happen to me? Why am I so afraid? Why don't I speak my mind? Why do I care so much about what people think? Why do I stay in this job that I hate? The answer to the question "Why?" won't help you. Knowing why may satisfy your curiosity, but *knowing why isn't very useful for changing the actual internal formula that sabotages you.*

It's really a booby prize, one that people point to as the excuse for, "Why I am not at fault for being neurotic and anxious and just plain unhappy." OK, that's dandy. You are not to blame. What if no one were to blame and you (and *only* you) were now responsible for HOW your thoughts, beliefs, and expectations drag you into the brambles? Ah, yes. Then you could actually do something to stop the process.

Knowing WHY you do what you do doesn't change the wiring, the unconscious biases, reactions, and decisions behind the behavior. In fact, figuring out why may just give you a scapegoat and a rationale for staying a victim.

Most of us get stuck in the idea, the illusion, that if we only knew WHY we do that dumb thing we do, we'd just stop doing it. How many times have you said, "Wow, I'll never do THAT again!" only to find yourself in the middle of the same bad movie script (crappy job, unhappy relationship, fight with your family) again down the road. Suppose you absolutely knew that you learned how-to put up with crappy jobs from your father, or that you avoid staying married to prevent yourself from experiencing the pain your mother experienced when your dad died. Great, you know why. That and five dollars might get you a latte or a gallon of gas. But that knowledge alone *does not inform your awareness about the thoughts, inner rules, and scary emotions that keep you running on that hamster wheel.* Knowing HOW does. It gives you a set of clues that can lead you towards new and different thoughts and emotions, ones that can deliver a new result.

One way we get stuck is by pretending that if OTHERS would just shape up, our lives would be easy, so we obsess about WHY people do what they do. Let's face reality—you don't really want to hear that your ex cheated on you because his father cheated on his mother as a way of avoiding sharing his fear of inadequacy with her, do you? Nah, didn't think so. What you REALLY want to know is, why did he do this *to me?* Aha! Well, the answer is lack of self-awareness, bad communication habits, and an implicit learning from his parents that this is how relationships are, and you remind him of his mother. There, did that help? Not so much, right? Knowing WHY doesn't matter a fiddler's fart when it comes to getting over the upsets we keep in place by looking everywhere else but at our own thoughts and behaviors for relief.

What if you knew HOW his behaviors triggered you to withdraw (like his mother did) and what if you knew HOW your own fears had you feeling anxious, always expecting that he will cheat? What if you were able to interrupt your part of the dysfunctional dance and unhook from what your own mind is doing to you? Could you have a less stressful relationship? Yes. And maybe even learn to get along, and if you parted anyway, you'd also know how to part with compassion instead of animosity.

Knowing *how* you produce a given result gives you the power to produce a different result. *Knowing the formula for persistent irritation gives you the insight you need to create a formula for persistent satisfaction.* And that's the real power of HOW.

So, for all time, the answer to every "Why?" question you may come up with related to feeling derailed by your repeating thoughts and behaviors is this: Why? Because someone or something in your past triggered your mind to set up a filter (blind spot, program, pattern, loop, take your pick) that once was useful but now repeatedly produces this undesirable result. That's all there is to "Why?" Period. And, by the way, many of the good and useful things we experience are also created from automatic thoughts, beliefs, and actions that are a result of filters and patterns created long ago.

Meet Your Subconscious Mind in Action

From our oldest evolutionary ancestors we have inherited a brain that is, at its most basic level, a survival tool.[1] Below the level of conscious awareness, our mind quickly learns to ignore unnecessary input that is not a threat to survival. There is so much information coming at us every second that we'd hardly function without the mental shortcuts and filters that keep our attention on what is important. Most of the time, this ability serves us perfectly. Based on your hardwired survival instincts plus what you learned as a child to pay attention to, your mind quickly recognizes patterns and chooses what is important to focus your attention on, and what to ignore. Notice the truck coming at you, ignore the airplane flying overhead. If you get that automatic response switched, it's Good Night and Good Luck.

For example, if you move next door to a train station, at first, every time a train goes by and the windows rattle and the teacups dance in the china cabinet, your mind directs you to pay attention, so your heart rate and breathing rate speed up a little and your muscles tense. In the most primitive part of your brain, you are unconsciously asking: What is that, and is it a threat to my survival? It doesn't matter that logic tells you that the train's not coming through your living room, you will still notice and physically react, at first. Every time a train goes by, after a few minutes of noise and vibration everything returns to normal. Within a few weeks your brain adjusts, automatically registers the sound as "not a threat" and it literally turns down the volume for you. You don't hear the train at full volume anymore. You barely notice it. First time visitors ask "How can you stand that noise?!" and you say, "Noise? Oh, the train. Y'know, it used to bug me, but I got used to it." Your brain has dismissed the sound as not significant and it's no longer commanding your attention. As far as your conscious mind is concerned, the train sound is minimal and maybe even soothing.

This is a filter in action. It has modified your senses to dismiss the train sound. We have plenty of these filters. Some are useful, others not so much.

Based on your experiences, your mind has created a host of filters and subconscious patterns of behavior that have long ago faded certain things into background. Think of the daily activities you perform almost unconsciously: brushing your teeth, washing your face, driving to work, crossing a familiar street. Throughout the day we perform tasks and even make choices ("I'll have a medium latte with skim milk. . .") without paying much attention and while thinking about a half dozen other things—what's happening at work, who's picking up the kids, what movie to see this weekend.

Close your eyes and imagine you are stepping out of the tub or shower. Where do you start drying yourself? Do you even have to think about it? No, of course not. That's a useful subconscious pattern formed long ago.

You have subconscious filters, with their habitual thoughts and behaviors in every area of your life. Some of these patterns work for you, helping you automatically make the right choices and decisions without a lot of thought. Other filters may cause you a lot of grief. You may filter out compliments, seek out criticism, miss seeing that $20 bill on the sidewalk, turn your nose up at potential mates who want to commit and instead be drawn to potential mates who are losers. You may filter out opportunities, "forget" important meetings, drive people you love away by being critical, or walk off from job after job because you manage to create the familiar pattern of feeling like a victim at work no matter what.

The good news is that you can develop the skill to recognize and revise the filters that keep you from having what you want or from feeling the way you want to feel. When you recognize how your mind is working for and against you, then it's easier to stop beating yourself up, feeling stupid or bad, wrong, and resigned. You didn't consciously choose the filters, so you are not to blame. It's wasted effort to do anything other than wake up enough to revise the filters that get in your way.

Try this at home: You (and your close friends) know a lot about what you're good at and about how you sabotage yourself. Assess your repetitive thoughts and beliefs honestly, with an honest friend who's not afraid to really tell you the truth, and you're off to a good start. Using the practices described later, you will begin to discover when you are using your mind compared to when you are on auto-pilot and your mind is using you.

Your Plastic Brain

One of the most revolutionary discoveries in brain science in the past 50 years is the finding that, even as fully developed adults, our brains are "plastic"—meaning that our brains are malleable, constantly changing and remodeling, forming new connections and breaking old ones as a result of input from our senses and our experiences. In terms of how your brain functions, you are, quite literally, not the person you were ten or twenty years ago. You aren't even the person you were five years ago. The people you hang out with, the work you do, your daily routines and what you repeatedly pay attention to has altered your brain's wiring, and so has changed your mind.[2]

We also know that the mind is not much of a logical instrument. Rather, it is a great pattern recognition device that can with extreme speed fill in missing pieces to identify a person, circumstance, or event. This is a fantastic tool for survival, allowing us to extrapolate potential threats to our safety and survival from a few clues, giving us time to escape. But it also works against us when, without thinking about it, we reflexively slap an inaccurate and illogical label on people and situations out of habit, and then respond out of reaction to the label rather than the actual situation at hand.

In their book *Sway: The Irresistible Pull of Irrational Behavior,* Ori and Rom Brafman provide several examples of how filtering has an impact, sometimes a negative impact on everything from the performance of sports teams to advances in science and medicine. They offer this great example of how value attribution (essentially, how we give things value based on what they cost and where and how

11

they are sold) clouds our thinking. The Brafmans state: "Once we attribute a certain value to a person or thing, it dramatically alters our perceptions of subsequent information." Here is a stark example of value attribution at work.

Joshua Bell, one of the finest violinists alive, regularly plays in top concert halls to standing-room-only crowds who bought high-priced tickets for the privilege of hearing him. In 2007 he accepted a challenge from *Washington Post* reporter Gene Weingarten. Bell took his $3.5 million Stradivarius and brilliantly performed one of the most difficult pieces composed for a solo violin while standing in a Washington, DC subway station during the morning rush hour. He played for 45 minutes, and in that time seven people stopped to listen. Twenty seven dropped money in his tip jar (he made a total of $32 and change). One woman recognized him and gaped in disbelief. The reporter counted 1,097 people who passed him by without appearing to notice he was there. Surprising? Shocking? His clothing—jeans, a t-shirt and baseball cap—and his location were enough to create an instant judgment in the onlookers. This was a nobody, some loser looking for a handout, and certainly not a world-famous violinist. And, therefore, according to a thousand people he was not worthy of attention. Even more interesting, Bell himself fell into the value attribution trap. He reported that before he began to play, he was nervous. "When you play for ticket-holders," Bell explained, "you are already validated. I have no sense that I need to be accepted. I'm already accepted. Here, there was this thought: *What if they don't like me? What if they resent my presence[?]*"

All of us are subject to these kinds of biases, which operate below our conscious awareness. However, once we become aware of our typical and habitual biases we can interrupt some of the behaviors and choices based on them. We can even revise them. The plasticity of the brain gives us the fantastic ability to freely create our lives and experiences according to our desires, beliefs, and expectations. We also have the capacity to observe ourselves, and our observations then affect how our experiences unfold. By cultivating these abilities, we can re-create ourselves and our lives. By catching and interrupting our repeating thoughts we can diminish the powerful loop of emotion, reaction, and behavior that would typically unfold subconsciously. We can catch ourselves in the act of self-sabotage and prevent the old outcome from repeating.

We are extraordinarily powerful. We have the ability to take actions based not only on our learned behaviors and history, but to literally "think outside the box" and create or encode new patterns from the many bits of information we have access to. We can learn to play chopsticks in first grade, and while some of us never play more than chopsticks on the piano, we have the power to use that knowledge to help us play Chopin or to become a rock star. What makes the difference?

HOW to Get Started on Self-Awareness

We imagine that we go through life making conscious choices every day. Ha! Truth is, the vast majority of our decisions are made subconsciously, with our reasoning mind only kicking in after the fact to add reasons and rationalizations that keep us thinking we know why we did whatever we did, be it brilliant or bizarre. (For more on this, see Shankar Vendatem's excellent book *The Hidden Brain.*)

Those subconscious decisions are made quickly using the patterns and filters based on assessments from long ago, the source of which has been long forgotten. What does it take to move beyond the habits, filters, and behaviors that underlie those subconscious decisions? It takes being able to quiet your noisemaker mind and be present in the moment long enough to sort out what is really going on.

We hear about self-awareness and the benefits of being more "in the moment," more "mindful," more "present." What does that mean, exactly? There are three levels of conscious awareness. We can be aware of what we think, we can be aware with all of our senses of what is going on around us, and we can be aware of the inner "weather" of our bodies through the shifting sensations that include temperature, heartbeat, breath, and the tension, pressure, twitches, and unconscious movements and of the packages of sensations that we label as emotions. Yes, the sensations happen first, and we name them emotions.

The more consciously aware we are of the world around and within us, and the less we live in the world of our own thoughts, the better able we are to relax and respond to whatever may happen. The more "present" we are, living in and experiencing the world, the more able we become to notice and act on the many signals and deeper layers of information that are messengers from our subconscious. The alternative, which many of us suffer with, is to live much of life in our heads, trapped in thoughts , worries, and assessments (many of which are compulsively, annoyingly repetitive) while missing important clues around and within us. We are tightly wound, tense, and reactive in much of our lives. Imagine being so lost in thought in the worry that a flowerpot may fall on your head that you neither see the falling pot nor hear the guy across the street shout out a warning. Not only might you get beaned, you'll also fail to notice that you dropped your wallet and then stepped right over that dollar bill lying right in the street.

I have worked with people who so buried in their own thoughts that when asked the question, "What do you notice in your body?" they say "Nothing." Well, unless you are dead or knocked unconscious, you have plenty of sensations to be aware of. Check into your body right now, as you read. Can you feel that you are breathing? Sure you can. Now notice the feel of your clothing, the temperature of your face, feet, hands. Notice the pressure of your bottom against the chair, the changes in pressure in your shoulders caused by breathing, notice the muscles in your face. Are your lips pressing together? Are you smiling? Frowning? Are your eyebrows furrowed in concentration? OK, as you see, there are plenty of sensations in your body available right now that give you information about what is happening in the moment.

Becoming more aware of your surroundings and more aware of the sensations and emotions in your body is one of the most useful practices you can develop. This awareness is packed with information and serves as a powerful guide to action. When we mostly live in our heads we invent a version of reality that we then confuse with what's really going on in the world around us. We can even become radically out of touch with our own actions and motives. Surely you know at least one person who operates like this. Maybe it is you.

Each of us has had days in which we felt "out of it" and days in which we think we can't even find our own ass with both hands. Interestingly enough, finding your ass with both hands is exactly the right place to begin. Whether you are anxious, annoyed, tired, or just having an "off" day, if you deliberately turn your awareness to your body for even five minutes, and notice your breath, notice your thoughts but let them pass through without following the train of thought, come back to your body, feel your feet on the ground, look up and see the sky, literally allow yourself to be aware of the moment that you are in and aware of yourself as a being with sensations, you will "wake up" a little. Your mind will become quiet after a few minutes. You will feel calmer, more able to focus. You may even have an insight about something or feel an urge to do something particular. Or not. You may just feel alive and at ease and maybe a little grateful in this world. Congratulations. That's mindfulness. That's how to Be Here Now. You don't need chanting monks, a special room, or nag champa incense to be mindful. Just a little patience and discipline.

When we are mindful, we can be aware of our thoughts without being abducted by them. With awareness, we know that our thoughts are not automatically "facts," but that they create context, meaning, and a story about life. We can reflect on and change our thinking and our emotional weather in new and useful ways, giving ourselves a way to break through repeating unconscious patterns of thought and behavior that might otherwise muck up our lives. When we revise our thoughts, our emotions and behaviors follow. We can create new stories, new personal myths that serve us and those around us. We can become hero instead of victim, success instead of failure, smart instead of stupid, loved instead of loser, all by changing our minds.

CHAPTER 2

Filters and Freedom

"One's real life is often the life that one does not lead."
—Oscar Wilde

Most people, much of the time, think they are making free choices when they are not. Like Charlie Brown, we run to kick that football, only to end up flat on our backs again and again. It takes time, attention, and energy to engage your will and to recognize, redirect, and revise those old subconscious habits. To use your will, you have to use your intelligence to override the seemingly reasonable thoughts and rationales that consistently lead you astray. Some of your old deep-seated ideas about who you are and what you do may work for you, while others work against you. Knowing how to alter those webs of thought, feeling, and behavior so that they work for you more often than they work against you is key to living a conscious life and making real choices based on preference and desire.

Here's HOW Filters Are Set Up

The part of your brain that sets the filters up doesn't "know" when filters and programs that once served a useful purpose have outlived their usefulness. That is for you, as a conscious being, to figure out. For example, the filter of being silent and therefor "invisible" to avoid an angry parent is a great survival pattern when you're three years old, but it is an awful thing to still have that pattern controlling the way you relate to a boss or other authority figure as an adult. Keep repeating that childhood survival pattern and there goes your recognition, promotion, and well-deserved raise.

The childhood ability to be an excellent "reader" of our parents' and teachers' mental and emotional states can be a good survival filter, even in adulthood. The ability to notice and react to subtle behavioral cues may make you a great negotiator, steer you away from con artists, and land you an excellent job in sales and marketing. But a similar filter may also lead you look for (filter for) subtle cues that in childhood indicated incipient disaster, like the ones that told you mother was angry and about to explode even though she said everything was fine.

In adulthood you may misinterpret certain cues in others, causing you to overreact and be suspicious and accusatory in your relationships. This may, for example, prevent a man from finding or sustaining an intimate relationship with a woman, unless he finds a partner who interprets that behavior as love because it mirrors her parent's relationship. It feels like home to her, because that's how dad treated mom. And since at least he doesn't beat her (the way dad beat mom), she talks herself into staying even though she may feel as worthless as a dishrag. Not a pretty picture. And it is happening, just like that or worse, in a million variations all around you every day.

Less destructive filters can still be bothersome and limiting. Your filters may cause you to ignore constructive criticism, leaving you vulnerable to insincere flattery, and giving you a sense of superiority that will eventually lead to failure—think of all those contestants on American Idol who can't carry a tune in a bucket. Conversely, you may dismiss compliments and seek out criticism, causing you to choose partners who pick on your every mistake—just like your father did.

Your subconscious processes incoming information, then presents that processed (filtered) information back your conscious mind. This is the primary source of your thoughts, emotions, and behaviors. Your filters create the context of your experiences. Your filters—which include biases, expectations, beliefs, and habits of thought and behavior—are responsible for your interpretation of events and your emotional reactions, and are the ultimate source of your current circumstances. *Instead of wasting time and energy trying to make your circumstances (and other people) change, your time and effort are better spent learning how to amend the associations and beliefs that have become your filters. By doing this you will learn to choose new circumstances, and reject what is not working for you, with much greater speed and ease.*

You may have turned yourself inside out, desperately trying to find the "right" job or the "right" mate or to put away enough money to "feel secure." Yet, all the while, what you say, the people you associate with, and what you do consistently produces results you don't want—crappy jobs, lousy relationships, empty bank accounts. You get angry or confused, blaming fate, circumstance, and other people rather than looking at the real source of your misery. To an objective observer the fact that you are the one hitting yourself in the head with a brick is obvious. The person responsible for your circumstances is—YOU.

You Can't Always Trust What You Think You Know

Because your filters literally determine much of what you see and hear—what you are consciously aware of—you can't always trust what your mind tells you and the conclusions you come to. Remember that our brains are pattern recognition systems, not logic machines.

It is estimated that about 95% of our seemingly conscious "choices" are not choices at all, but behavioral decisions predetermined by our past associations. This, combined with our tendency to skip over or dismiss the information we receive as hunches, intuitions, and impressions, keeps us stuck.

Our brains filter all of our experiences—the neurological signals that constitute our senses of sight, hearing, smell, touch, and taste—through many layers. *We see and hear what fits the pattern we expect to see, whether it's there or not, and we delete things we see and hear that do not fit.* Your intuition—those subconscious perceptions that add up to a "feeling" about a person, place, or situation—is an important resource. More than rules, laws, expert advice, or technological advances, the solution to problems most often lies with this grand resource that we each carry within.

"If intuition is used by a woman to explain a choice she made or a concern she can't let go of, men tend to roll their eyes and write it off. We prefer logic, the grounded, explainable, unemotional thought process that ends in a supportable conclusion. In fact, Americans worship logic, even when it's wrong, and deny intuition, even when it's right. Men have their own version . . . theirs is more viscerally named a 'gut' feeling" but it isn't just a feeling. Intuition, regardless of the name we give it, is a process more extraordinary and ultimately *more logical* in the natural order than the most fantastic computer calculation. It is our most complex cognitive process and at the same time the simplest." From *The Gift of Fear*, by Gavin De Becker. Do read his book. Although De Becker, the nation's leading expert on violent behavior, is writing about how we override our intuition and so put ourselves at risk of violence, his work is extremely powerful in demonstrating how the voice of your subconscious constantly provides information worth paying attention to in your everyday life.

Your survival depends on your mind's ability to assemble and compile information rapidly, away from your conscious awareness.

When you "instinctively" leap away and miss getting beaned by a falling branch while you were in the midst of an engrossing conversation and otherwise unaware of your surroundings, that is the unconscious mind at work, talking directly to muscles and nerves without bothering to contact conscious awareness. The mind is able to take in and correlate many more bits of information on the unconscious and subconscious levels, levels that are just below your normal awareness. You experience that awareness as sensations, as fleeting glimpses of knowledge and sudden feelings, as well as in dreams, forebodings, and other subtle ways.[1]

You Know More Than You Think You Do

Your subconscious helps you by assessing a tremendous amount of sensory data and processing it to give you a pattern you can recognize. It's not just about the past. That's only one layer of what subconscious processing can do for you. Another layer, the instant assessment of data that gives us accurate immediate information about in-the-moment observations is also available to you.

In his book *Blink: The Power of Thinking Without Thinking*, Malcolm Gladwell describes the ways that very accurate decisions can be made rapidly. Indeed, our initial, intuitive response to a person, object, or event—the one that transpires in the first few milliseconds of our exposure to it—is often the one that proves to be correct. This is predicated upon what Gladwell terms "thin slicing"— the ability of the human mind to examine a situation and skim all of the information that is necessary to make a correct decision and plot a course of action almost instantaneously. The most accurate "thin slice assessments" are often those that involve assessment of the emotional or mental states of others. Apparently, over the course of many millennia we have evolved a mind that can accurately evaluate the actions and motives of our companions with a split-second glance.

Although the human mind's ability to thin-slice is remarkable, its utility is tempered by a number of distinct characteristics. As Gladwell points out, we often don't know what our unconscious knows or how it has helped us to make a decision or choose a course of action. Gladwell also recounts the ways in which our sociocultural context can impede our ability to benefit from the thin-slicing skill of the unconscious. Most significantly, he asserts, our vast stores of prejudices and biases can often override the unconscious signals and disallow access to our thin-slicing, intuitive abilities. However, we can develop and incorporate solutions that will protect our thin-slicing unconscious from the undue influence of prejudice. In his book, Gladwell suggests techniques that will short-circuit prejudices in our everyday lives. In this way, he contends, we can reconnect with and benefit from the power of the blink.

Now let's take a look at one way we inhibit our ability to get to that "thin slice" information and miss the reality under our noses.

In *Sway: The Irresistible Pull of Irrational Behavior*, the Brafmans quote Franz Epting, an expert in the field of meaning and interpretation and how it affects our experience, "Once you get a label in mind, you don't notice things that don't fit within the categories (you have created). . . . It literally prevents you from seeing what is right in front of your face. All you can see now is the label." (Hey, we'd call this a filter!)

The Brafmans report on studies that clearly demonstrate that the way in which a person is labeled by others clearly affects the behavior of that person. As we mentioned earlier, with enough repetition, or with enough emotional impact, the labels we assign people will elicit at least some behavior to support that label. In other words, we literally show, teach, and train the people in our lives how to behave to meet our expectations, and they (usually unconsciously) deliver according to the label we slap on 'em. So when you are with a man who never used to be considered a jerk, but you strongly believe that all men (or Steelers fans, or meat-eaters) are jerks, your suspicion and emotionally charged assessments about him will be felt, seen, heard, and reacted to by that guy's nervous system, and voila, a jerk is born.

That's not to say that there are no jerks or that what people do is all your fault. We are saying that it's clear that each one of us, both implicitly by what we believe and explicitly by what we say, what we do, and our body language, tell the people around us exactly how we expect to be treated. We contribute to their behavior towards us. And since we're not in their heads and we can't change anyone but ourselves, that's the place to begin if we want to stop finding jerks around every corner.

Every aspect of our lives reflects our subconscious beliefs. The background thoughts and beliefs we hold about relating, age, life, money, How Things Are, and How Things Should Be affects everything from our reactions and experiences to the way our bodies fight infection and the rate at which we age.

Now don't get yourself worked up. The skill of uncovering and redirecting these thoughts and beliefs just takes some practice. It all begins with sharpening your innate ability to break through the trance of belief and notice what is really going on in the moment. Once you realize the basic background beliefs you have, it's not rocket science to figure out how to shift from perpetuating the life that you have to creating the life that you want.

Subconscious levels of awareness hold a great wealth of information that is vital to your wellbeing, and when you are open to the information, your subconscious will take very good care of you. Your subconscious is, in essence, your guardian angel, your genie, genius, and guide. Often, your mind's filters—your beliefs, habits, and thought patterns—keep that information hidden or lead you to ignore it. It's a handy and beautiful thing. Except when it isn't.

A filter and the reaction it causes that was useful when you were young can stop you dead in your tracks when you're an adult. You can repeat the same thoughts, and have the same story and reaction for many years without knowing that it is your inner "security" system stopping you. Once you learn to see it, a new road can be built and the security team can be retrained or retired.

CLUE: When something you strive for eludes you repeatedly, you are probably paying attention to the wrong things and filtering out the right things.

That's your first real clue: realizing that something you have tried repeatedly to make happen stubbornly or mysteriously fails to materialize. Your mental filters need cleaning! Once you know how you are filtering you can revise the thoughts, beliefs and actions that now drive that bus over the cliff. You will stop overlooking what will get you that job or life-mate or the income you say you want, and your revised filter will as reliably bring you towards what you desire.

Filters in Action: A Fable

Paul and Jack are walking together down a busy Manhattan street. They both came to New York with the same amount of money saved up. They both grew up in very poor families. Both of them grew up with beliefs, assumptions, and expectations that originated with the attitudes and circumstances of their parents. That's where the similarity ends.

Paul believes that life is hard, money is scarce, trying hard doesn't necessarily pay off, and that when he doesn't get what he wants, it's not his fault, it's just How Things Are—the rich get richer and the poor get screwed. Paul figures that if he has any luck at all, it must be bad luck. That's something his mother always said, especially when trying to make his dad feel better after he got fired yet again.

The other guy, Jack, grew up believing that you make your own luck, things usually work out for the best, success is about enjoying what you've got, and friends and family are more valuable than money. Jack expects the best from life and from others. Though both of Jack's parents worked hard and stayed poor, they were always kind and generous to others and often invited Paul to have Sunday dinner with them, even when all they could afford was soup.

Paul and Jack are walking along, side by side, on the same street, hearing the same sounds, smelling the same scents of pizza and exhaust fumes, and feeling the same warm breeze as they walk through dappled sunlight on this lovely afternoon. Jack is paying attention to his surroundings and he feels excited about the new adventure before him. Paul is feeling a little edgy, thinking about how hard it will be to find a job he likes, and when he does it probably won't pay enough for him to afford a decent place to live in the city. People are shouting. The cabs are honking. It's a typical vibrant New York day.

On the sidewalk in front of them lies a $20 bill.

Which one sees it, Paul or Jack? Jack sees it—*but of course, you already knew that, didn't you?*

Do you know HOW Jack's mind was directed to notice the $20 and HOW Paul's mind skipped over it? Sure you do. Most of us can see how somebody *else* shoots himself in the foot pretty easily. But that's the information you need to get off the road to frustration and on the road to satisfaction. You need to learn how to recognize when you're doing that to yourself.

One of the many filtering mechanisms that our short-cutting brains develop comes from what we were taught to believe when we were young. In some ways, those beliefs determine what we regard as reality-whether or not it is true. Our beliefs and expectations serve as filters that identify, then either overlook or make us consciously aware of what serves the idea of "reality" we have acquired. This is why some filters cause "Reality Blindness" that consistently creates seemingly unwanted results in our lives.

Paul walks right past the $20 without even seeing it. His long-held belief that life is hard and that he has to struggle for every penny has primed his brain to filter out things that look like luck or good fortune. He might not get the money, but he does get the satisfaction of thinking that he's right about his rotten luck, and like his father, he can make himself feel better by imagining that he has little or no responsibility for the results he gets. He won't see the money but will still get the booby prize. He gets to be right. His brain has substituted being right—and its guaranteed limitations—in place of the risk of failure we face when we own responsibility for our lives. In the process of filtering out what his brain has been trained to overlook, he is literally blind to the money on the sidewalk. Oh, the image of the money reaches his retina, and those signals make it up his optic nerve, but they (along with thousands of other signals that his subconscious deems to be of no use for his survival) never make it into his conscious awareness. His mind just doesn't see it.

Jack's brain, meanwhile, is also scanning through the filter of *his* beliefs and expectations. His brain seeks out evidence that seems to prove the inherent generosity of the universe, and he spots and picks up the $20. Both Paul and Jack get to continue being right about How Things Are and how the world treats them. Paul can continue to blame circumstances and avoid the reality that he is creating his own "luck" (or lack thereof) with his beliefs, thoughts, and behaviors. Jack gets to reinforce his beliefs and feels grateful that the universe is indeed friendly and generous—while also remaining unaware that the experience of a "friendly and generous universe" is mostly a product of his own beliefs and actions.

For Jack, the subconscious filter in this case works in creating a pretty good life, so he may never need to give it a second thought. If it ain't broke, don't fix it, as the saying goes. Jack's beliefs and actions have done their work on the chemistry in his brain, and he focuses his awareness on noticing his "good luck" experiences and synchronicities. You probably have some success filters working for you. Excellent. In fact, if you identify things that "just seem to work out" for you, and feed them with a little gratitude and recognition, they'll work even better for you!

Paul's brain, flooded with the chemistry produced by anger and jealousy, further dims his awareness to anything that may seem like "good luck" or ease in being successful. If he can't have what he says he wants, at least he can hang on to the belief that he's right and he is just a victim of circumstance. Missing a $20 bill on the sidewalk is small potatoes, but there are other ways that Paul's brain reinforces his old childhood belief that bad luck is just his lot in life—ways of filtering reality that have not-so-trivial consequences.

Six months go by.

Paul has not been able to get or hold onto a decent job. He repeatedly forgot to set his alarm and sometimes got lost on the way to job interviews. Yet, when he arrived late, unshowered and with hair that looked like a cat that's facing off with a bulldog, he was shocked that people wouldn't give him "a break." In his mind, none of this was his fault, of course. It was the cheap alarm clock or the crappy bus schedule.

Still, Paul's résumé looked good and his references said that he's really quite intelligent, so, despite his screw-ups, he did eventually land a job. Which, as you may have expected, he quickly lost. Even though when he was there and actually worked, his work was very good, Paul's chronic lateness, slow pace, snide remarks, and "the look" he had that conveyed entitlement certainly didn't endear him to the boss.

Jack, who would be the first to admit he is neither as skilled nor as experienced as Paul, always confirmed interview appointments, arrived on time, and showed up comfortably well-dressed. He was at ease and personable and even when the company was not interested in hiring him, they liked him and often gave him a tip about who else might be hiring. Jack was able to select a job from three separate offers. He was successful at a series of jobs, each at a higher level of pay, and with greater creative freedom than the one before. Then he landed a permanent position in one of the companies that had rejected Paul. Uh-oh.

Paul secretly begins to resent Jack for his success, and uses it as further evidence that his misery is not his fault, the world just isn't fair, and that ass-kissers like Jack always get what they want. Never mind that Paul knows Jack is headstrong and assertive, and not even close to being an ass-kissing submissive type by any stretch of the imagination. Paul starts to avoid Jack and doesn't answer his calls for two weeks because he can't stand to be reminded of his bad luck. Meanwhile he misses two job leads that Jack left on his voice-mail. He deletes the messages without listening to them because, as he told his mom, he "just didn't want to hear any more of Jack's goddamn good news."

The moral of the story: Neither Paul nor Jack are conscious of the choices they are making, minute by minute, that help hold in place their stories about How Things Are. Their subconscious processing keeps their thoughts, emotions, and actions in alignment with their expectations, the circumstances conform, and they both get to be right.

Now, there's nothing wrong with being right, especially when survival is at stake. For our distant ancestors, being able to quickly notice that the cave holds fresh mountain lion tracks and that means "run the other way NOW!" increased their chance of survival and guaranteed they'd live long enough to reproduce and, ultimately, produce us. Today, being right when judging the speed of a car when crossing the street is vital to your survival.

However, not every pattern your mind has created keeps working for you. When that happens, you may have to choose between being Right or being Happy. You may have to choose to change your stories about How Things Are. What you consider to be "fact" and "real" is, in many cases, only an interpretation, a convenient story designed to give you a shortcut through the myriad of possibilities before you.

Having a mind that creates and runs subconscious programs as a shortcut strategy for survival is remarkably helpful, except when those programs, once designed to steer us away from threat and discomfort, now keep us from getting beyond discomfort to where we want to go. You may be smart and strong, logical and intelligent and yet sometimes you just can't seem to get some aspect of your life on track. And all while you think you are making real choices and seeing reality as it is. You think your consistent failure is random, fate, God's will, bad luck, or some other delusional thing or another. Yes indeed, the consistent factor in your re-runs is you.

CLUE: If you are playing the blame game (even if you are blaming yourself) and feeling like the victim, take note, your filters are showing!

Your subconscious mind is designed to take very good care of you, so don't think that you are stuck being the victim of your subconscious decision-making and that's all there is to it. The self-awareness that occurs when we stop to really notice how life is unfolding is the first step in revising old filters and behavior patterns that are no longer bringing you the protection and pleasure they once did.

Obviously, that your brain once wired together "car is large and hard and moving fast + body is soft and squishy = do not cross street in front of car" is one hell of a useful filter, and we strongly suggest you hold onto that one. On the other hand, your brain has also wired together other early experiences that once threatened or seemed to threaten your survival. Today some of those old decisions about what is important to notice, and what is better left unseen, may still be operating, but may no longer be relevant or useful. In fact, these filters may be what is getting in your way.

In Paul's case, he got his beliefs and expectations (the story) about How Things Are (reality)—from his parents' beliefs and behaviors, particularly those that helped them to avoid feeling the pain and shame of being a failure. Paul heard mom and dad complain regularly that hanging onto money is based on luck, and dad just wasn't the lucky sort, and that is How Things Are. Today when it comes to getting and keeping a steady income, Paul relies on luck, and "hopes" for the best rather than planning and making his own "luck" by relying on consistency at work and other useful habits. Certainly his parents did not intend for Paul's mind to use their words and emotions to create filters that sabotage his success, but that's exactly what happened.

As a child, those filters also probably worked pretty well to alleviate Paul's own pain or shame around having less stuff than his friends and not having the coolest clothes, and probably also gained him a few perks from teachers. The neighbor that gave him cookies and told him how awful it was that no matter how hard his parents worked they couldn't get ahead helped reinforce the "victim" program. The "hard work makes you a victim" belief was reinforced when his father worked overtime at a job that he hated, even after his first heart attack, eventually leaving his mother a widow as a result of more "bad luck." Of course, mom never mentioned the drinking that contributed to dad's early death and their ongoing financial predicament. Paul was bright enough to get a college scholarship, and to stay sober, but his mind still carried the old filters and he never became as successful as he said he wanted to be.

Not everyone completely absorbs their parents' world view the way Paul did. Some of us reject our parents, thinking "there but the grace of God go I" and accidentally or actively find people that show us other useful beliefs to adopt. However, most of us do absorb some of our parent's beliefs and patterns, and then find ourselves living out a rerun or an adapted version of our parents' lives.

It would be a lifelong and virtually impossible job to decode every filter your mind uses to help you run your life. Nor do you want to. Remember the notable difference between the filters that Paul and Jack have "inherited" from their parents—Jack's are working FOR him while Paul's are working AGAINST him. Most of your filters are useful and provide you with experiences that are favorable and life affirming.

CLUE: What background beliefs are the soil in which your desires grow (or wither)? What do you believe about money, relating, the world, relationships? What did your parents believe?

CHAPTER 3

Time to Change the Filters

"We don't see things as they are, we see things as we are."
—Anais Nin

Filters Start With Survival

The human brain evolved from the simple instinctive and re-flexive systems of pattern recognition-and-reaction found in amphibians and reptiles. The more complex nervous systems of birds and mammals were formed by layering new brain structures on top of this primitive system. Your brain still contains the "lizard brain" that runs the functions you never think about, and that continue even if you are knocked unconscious or pass out: breathing, circulation, digestion, elimination, and reflex reactions, also called "autonomic" functions. (And thank goodness for that! We all occasionally forget to put the milk away, lose our keys, and go to the post office without the mail—If we had to remember to breathe, we'd be goners!)[1]

Unlike most other animals, the human baby's brain is still relatively unfinished at birth—still growing, developing, creating and destroying connections between brain cells until we're finished at

32

about age 20-25 (sooner for women, later for men). Newborn humans are extremely vulnerable, and require a much longer period of parental contact and protection than many other species. The human brain evolved to ensure our survival in the context of this harsh reality, and as infants we quickly become vigilant for signs of potential abandonment. This is the beginning of our filters.

In infancy and early childhood your life would be at stake if adults (particularly your mother) were to abandon you before you can survive on your own. The human infant's mind is superbly focused on recognizing and reacting to the threat of physical harm, neglect, or potential abandonment. Our brains quickly and accurately decode (among many other signals including sight, smell, touch, proximity) the tone, rhythm, and pitch of adult voices; we experience emotions triggered by those changes; and we react to those signals instantly and instinctively by sounding an alarm—by crying. A human mother becomes well-versed in recognizing the various cries of her infant, and soon knows the difference between the cries that mean wet, hungry, tired, or afraid and in pain.

As the human mind develops in early childhood, children learn to compensate for and protect themselves from the threat and danger of abandonment, whether it is actually imminent or a product of their inexperienced mind jumping to conclusions. After all, it's better to jump at shadows than be eaten by a tiger. *As children we adapt our behavior to avoid situations that are, or that we interpret as, a threat to survival.* We learn to react so quickly and unconsciously that when we are similarly triggered as adults we may never stop and notice how illogical and childish those reactions are now that we are fully grown. Instead, we come up with rationalizations and judgments and explanations to help hold those protection devices in place, just like Paul's lament, and subsequent "evidence" that he just can't catch a break. When you lend your mind's logic and rationality to support an old pattern rather than investigate HOW you might be contributing to some repeating outcome, you are pretty much screwed. It's a clear case of the asylum being run by the inmates, and in the real world where these old patterns play out like broken records, you only need to look around you to find children in adult bodies reacting like tantrum throwing five-year-olds, painfully self conscious 11-year-olds, or sexually intoxicated teens.

HOW to Recognize Your Filters

Like spam filters and water filters, like your personal shopping suggestions on retail websites and the ads on your Facebook page, your mind's filters are based on pattern recognition. Filters are created throughout our lives, any time repetition and emotion fuse beliefs, expectations, and reactions together. These packages of associations serve to let some perceptions in and keep others out. They insert meaning where none exists, eliminate what does not fit the pattern, and provide us with shortcuts, some of which are useful and some of which are not.

The filter that allows you to rocket down the highway while listening to the radio and talking to a buddy about tomorrow's big presentation is a fine, fine piece of work. You can even recognize with split second accuracy when to change lanes to avoid the guy who is driving like a crash-test dummy without even breaking a sweat. If you were aware of your body, you might have noticed that your breathing and heartbeat went up a notch as your brain chemistry changed in reaction to the potential threat, which made you even more able to see and avert danger. Yay for your subconscious!

Filters determine what we see and hear, seeking out some things while ignoring others, and so affect our every experience of the world. The thing you want to know is that your filters may keep you from seeing and hearing good stuff as readily as they filter out what is useless.

Many of us have complex filters that were set up in early childhood and linked to events that, at the time, registered in our brain as life threatening, such as the fear that our parents or other adults would abandon us. Many filters, while originally generated to protect you, to limit your suffering, or give you a better chance of survival, are counter-productive in adulthood. For example, "don't talk to strangers" or "speak only when you are spoken to," need to be revised if you are to become a happy, fulfilled, and successful adult.

Sometimes we grow up assuming that the filtered reality is "how the world is" and "how life is." We can stay trapped, unable to see beyond those assumptions unless we have repeated contradictory experiences that wake us- even for a moment—and make us question, then revise the filter and alter our experience of what is possible. Sometimes this revision can happen seamlessly and other times, "changing the filter" requires vigilant attention. As our adult capabilities develop, we may replace a childhood filter such as "all strangers are dangerous" with a more evolved filter as our adult awareness evolves.

The subconscious consistently provides sensory clues that can help us revise what isn't useful. Without heeding those clues, we stay stuck in our filtered reality—as if being born wearing orange-tinted contact lenses, we simply believe that the world is orange and don't imagine that life can look any other way.

Because these filters were incorporated into our early identities as a means of protection, we often feel threatened when those old beliefs and expectations are challenged. Since our own assumptions become the source of our suffering, we must learn to challenge them. "If the world is not orange, then HOW do I act in a world with blues, greens, and yellows?"

The old familiar, if unwanted, reality can seem less frightening than the idea of reinventing your idea of yourself or admitting that your version of "how things are" and "how people are" is inaccurate and, by the way, also the source of your stress. The old familiar pain and disappointment is something you at least know how to handle. If things become desperately unpleasant, you may suddenly reach a breakthrough point and think "anything is better than this!" But you don't have to wait for misery to motivate you.

For example, you may find a kind of familiar comfort in being rejected by potential mates—you know how to be alone and lonely and the prospect of negotiating a long-term relationship feels terrifying. You may think you want it (or think you should want it)—but more as an idealized fairy tale experience, not the messy and challenging relating and intimacy that requires listening, sharing, and getting over disappointments. With the logic of a child you avoid the fear of discovering that you may, like your mother, marry a mate that starts drinking and dies an untimely death. Instead, you become expert at finding people who are unavailable and those who will reject you again and again. You have little or no conscious awareness that your filters keep directing you towards people who, like you, are unconsciously committed to staying the hell out of a relationship and the potential pain it may bring. Your filters, after all, are doing their job—protecting you from pain and threat, whether real or imagined.

So, when someone asks you why you ditched Joe, who clearly adored you and treated you like gold, and dated Jim, the jerk who left you for the bartender at the Paradise Club, you will say: "Joe was nice but he was boring. I guess I just go for the exciting and funny guys (translate: immature risk-taking charming drunks like your dad) and they don't work out. I felt so comfortable around Jim. (of course you did) I guess (here it comes...) that's just the way I am." Um, nope, not even close.

Familiarity and comfort are THE favorite and most common bogus rationalizations for doing the same things again and again, even though the outcome is as pleasant as eating a bowl of sand. While feeling unlovable, fearful, and rejected is just slightly more fun than being hit in the head with a brick, at least it's familiar and you know how to survive it. The risk of stepping into the unknown, even if that unknown is filled with the possibility of better times, greater ease, and improved circumstances, triggers fear and resistance.

The good news is that you come well equipped with everything you need to get through to the other side of the fear/resistance mudhole. The natural curiosity and resilience that once inspired you to get back on that new bike when you fell off, or swing a bat again at the ball that hit you in the face, or finally kiss the boy you pined after for the entire school year are the right tools for the job. Growing up, you watched the older kids, asked adults, watched sports on TV, chatted about kissing with your friends, and so your world opened up despite your fears.

As you become more and more aware and self-observant, you will be able to, with increasing speed and skill, notice the background thoughts and beliefs that run you off the road, and revise them to bring you to the creation of a more pleasurable life.

HOW to Start Re-Tuning Your Filters

Each filter contains a pattern of beliefs, expectations, reactions, emotions, and behaviors that fit a predictable overall pattern or "frequency" like a radio station. So, if you are preset for the "Classic Rock", or "Country" or "Classical" or "Oldies" you will only hear (and see and think) in the nuances of the music coming in on that frequency. Makes sense, right? If you grew up hearing only Country, it would become the background music of your life and would keep playing in the background without your even being aware of it. Until you tune to another station, the choices you make and those you avoid will keep giving you the same experiences—comfortable in their familiarity, even if they aren't what you really want. I mean those country tunes are usually about cheatin' men, broken hearts, makin' do, and a sad old dog named Blue. That radio channel gets awfully old.

The hardest part is waking up to the reality that the life you are living isn't written in stone, is not the product of "the way things are" (or the way you are), but is a product of the station you're tuned in to—your filters—that pick the music you hear. It is possible to become conscious of this entire process, and to break through the fear to the giddy freedom of experiencing what were once only hopes and wishes. Interrupting your assumptions opens your mind to new possible ways of interpreting events, new ways of relating to others, and new expectations. Conscious awareness of how your mind operates opens you to new ways of seeing, new ways to relate, and new ways to interpret experiences. When you examine the preset automatic assumptions you now confuse with reality, you can sort which ones are useful (people find me lovable, I always make good money, things always work out for me) from the ones that create dissatisfaction or suffering (men always cheat, women are gold diggers, I never get the promotion I deserve).

CLUE: When you hear yourself saying "always" or "never" that's a clear sign pointing to a filter.

Here's an example.

Eric has a job interview tomorrow, and tonight as he tries to fall asleep he repeatedly runs through his stories of how bad he is at interviews and how he never gets the really good jobs because he just doesn't make a good first impression. His thoughts and emotions are triggering biochemical signals, cranking up the input of adrenaline and cortisol—"stress hormones"—that are making his mouth dry, his heart race, and relaxation and sleep nearly impossible.

The next day, his lack of sleep makes it harder for him to focus his attention and he misses a turn and ends up arriving late, then forgets the interviewer's name. His fears about fumbling the interview and not getting the job offer come to pass. And he has increased the likelihood that the next interview will go as badly if not worse, because his expectations of failure have been reinforced and his beliefs more entrenched. Well, at least he gets to be right about being a screw-up.

Eric could change the outcome if he were aware of the thoughts and physical discomfort. If he just took a moment—a breath—to be an observer of his own thoughts, he could catch himself and do something new, different, and useful. Eric might be able to catch himself on the third or fourth re-run of the "worry express" and interrupt some of his suffering. He could go to the gym, or have a beer with a friend, meditate, masturbate, do something to interrupt that train ride to hell, and then get some sleep.

Even if he had the same experiences of missing the turn, arriving late, and forgetting the name, he could still get some relief by taking a few breaths to settle down. He could do something new, by simply reporting all of that out loud at the start of the interview, "I'm pretty nervous about this interview—and on the way here I missed a turn and got lost and at this point I can't even remember your name. Will you please remind me?" The truth would let the interviewer know exactly what's going on and that's certainly preferable to having his distracted and edgy behavior misinterpreted. And it's possible that being candid about his nervousness will be the thing that sets him above the other candidates for the job.

We know that as "grown-ups" we can use knives, light matches, and easily do plenty of things that were forbidden territory when we were children. However, when it comes to the filters, stories, and strategies that our minds have created to avoid potential but undefined threats (like someone yelling) then revising old taboos takes a little more awareness. Those emotionally charged habits don't just vanish when presented with logic. Unlike using a knife or lighting a match, which becomes part of everyday adult life, speaking up and telling the truth carry a different layer of emotion. Rather than just physical danger, these kinds of habits are meant to remedy the fear of abandonment, rejection, being shamed, (or even hit) for no reason at all.

We know enough not to try to squeeze ourselves into the clothes we wore when we were toddlers, and we certainly don't ride around on our ancient tricycle. But because we have filters and blind spots that keep us from easily knowing how to rewire our child mind's defense system, many of us react with the same habitual fear of rejection we experienced as children, or we hold a view about money, sex, or getting what we want that's only a leftover and unconscious childhood program. In addition to these old dead-end roads, our daily decisions are also influenced by societal filters that sway our thinking away from the pathway and roads that will take us directly to the places we want to go. Once we know how to recognize dead ends and the lost highways, we can revise the roads. Out come the red flags and orange barrels as we begin to create useful detours around those reactions that no longer serve us.

HOW to Notice, Interrupt and Revise a Pattern or Filter

Sounds easy, right? Well, you used to be a great little noticer, but somewhere along the way you, like most of us, were taught to behave as if we believed what we were told (stories) rather than believing and acting on what we noticed (reality).

Most of us as kids had to choose between what we noticed—that mom and dad are mad at each other, daddy's drunk, mom is crying, Aunt Jill is fat—and what we were told and expected to believe—that everything is fine, daddy is tired, mom has an allergy, Jill is big-boned. At first, we got confused, then annoyed, when we learned to ignore the obvious in favor of pretending just to avoid unpleasant scenes and keep the peace. Instead of saying what we thought or asking for what we wanted, and instead of asking for clarification because we assumed we'll be lied to, we learned to clam up and just repeat what we were expected to say.

As adults, we often start out to say what we think or feel, then begin to have the physical sensations of those early experiences that involved punishment, shame, and /or embarrassment for reporting what we noticed, so we stop ourselves to avoid those strong physical sensations.

We avoid discomfort and fear. We inhibit ourselves from expressing and, therefore, from getting over hurt and anger. We put off of asking for that raise or that date to avoid the discomfort we generate by thinking of rejection. We end up with a life ruled by a subtle but pervasive sense that saying what we see and asking for what we want will only leave us feeling frustrated or depressed. And then we invent reasons to explain why all of this pretense and inhibition is necessary and right.

CLUE: If you hear yourself defending, explaining, and rationalizing, your filters are showing.

Repetition and emotional intensity are how filters and patterns get set up in the first place and are also what creates new ones. The good news is that we can use this same process—repetition and intensity—to alter even complex deep-seated behaviors. In the next few chapters we'll give you some practices that will get you started.

Imagine, as a young kid, you are playing with a ball and without looking you run into the street after it. The intensity of your mother's fear and anger comes through in the sound and volume of her voice as she races into the street and grabs you painfully by the arm, screaming "Stay out of the street! You'll get yourself killed!" That moment may set up a filter that makes you—almost involuntarily—stop dead at the curb and look for cars forever after. It's the combined force of repeated experience + intensity that carves a road into your awareness. It's a shortcut, and often a useful one.

So when you are replacing an old rutted road, that same formula of emotional experience + intensity must be invoked, or nothing new can happen with any consistency.

HOW to Persist in the Work of Amending Your Filters

Creating greater freedom from the automatic reactions and assumptions that drive our decisions is an ongoing process. Overlaid on whatever happened in the past is our culture's denial of the importance of pleasure as a part of being human. We end up with a background belief that sabotages our ability to accept more pleasure in life.

We gain larger and sweeter doses of pleasure and happiness with every layer of false assumption or misplaced motive that we peel off. We have to build up our tolerance for enjoyment and pleasure, so that rather than reject the good that life offers us out of habit, fear, or mistrust, we can keep saying "yes", finding and taking more opportunities to enjoy the intimacy, wealth, and satisfaction available to us.[2]

Understanding HOW something undesirable repeats in your life is like finding the recipe or formula for an inevitable result. As you figure out the recipe for HOW you get what you do not want, you can then alter the ingredients and make something new happen. Substitute new ingredients (thoughts, interpretations, beliefs, and behaviors) that will create the experience you want. Sometimes you'll need to be a detective, sometimes it will be obvious. Either way, knowing how the ingredients are mixed together is the first step.

My Story: Filters Pop Up When You Least Expect Them

Though I have done plenty of work regarding my family and my issues, I can tell you that I am still (at age 57) uncovering and taking responsibility for remnants of my childhood filters. Recently I uncovered a long-stored deeply rooted filter that certainly wasn't doing me any good. It was late at night when I woke to use the bathroom. I'd been in a very deep sleep. While I was sitting there I found myself reflecting on what was going right in my life—a CD project that was coming together, this book, a trip coming up to visit my daughter, a music project coming to completion in two months—and suddenly, just as I stood to flush, I had a bone chilling thought. "That means I'm going to die." What?! As I shrugged off the little surge of adrenaline and came fully awake, I said out loud, "Where the hell did THAT come from?" and in that moment, standing in the dark in the bathroom I was deeply aware of my father's life. He reached a point in his life when things he had been working on for years were finally coming together, and he was about to achieve a new level of success, when he died suddenly from a stroke. In that moment, it was as if a thread opened between the past and the present. I flushed, telling that filter to go on down, thanks for the warning, but that's so *not* happening. In the following weeks I was able to recognize the products of this belief, a filter that had been invisible to me before that night. This subconscious filter had been guiding me to make choices that sabotaged my ability to fully succeed in a misguided attempt to "save my life." Now that I am aware of this "success = death" filter, I have been noticing that I have plenty of options and opportunities that had been hidden in plain sight. It is both exhilarating and disturbing. "Holy crap." I thought, "Here is the roadblock that has continued to distract me from clearing out the remnants of "making do is good enough." Since that night, I have become aware of at least a dozen ways that this had been operating in my life. The best thing I can tell you is this: When your subconscious speaks, take notes! I have successfully identified and revised some old habits that kept that "don't accomplish too much" feedback loop in place. I am happy to report that I now easily recognize where and how many of those filters were affecting my decisions and that I am taking new actions and making progress.

Facts About Filters: A Review

- Filters are pattern identification programs that are mostly unconscious.
- They trigger thoughts and actions that once served or still serve survival and wellbeing.
- Filters help determine what sensory information we pay attention to, literally altering what we see, hear, interpret, and remember.
- Filters are revised or reinforced every day.

- What you filter for is what you get.
- Filters prevent sensory overwhelm by subconsciously tracking many things that we cannot consciously be aware of at once.
- Some filters are still useful in creating the life you want, and can go on subconsciously leading you in the right directions.
- Some filters that were once useful adaptations no longer serve you.
- Other people can see and identify many of your filters, sometimes quite easily.
- Your subconscious provides information from filters as impulses, instincts, and gut feelings to alert your conscious mind.
- Filters are interpreted as "reality," which may work for or against you.
- Filters dictate most expectations and reactions.
- Most (90%+) decisions are made unconsciously through filters.
- When reality and filters conflict, filters win.
- Your current circumstances are "status reports" about your filters.
- Filters can be amended by redirecting your thoughts and actions.
- Filters are reinforced or amended by the company you keep.
- Emotional intensity plus repetition builds filters.
- Emotional intensity plus repetition revises filters.

CHAPTER 4

Unconscious Commitments and Dueling Beliefs

"Brain: An apparatus with which we think we think."
—Ambrose Bierce

Most of us most of the time imagine that the choices and decisions we make are conscious free-will choices. If you're asked why you took this job, bought that car, or married this man, you have a boatload of reasons, and very few of them would be true. Not because you're a lying creep, but because your conscious mind is always spitting out rationalizations and justifications for why you do what you do. It is digging through your mental files and tossing out possible answers to any question you ask. That doesn't mean the answers are accurate. When filters are working against you, it's often because you believe that your filtered experience is objective reality. *You can't trust everything you think.*

The way our brains work gives us an illusion of control that is so impenetrable that we can justify and defend even the dumbest, most illogical and self-destructive things that we do. We do the same things and make the same choices over and over, errors in judgment that make us miserable and cost us health, relationships, and financial stability, all the while thinking we are being logical and rational. Ha!

Sometimes we end up with "dueling beliefs." This happens when we are unconsciously committed to one outcome (staying single avoids marital woes) and consciously wanting another (to get married). The unconscious commitment will win here, and we will end up with a story that might look like "there are no good men left" or "I always pick creeps" or "I'm not meant to get married."

We all have unconscious commitments that are rooted in old, unexamined beliefs about How Things Are. Sometimes those unconscious commitments almost magically help us get what we want, while others keep us from having what we want. Here's how to sort things out when you have dueling beliefs.

HOW to Become a Better Observer

A good first step is to establish some practices that, done regularly, will bring you some freedom from the same old, same old and will help you feel good, have energy, think more clearly, respond faster, and stress less. You may already be doing some of these things. Great, keep going. If this is all new, start with the first three and practice regularly. Schedule them in. Once those become habits, add the other two. This may be the way you actually start being able to find your ass with both hands.

Pretend this list is a bunch of free prescription drugs with zero side effects that cure malaise and reduce stress, improve your sex life, and prevent a good chunk of all lifestyle-related health issues. As the shoemaker says, "Just do it."

- Exercise for an hour five days a week.
- Meditate every day. Something meditation-like counts—dance, tai-chi, yoga, drawing, playing an instrument—whatever gets you off the mental hamster wheel and shifts you into "timelessness"
- Give your fridge and pantry a makeover. Get rid of the crap (junk food, overly refined foods, sweets, high-salt and or

high-fat snacks, etc.), and increase the amount of whole foods in your diet, since what you eat directly affects your ability to think clearly, and feel emotionally stable

- Stop so much multi-tasking. Do fewer things at once so you can experience what you are doing rather than thinking ahead. In other words, slow down. Do less, live more.

- Hang out with people whom you like and who "get" you, and have fun regularly. Do this not as a reward for working hard or as if it is time off for good behavior, but because you NEED consistent regular contact with your tribe to stay mentally and physically healthy. Do these things as if they are the magic formula for happiness and longevity (because they really are).

Think of this as a three-legged stool: decent nutrition, meditation/mindfulness and exercise/fun. These are the three things you can manage consciously and that have a huge (yes, huge) impact on your ability to stop your freight train mind when it's dragging you into a dark place, or when it's on an endless loop of rerun thoughts. It's a three-legged stool, and needs all three legs to stand. If you're living on coffee and power bars, sleeping when and if you can, and think that walking to the mailbox is exercise, your ability to make good conscious decisions will be zip, nil, nada. You get my drift?

Here's what one woman said to me after making a decision to end a relationship:

"It was as if, after I really started observing what I was thinking and how I was acting more objectively, I suddenly woke up. I realized that not only was I unhappy but that I had put my attention on making him happy, as if I could, and ignored the fact that the few things I did ask him for were ignored. I realized that it was like waiting for my father to see me, to get me, and that it just wasn't going to happen. That's when I told him I was leaving. And what was especially interesting is that I wasn't mad at him anymore and I wasn't interested in trying to get him to change. I knew that, like my dad, that's the best he could do. So I moved on."

The first step in catching your mind in the act of automatically leading you down dark alleys and dead-end roads is to use meditation and other mindfulness practices to slow down your automatic thoughts, and become an investigator in your own life. This doesn't mean you need to constantly analyze yourself—simply observe what you're feeling, thinking, and doing. Plenty of information is available in those sensory clues, and self-medicating behaviors.

"Hmmm, seems like almost every time I see my Mom I come home and pick a fight with my husband." Or,

"Hmmm, when I get upset at my kids I notice I eat a lot more." Or,

"Hmmm seems like I feel kinda sick almost every Monday morning." Or,

"What a knot I get in my stomach when my wife mentions her ex."

Then you can ask yourself useful questions to get under the experience,

"How do I get myself charged up around Mom? What assumptions am I making? What could I do or say differently?"

"Is there a pattern around when the kids act up? What can I do differently?

How can I soothe myself without eating junk?"

"What thoughts do I have on Monday mornings? How do I stress myself out about work?"

"What is my story about my wife's ex? How am I distressing myself with it?"

Your conscious mind must learn to dance with your subconscious, and your subconscious is the partner that always leads.

Filters and the patterns that they generate are made and revised throughout our lifetimes. Not all of them date back to childhood, and not all of them come about through lots of repetition. Sometimes the emotion itself is powerful enough to create one of these programs instantly. After my cat of 18 years died a hard death at a time in my life that was filled with unpleasant change and loss, I developed a filter that prevented me from having a pet. I was 47 at the time. By observing my thoughts I realized that the seemingly "logical" and "rational" stories I told myself were all a cover for the reality that not getting another pet really meant not suffering the inevitable loss. So new patterns do pop up.

Often though, the filters that haunt us most are the old childhood strategies designed for keeping us from repeating unpleasant experiences. Our own and our parents' unpleasant experiences both served to trigger our hardwired survival button, and our minds adapted to protect us and ease our discomfort. To avoid having a "rotten marriage like my parents had", one mind may become adept at reading people and seeking role models that demonstrate happy healthy relating, while another mind may create a strategy for avoiding commitment at all costs, and another may unconsciously choose potential mates with whom it is impossible to create a marriage.

Remember that most of our filters are good and useful. For tens of thousands of years, this ability to react without a lot of conscious thought worked effectively to keep our ancestors alive. The awareness that we experience as "intuition," "hunches," "gut reactions," or a seemingly instantaneous sense of ease or unease provide useful memos from our subconscious awareness. It is the linear, intellectual reasoning capacity of the human brain that deludes us and convinces us that we are reacting based on "rational thought" and "free will."

When we listen to what our reasoning mind tells us and take it as real and true, while ignoring the "tells" that rise from our subconscious as sensations and unbidden ideas, *we are missing at least half of the information available to us at any given moment.* Who wants to drive across the country with only half of the directions—oh, and some of those will be made up just for excitement?

Your subconscious mind is responsible for the vast majority of all the decisions you make. That's right. You are not in conscious control. This is the good news, since it frees your higher mind up to do the things it does really well—invent, explore, analyze, strategize, plan, create, and interpret. The conscious and subconscious do best when they work as a team, and most of the information we take in through our senses is interpreted by our subconscious. By ignoring and overriding the signals you get from the subconscious, you stay ignorant of the very things you need to know to create the health, relationships, jobs, and future that you say you want.

For Example: You have background beliefs and expectations about how the world is and how people are. Your mind absorbed and adopted these beliefs and expectations throughout your childhood. Some grew from your experiences, but most background beliefs came from observing the expectations and reactions of your caregivers and other authority figures. These background beliefs now function as filters that unconsciously make choices for you. If you have a learned race, gender, or age bias for example, you may overlook the qualifications of a potential employee (or mate!) without knowing on a conscious level what you did.

Some common limiting background filters:
- I have to be "nice" no matter what I think or feel.
- Wealthy people are selfish, superior jerks.
- You can't trust anybody.
- Men always cheat.
- Women are bitchy and controlling.
- You can't trust any politicians
- Fat people are lazy gluttons

You can add to this list many other race, gender, appearance, or age biases.

Here's a way to identify some of your personal rutted roads, check the background, and see if what's already in the system is working for you or against you. Fill in the blanks right off the top of your ahead. Don't think. You may have two or three ways to complete many of them. Go ahead, jot your answers down. Notice the ones that come to mind with some conviction, you'll be able to make use of it in a few minutes.

Relationships are _____ .

Getting what I want is _____ .

I am _____ .

My life has been _____ .

Money is _____ .

Work is _____ .

Men are _____ .

Women are _____ .

My parents _____ .

I can't seem to _____ .

People are _____ .

The World is _____ .

The Unknown is _____ .

What I'm afraid of is _____ .

I should _____ .

People should _____ .

My childhood was _____ .

My luck is _____ .

Marriage is_____

If only I _____then I _____.

If only people would _____then I _____.

If only my parents had ____, then I _____.

You now have a list of some background beliefs, biases, and unconscious commitments that, when woven together, subconsciously direct your decision making, build your "story" about your life, and generate experiences to prove these beliefs are correct—even when they're not, and they're costing you big time.

What if you were offered a great job working for a wealthy local Irish Catholic politician, a man, a redhead, and you had these background beliefs hidden just under the surface of awareness?

Women are nicer than men. All politicians are corrupt. People with plenty of money are all jerks. Work always sucks and is never fun. Redheads are sexy but hot tempered.

My religion is the only one that is true, the rest are all delusions, especially Catholicism.

Whoa! What a mess. What might happen? If you somehow actually talked yourself into taking the job, chances are very high you wouldn't last. And you probably wouldn't even be sure what the hell happened.

OK, now you give this a shot: pick an area of your life (for example, relationships, career, family, health) in which what you have is clearly not what you say you want. Without thinking too hard about it, come up with a list of statements (beliefs) that may be related to that area. These beliefs may seem trivial, or you may be embarrassed to admit you even have them. (Don't worry, you don't have to show them to anyone. Yet.)

These beliefs and thoughts in the background color your interpretations of events, and are responsible for the way you create the story out of events. A rich man who is penny-wise may be thought of as a "cheap jerk" but you'll label someone that's not rich "thrifty" when he has the same behaviors. You may call a loud woman a "bitch" but think of a loud man as assertive and outspoken. These are clues to how your implicit expectations are guiding you. Your subconscious will faithfully reflect your inner world back to you in your experiences, and your daily experiences are powerfully influenced by the beliefs as they filter your experience of reality.

Other people will have completely different experiences of men, women, religion, rich people, politicians, red heads, and religion, even though we live in the same world. Other people who have the kind of life you desire are not better, smarter, lucky, or predestined, nor do they have superior brains or superior DNA. But they DO have thoughts, beliefs, emotions, and actions that support the lives that they have.

Becoming conscious of these not quite hidden assessments are a good and useful place to begin. Not that you can (or want to) unearth every bias you have, but uncovering the ones that prevent you from making good choices is the first step toward getting honest with yourself. By becoming more conscious of the labels you carry around, you will be able to redirect those that sabotage communication and relating.

CLUE: If there is a contradiction between your unconscious commitments — the kinds of beliefs and convictions that showed up on this list — and your conscious commitments, then the result that you persistently get tells you which one is driving the Reality Train.

You now have a place to start. Bring your unconscious commitments to the surface, and make a conscious commitment to reinforcing the ones that work for you, and notice, interrupt and revise the ones that work against you. If you have some filters that shape your "luck" by giving you great instincts to pick the right job, fall into the best financial deals, meet people who have the answers you've been searching for and if you have background beliefs that steer you towards wealth or health producing thoughts and actions, then reinforce them every change you get. Even the small ones are great — things like having a knack for always finding a parking place, walking into a store and finding the thing you were just thinking of last night, or discovering that the friend you haven't heard from in six months left a message on your voicemail while you were at the gym. Say "thanks, nice job!" to your subconscious. *The more you acknowledge a result, the more deeply it is reinforced and can reproduce a desired result.* Report the experience to someone so you can hear yourself say it out loud. This overt recognition of the process will encourage your mind(s) to communicate more easily, and your conscious mind will begin to understand with greater accuracy how the subconscious memos break through. This will help you catch and revise the stuff that's not working for you.

REMINDER: Why "Why?" Is Worse Than Useless

Suppose you have beliefs and expectations that limit your ability to become wealthy and get ahead. It may become a duel to the death if you keep going down that victim road of: "Why? Why is this happening to me? I work hard, I do all the right things, and nothing ever works out. Life is hard, people are rotten, what's this world coming to, even my friends are idiots!" You will continue to find yourself thwarted at every turn, not by "life" but by your own miserable thoughts, beliefs, and the emotions and actions they spawn. *The more you acknowledge and reinforce a belief and its results, the more your subconscious will seek out those same results, over and over.*

CLUE: The battle cry "Why me?!" is really a road sign that says "Stop! Turn back!" and can show you how to begin noticing the thoughts and actions that stop you.

HOW to Notice Dueling Beliefs

If you have dueling beliefs, you will sabotage what you say you want in order to avoid the potential pain of the subconsciously anticipated result. Sometimes it will seem as if the universe is conspiring against you. That's a clue.

What you believe on the surface (I'd love to be rich!), and what you deeply believe (If I become rich I'll become a selfish jerk and will lose my friends and end up alone and miserable with my money, and I know you can't buy happiness.) are in a tug of war. The subconscious protector will trump your desire to succeed, to "save you" from the terrible consequences that may come with having it. As you notice and redirect that faulty thinking, you will literally be building a new road in your brain.

The tug of war process between the beliefs is not very well hidden to begin with. It's pretty easy to see in others, and sometimes people DO break through these issues when they are faced with enough contradictory evidence AND they are willing to accept it. If you're working for a great guy that you've formed a fatherly bond with and he's got a track record of kindness and generosity, and THEN you discover he's incredibly wealthy, you may wake up. If there's one white crow in the flock there may be more—and you can be one of them.

Meanwhile, you will be BOTH attracted to what you want AND stopped by your mind, caught in an endless dance of one step forward, one step back, until you either find a way to break the cycle or become resigned, believing that you simply can't have, or aren't destined to have, what you say you want. That's the nature of dueling beliefs.

Now, It's likely that if somebody asked you, "Do you think rich people are mostly jerks?" or "Do you think all marriages suck?" you would honestly say, "No. Of course not." Yet, when people complain about the greed of the wealthy, or the awful stress in their marriage, you may also find yourself wholeheartedly nodding like a bobblehead doll on speed. So how can you have it both ways? Which belief dominates? The experiences and circumstances of your life answer that one. What you filter for is what you get.

CLUE: Look for any place in your life where what you say you want opposes what you actually do and you will find dueling beliefs.

If you say you want a mate yet avoid dating, are overly cautious, or pick mates that all have similar undesirable traits, then Bingo! There's a filter at work. If you say you want wealth but make bank errors, invest unwisely, screw up job interviews, make mistakes that cost you promotions, refuse to find a financial advisor, and have a slew of other wealth-depleting behaviors, there's a filter running the show. Oh yeah, they can be cagey little bastards. They are designed to protect you and they play for keeps, even if that means locking you in a proverbial tower to keep you from harm.

You get the point. Now here's a quick way to get some "enlightenment." Check in with your friends—the ones who will tell you the complete truth—and they will be able to point out places where your words and actions do not match. When you feel that urge to resist what they are saying (and you will), zip it and listen. All of that drive to defend and justify why you do what you do is that filter at work. Breathe. You are one step closer to getting out from under its spell.

It's amazing how many self-sabotaging thoughts and behaviors we repeat unconsciously. The good news is that although our filters are mostly invisible to us, they are usually pretty obvious to others.

Rhoda's Story: Dueling Beliefs

Rhoda repeatedly experienced being attracted to men who were unemployed, or who could not manage or save their money. In her work with me, Rhoda unearthed the following beliefs, handed down to her unconsciously by well-meaning parents. Logically, at first, she did not believe that she had these beliefs until she saw and felt how quickly she agreed with people who overtly held these opinions.

- Educated people think they are better than you and will hold your lack of education against you.
- Wealthy people got wealthy by using others and are neither generous nor trustworthy.
- Woman who marry educated, wealthy men always end up alone, manipulated, and cheated on.

These ideas were expressed both implicitly and explicitly by Rhoda's parents, because they wanted to protect her from a bad experience her mother had before she married Rhoda's high school-educated, hard-working father. Once she recognized

56

these filters, Rhoda, by now in her late 30s, had a few conversations with her parents. She told them what she was doing over and over again. She did not blame them. She simply revealed how the messages they gave her were well meaning and no longer useful. Her parents were pleased that she felt able to break the old cycle and find a good man. They reminded her cheerfully that grandchildren would be nice.

Next, Rhoda deliberately befriended and started hanging out with two wealthy girls in her neighborhood whom she'd met at the gym. Her thoughts changed as her views of wealthy people softened. After a few months, she started dating again. She went to new places with her new friends and met men that she typically would have avoided or criticized. Rhoda expressed amazement and relief when she told me that she actually had made friends (just friends—something she previously believed impossible) with two wealthy men who helped her with some business decisions and taught her to play golf. Eighteen months later, she met (and then married) a college professor who wasn't exactly rich but was indeed educated, good with money, had a steady job, and a good heart.

You probably have at least one friend who dates the same person over and over again—although that person may have a different name and face, the essential personality traits stay the same. Maybe you know a guy who dates women who want to be rescued and then dumps them, complaining to you that every new woman wants him only for his money, just like all the rest. Maybe you know a woman who dates "bad boys"—men who are emotionally distant risk takers—thinking that her love will magically change them into the "good boys" she really wants. The men don't change, and your friend keeps on complaining about what dogs men are. Let's face it, when you kiss a toad, all you get are slimy lips. Yes, sure, people can certainly respond positively to love and appreciation and people do certainly have the power to transform their lives, BUT the repeating pattern is a dead giveaway that these events are unconsciously designed to lead to the same unpleasant end. Wake up and smell the repetition. It stinks.[1]

Thirty Second Review

Now you know how your brain's drive to keep your being alive—your survival instincts coupled with childhood experiences—has provided you with a set of pattern recognition–reaction packages that we call "filters." When it comes to creating the life you want, some of those filters may be useful and worth hanging on to. Others have outlived their usefulness and have become obstacles, holding you back and giving you a bad case of "same crap, different day." To create and have the life that you want, you have to revise your filters.

CHAPTER 5

Take Responsibility (Response-Ability) for Your Life

"It is never too late to be who you might have been."
—George Eliot

Whether or not you have childhood issues that haunt you, you may never have consciously made the decision to become your own authority in life. You may still be relying on your parents, or unconsciously on your boss or your mate—to make decisions for you or fix your life. Sometimes as adults we start to blame circumstances or others instead of blaming parents, but the blame game is still a dead end road.

Your parents, teachers, and other authority figures are not to blame for whatever behavioral dead ends you may still end up in. You are capable of using your intelligence, present in mind and body, to notice what is and is not working for you now, especially once you have some practice identifying the habitual knee-jerk reactions. It's not rocket science or brain surgery. Hell, it isn't even as hard as learning to work the apps on your smartphone!

The first and absolutely necessary step in getting where you want to go is to make the decision to accept 100% responsibility for everything in your life right now. No, you don't control the weather or the state of the economy. But your assumptions, how you express emotions, and your interpretation of experiences are all yours. You are the source of your beliefs, assumptions, experiences, thoughts, expectations, emotions, and actions. You are responsible for the vast majority of the things that determine whether or not you have what you want, and whether or not you live with ease and a sense of mastery, or live a life dominated by stress and suffering. We're not talking about past lives and karma here, just the cause and effect that our thoughts, biases, beliefs, and actions generate.

This one realization can change your life completely, and for the better. *As long as you continue to believe that other people and outside forces are the cause of your unhappiness, nothing will change.* Do events and people contribute to your pain and pleasure? Of course they do, but your mind and your associations are the last stop, the final say on what you do with the input you get from the outside world.

This is not a suggestion to minimize disturbing events or to blame yourself. *Blame and responsibility are completely different things.* By taking 100% responsibility for your thoughts and emotions, today and every day, you generate the power to alter your circumstances. That power, the ability to act or take action, starts at the level of your thoughts and expectations. When you are clear about what you can change and what you can't, your actions become more directed and productive, issues take up less time, and circumstances have less emotional charge. In other words, you get less drama and more ease in your life. Response-ability, then is essentially the skill of noticing and redirecting automatic, knee-jerk reactions to minimize drama and maximize the outcome of your communication.

This responsibility for our own inner lives is what allows women who have been raped to recover without becoming perpetual victims, allows POWs to survive captivity, allows people to get over betrayal, affairs, and other disturbing events. The ordinary events in our ordinary lives are much easier to own responsibility for and yet we often react as if we have nothing to do with our own inner lives, blaming others and demanding that they change so we can avoid having to manage our own thoughts and emotions.

There are plenty people who waste their potential for happiness and satisfaction by holding on to the past, constantly referring to what they do not have, lingering over regrets, and wallowing in resentment. You may even know a few. We can and often do become prisoners of our own minds, when we tell ourselves that there is nothing we can do because some things in life just make us miserable. Of course you don't have control over everything (or anyone) that happens around you! *But how you react to what happens and how you interact with other people ultimately creates your experience.*

CLUE: When you find yourself living in the past or reliving a hurt ask the question, "HOW am I making myself (sad, angry, miserable)?" Then take responsibility for interrupting and redirecting the thoughts that you are using to torment yourself. If there is an action to take, or a conversation to be had, just do it.

HOW to Stop Playing the Blame Game

Owning responsibility for the events in your life does not mean accepting blame for bad things that happen. Blame and responsibility are not synonyms, and one of the biggest mistakes we make is confusing the two. We take the blame for things we did not cause and fail to take responsibility for circumstances we engineered. Blame comes with intention, a conscious awareness of cause and effect. If you point a loaded gun at someone's head and pull the trigger, yes, you are to blame for that particular hole in that person's head. If you walk down the street and a flower pot lands on your head and knocks you silly, are you to blame? Of course not. Are you responsible for your decision to walk down that street? Definitely. If you get food poisoning are you to blame? No. Were you responsible for picking the restaurant? Yes. Responsible but not to blame. Got it?

When you interpret what people say and do through the filter of believing that they set out to hurt your feelings, piss you off, or make you crazy, you are dancing with the devil of your own thoughts. When you get stuck blaming people for the way you feel, you are assuming that they should have known how you'd react, or that they intended to get under your skin. Yes, it can be difficult to sort out what part of a complicated mess belongs to whom. If somebody tells you they feel hurt over something you did or said, you can say, "I am sorry that you feel hurt" without having to defend, justify, or explain what you did. Likewise, when you are hurt or angry, you can let people know what is going on with you without blaming them, by *revealing what you are thinking and how you are feeling, rather than accusing.*

You can say, with whatever heat you feel, something like this: "When you went in the other room I felt hurt. I wanted you to stay and hear about the rest of my day!" rather than, "You don't give a damn about my day! Screw you for leaving the room, you never listen to me!" (Remember, "You never . . . " is a pretty good clue that your filters are showing.) Want to know what someone meant by their behavior? The only way to find out is to ask. I know, it's an edgy and innovative idea. "What were you thinking when you went in the other room while I was talking? I feel dismissed and unimportant."

Isn't it interesting that we can easily judge and blame some people for certain behaviors, but accept the same behavior in another? You might get cranky about someone showing up late to your dinner party, but if it's John, who is late to everything, always, you're more likely to start without him and chalk it up to his "Johnness" without taking the late arrival as a slight or disrespect or intentional. John may be forgiven carte blanche, while you may criticize and complain about the same lateness when it's your mother or your best friend who's late. That's a blame game.

So before you get out that mental label maker and attach meaning to actions, slapping "disrespectful," "mean," "insensitive," and "rude" stickers on people's foreheads, ask yourself if you have a surplus of these labels in your back pocket. Is this judgment a usual part of your vocabulary? *If it is, chances are very high that you have a filter that makes your experience of that person, or maybe people in general, appear to fulfill that expectation.* Moreover, when they don't fit the label, you may do things to "encourage" them to fulfill your expectations with subtle and not-so-subtle behaviors of your own. I can tell you that more often than not, we do get people to behave the way we assume they will—they live up (or down) to our labels.

As an adult, you and only you are responsible for the way you treat yourself and for how you allow others to treat you. As you become aware of what you don't like about your life and about the way people treat you or the way your gut locks up around somebody, there is NO ONE ELSE BUT YOU that has the power to make the changes to create a new result. Noticing what you do to make a bad thing worse is the first step in doing something new. Just notice what you do, and let blame go. Treat yourself and others with some compassion and humor and you will find the life overall becomes more pleasant.

HOW to Interrupt Yourself The Step-by-Step Way

Ok, so you've done some of the practices recommended to sharpen your noticing skills, and you are ready to take 100% responsibility for your experience. How will you do that? Here's how.

To revise the patterns that stop you:
- notice the clues (and ask your honest friends for their input)
- identify the pattern (I think this, I feel that, I react by doing/not doing)
- interrupt your thoughts and your behavior as quickly as you can (whether it's within a minute or the next day)
- challenge your old story about How Things Are,
- relax your defenses,
- ask, "What else could this mean?" (get a new story that's helpful)

- revise your thoughts,
- take new action,
- and then REPEAT the process every time you catch the old pattern that runs you into a ditch.

THE SHORT VERSION OF THESE INSTRUCTIONS:
NOTICE, INTERRUPT, REDIRECT, REPEAT

Here's the simplest place to start, right this instant. Just take a deep breath. Right now, go on. Take another, they're free. Good. Now one more ... go on, take a deep one. Can't hurt, you gotta breathe anyway.

Now for future reference: Irritated? Take a breath. Feeling hurt? Take a breath. Anxious, pissed off, afraid for no reason, worrying? Take a deep breath. Or three, or ten. Deep breathing changes your chemistry by putting pressure on your diaphragm, which triggers a nerve pathway to your brain that signals "Chill. Relax. No threat here." And in that little space between your thought and your breath, you have an opportunity to observe. So take that deep breath.

Yes, it's one of those over-used phrases that may call to mind every cheesy stress reduction tape you've ever heard, BUT taking a breath or two **really does** change your chemistry. It gives you a second or two to focus your awareness and to take the exit ramp off the Road to Repeating Useless Thoughts and Behaviors. It is a key to making accurate thin-slice assessments. So just do it.

Now that you've taken some breaths and you have some space, notice what you're thinking. Yeah, that's right, think about what you're thinking and the case you are building to prove how right you are. Identify the interpretation of events (your story, the meaning you assigned to events, the motive you assigned to people) that has you off to the races.

Now interrupt that repeating loop. Challenge the validity and reality of that story. Ask what else could this mean? How can I check out this assumption? Tell those voices, be they fearful, worried, angry, blaming, or some combination thereof, to shut up. Pipe down. Thank you, but I'm changing the channel now.

Then insert a new, different, more useful thought and behavior.

Practice Makes Permanent

Repeating an unwanted pattern? Just:
- Breathe
- Notice
- Interrupt
- Redirect
- Repeat

Do this repeatedly, and the way you experience the same circumstances will change as those automatic thoughts and emotions are revised. Your "story" will change. You may eventually wonder how you ever got so worked up, so often, about something so insignificant. Now THAT'S what we're talkin' about! Getting over a pattern requires enough repetition and emotional intensity to amend an existing filter.

It's like getting the train to switch tracks, and when it does that seamlessly, you end up with lovely scenery rather than gazing at acres of the garbage dump.

Emotions are chemical and electrical signals that flow through the body. They usually reach a peak and fade, unless they embed in your body through repetition that keeps the emotional signals alive. With repetition, they "stick," literally causing muscle tension and mental stress as you "brace" against the threat—even though the threat is imaginary. Similarly, revising the direction of your thoughts and emotions through repeatedly interrupting and redirecting the Reality Train will diminish, then amend the triggers that make your body clench in unpleasant expectation. (Aunt Helen's annoying voice and constant corrections are, let's face it, NOT a threat to anyone's survival.) And yes, when you "insert" a new thought, challenge your story, and redirect your thinking, you will feel weird . . . odd . . . not quite right at first. That's OK. That will shift.

It is up to you. You can keep feeling anxious, angry, or afraid because it's familiar and habitual, or you can feel those new sensations rolling through your body as you generate thoughts that direct you to feel calm, confident, indifferent, or at the very least, less reactive about what once got under your skin.

This is what one client, who had been experiencing anxiety and paralyzing suspicion ever since she started working, told me:

Wow, I finally caught what I was doing and flipped it. I was feeling so suspicious of my husband (again) that I couldn't sleep and got up thinking that I'd scroll through his text messages to see if there was anything incriminating. I just sat there and took a few breaths and said Ok, what the hell am I doing? And first I thought, "protecting myself." And I asked, "Is there a better way? Something else I can do?" and my urge was to wake my husband. Then I thought of all the reasons I shouldn't wake him—he'll be mad, he needs his sleep, he'll think I'm nuts, blah, blah, blah. But then I noticed I still wanted to wake him. I'd done that before, but woke him accusing him of infidelity and we got into an awful fight in the middle of the night. So I asked myself, "Really? Do you really think he's cheating?" and suddenly, as if the sun came out, I clearly got it. What I felt was inadequate, insecure, too busy and afraid that I wasn't being "enough" for my husband, and I thought surely he must be looking for someone who was kinder, more attentive. So I woke him and said, "I'm so afraid that I'm not giving you enough attention that I'll drive you away. I'm making myself miserable thinking that you'd just be happier with another woman that was home and had dinner on the table every day.

He wasn't mad, even though he didn't like being awakened. He told me that he did want to have more time with me but that he wasn't in any way thinking of trading me in for another woman. He made me laugh. I told him I was gonna check his phone and he—I couldn't believe it—he got it off the night stand and handed it to me. Then, after we talked a little about the kids we snuggled up. Just as I was drifting to sleep I remembered that when my mother discovered my father was having an affair she took us girls aside and told us "If you don't just stay home and attend to your man he'll run off and get his needs met elsewhere." So yeah, now I have a little chat with Mom coming up this week. And I feel good.

Practice makes permanent. Without repetition, the old pathway will reassert itself. This is why we so often have great new ideas and insights, then go back to doing the same old dumb stuff. The new habits **must be installed if they are to survive** competition from the dug-in old habits. Repeating this process will literally create a new pathway in your brain; a new way to get from "here" to "there" mentally and emotionally.

HOW to Sort Fact From Fiction

Brain research has revealed that we can, literally, change our minds. Our brains are known to be plastic, malleable, capable of growing new pathways and circuits throughout our lives. We can choose, consciously, to change our programming, to turn the detours into new roads. We can choose, consciously, to dump the beliefs, habits, and patterns, the filters that sabotage our attempts at having a happy, healthy, fulfilled life. We can revise those patterns with new beliefs, habits, and behaviors that create what we want in our lives.

Sometimes the first step is to sort out reality from delusion. This will help you get to the truth of things rather than live as if your assumptions and judgments are facts. Sure, sometimes our assessments are accurate, but quite often they're just a product of our habitual biases. Sometimes there's more pleasure in being wrong than in being right. Here is one example.

Alice's Story: The Mean Boss

Alice complained about how unfeeling and nasty her boss was. Awful and mean, she said. Her evidence? Every Wednesday when she arrived 10 minutes late for work after taking her child to physical therapy (and he *knew* why she was late, and he *said* it was ok) her boss was nearly always in a cranky, door-slamming, order-barking mood. Alice assumed that he was angry at her for being late, that his anger was his way of punishing her for being "tardy" (her word, and there's a clue) and that this behavior (say it is ok, then punish me for it) made him a rotten person. After all, he knew what she was doing and why she was late, and she was less than 10 minutes late and it was only once a week. She was ready to quit and walk out. Oh brother.

I told her to have a conversation with him the following Wednesday, and to plan the meeting ahead of time so he knew she wanted to talk as soon as she came to work. When Alice arrived he ushered her into his office and then proceeded to slam the door and toss things around his desk. Before she could get out her well-rehearsed questions, he shocked her by saying: "Listen, I just hate Wednesdays! I play cards with the guys Tuesday nights, and then Wednesday morning I have to listen to my wife bellyache all morning long, while I nurse my hangover and pretend to be paying attention to her. Wednesday morning is her revenge for my boys' night out!"

Well, Alice started laughing, and then so did her boss. She clearly saw her filter and the whole tar pit of thoughts, emotion, story line, and behaviors that came with the package. She also got a good view of her boss's patterns! He was not her mother. He was not punishing her. She was glad she was wrong.

For Alice, the strategy of becoming still and silent when Mommy was angry may have worked well for childhood self-preservation, reducing or eliminating experiences of being rejected, ignored, yelled at, or hit when she was small. That same strategy, when employed as an adult, prevented her from learning how to resolve conflicts or stand up for herself, and frequently kept her from seeing what was really happening in the moment. If the experience became "too intense," she would just check out and think about anything but the present moment.

CLUE: If you feel frightened and get quiet rather than speak your mind, vent an emotion or reveal the truth, you've got a blind spot— you're running an old fear pattern and you've just found a filter, or maybe more than one.

As an adult, "vanishing" or becoming silent in the presence of assertive, loud, or angry adults, or when feeling rejected, is not a useful strategy for resolving conflict. That danger you react to is in the past, stored as a memory and very likely completely under the radar of conscious awareness. In other words, when the boss yells or the computer guy shows up cranky from being up all night with his newborn, you surely won't be thinking about your mother. Even though you may consciously understand the reasons why the boss is upset or the computer guy is cranky, when someone gets loud your emotional brain may still generate a chain of chemical messages that you experience as fear and stress. In that moment, you may react by clamming up and shutting down, and find yourself speechless or unable to move. Meanwhile, your conscious mind is busy using that powerful reason-making part of your brain to explain, justify, and defend your (six-year-old's) reactions and behaviors.

What to do when fear takes over? Feel the fear. Take a breath. Put your attention firmly on something concrete in the present (the feeling of your clothes, the color of the carpet, the steam rising from a coffee cup) and allow yourself to unhook and relax a bit. Do it again, and you might "wake up" in the moment, clear that the fear was a hiccup, or you might discover that you have something to say, a question to ask, a resentment to reveal, or a request to make.

We're focusing here on fear and anger because most of us don't handle those well, whether we're the one who is angry or we're faced with other people's anger. This will work in the presence of any strong emotion: feel it, breathe, focus on sensations in the present moment, and gain a bit of clarity. Practice this, and you will raise your awareness of HOW you keep yourself from being effective in your job or relationships. This is HOW you can begin the process of waking up out of that old trance, breathe, find your voice, and change the old program. With practice, we can disrupt the cycle until "angry" no longer represents an immediate threat to our survival.

Let's revisit the example of a yelling boss.

When you find yourself asking questions like, "Why is the boss yelling at me? What did I do to set her off?" " Why doesn't he/she like me?" interrupt your run-away thinking (taking a deep breath is a quick method), then ask "How am I scaring myself? " "What's the worst that can happen?" or even, "How is this familiar?" or maybe "How do I contribute to having this experience?" When you have the answers to some of those questions, then ask "How can I interpret this differently?" And, "What if this yelling has nothing to do with me?"

Now the absolute worst case (the boss beats you up or kills you) isn't gonna happen, and you KNOW it. What's the next worst? The boss fires you? OK, then would you live another day to find another job? Yes. So now you have a bit of space between the event—a raised voice—and your usual reaction—fear, getting quiet, hiding, yelling back and escalating, leaving the room and slamming the door, gossiping and getting others to agree how right you are, whatever it is you do that never gets you anywhere near what you want. *In that space you have a choice, and you can choose to respond consciously rather than react.*

That's not to suggest that you put up with someone whose idea of communication is yelling in your face. The point is that when you can create a space between your unconscious reaction and your actual situation you create freedom to consciously choose how to respond. You have a chance to accurately predict the level of threat (she yells, goes in the office, comes out later like nothing ever happened = no real threat) and you might do something other than wilt, throw a tantrum, or exit like a frightened child. ANY new behavior is a step up. You could simply request, "Please, lower the volume of your voice." You could quit, yell back, make an appointment with the boss to discuss how you feel, write up a formal complaint, laugh it off, ask for a transfer, or even suggest an anger management program! The choices an adult has are many, but the reaction of a child is only one note—knee-jerk survival.

The threat-fear-control reaction is only one example of many, many patterns of belief and behavior that can keep us from the life we want. You might react with anger and intensity when faced with the inefficiency (or imperfection or stupidity or disloyalty—fill in your favorite complaint here) of others, as if your life depended on getting someone to live up to your expectations. That's a reaction guaranteed to throw a wrench into the way you relate to others. Face it, an irritable judgmental perfectionist is about as much fun as a passive-aggressive control freak.

Remember, the way things get wired together is influenced by two critical factors: repetition and emotional intensity. Some patterns are pretty obviously linked to an old survival/protection cycle. Others may be just useless learned beliefs that may be more subtle, but just as likely to derail your ability to resolve conflict or have what you want.

Many beliefs, for example, have nothing to do with choice, or logic, but with the drilling in of an idea and the emotional intensity that gets passed onto us. Those beliefs (thoughts + beliefs = expectations) then generate pre-determined ways that we react to things.

Beliefs are very potent, because our minds have the ability to substitute our story about reality for reality itself. Even in the face of hard evidence, beliefs often trump reality. Those pesky filters blind us to

71

whatever does not fit our belief structure. Just look to history and you will find countless examples of this. There are STILL people who believe that the world is flat, that there was never a moon landing, and that Elvis is alive! While we may like to believe that only true wing-nuts are this delusional, we are mistaken. We do this in our everyday lives all the time. Every time we jump to a conclusion and act on an assumption as if it were the truth, we are inserting belief (imagination) in place of reality. We are seeing what we want to see rather than what is actually in front of us. This process even revises our memory to fit our beliefs.

Here's a concrete example of beliefs driving actions:

A young boy, living in poverty, is provided with a free education in the context of religion. The beliefs and behaviors he learns in school and at daily worship services provide him with comfort, a sense of belonging, some escape from terrible living conditions, and belief in an afterlife with God in Paradise as a reward for serving God on Earth. As an adolescent, he feels an overwhelming call to do God's work, although he also has an increasing streak of self-righteousness, and tries to prove his righteousness by making sacrifices that others lack the piety to make. Are you thinking "priesthood?" How about suicide bomber?

We all sometimes find ourselves in situations when friends, family, lovers, coworkers, or bosses trigger a strong reaction pattern. When we get stuck in these sudden emotional storms we stop listening to our gut, our inner guidance. We override both the current information available to us in our bodies and the evidence in front of us by distracting ourselves with rationalizations, justifications and judgments. *We then mistake other people's behavior as the source of our suffering*, when in fact it is our interpretation of their motive and/or our imagined version of what they are thinking about us, and/or our underlying fears and suspicion of others (and the stress it causes) that is the real source of our misery. As we do this over and over again, we also eventually train the people around us to treat us the way that we expect them to, although sometimes that takes a lot of work!

CLUE: When you think you know the meaning or motive behind a person's action or words without doing a reality check, your filters are showing. When you react to what they said or did based on your assumption, you are going over the cliff.

Don't believe everything your mind tells you. Challenge your annoying thoughts. When in doubt, check it out—by bringing your attention to the sensations in your body. Developing your sensory awareness will cure some of your reality blindness.

CHAPTER 6

Resonance and Revising: A Little Help from Your Friends

"One of the blessings of old friends is that you can afford to be stupid with them." —Ralph Waldo Emerson

Millions of years of evolution have given us minds and nervous systems that are in constant communication with the minds and nervous systems of other human beings. You may notice this when you are with family and friends and you experience subtle changes in mood or pick up on others' thoughts. We held on to this subtle communication because the ability to communicate quickly when there is danger or prey nearby is a valuable survival skill. We are not alone in this. All mammals have this ability, which is what is going on when you feel sad or sick and your faithful though usually aloof kitty suddenly curls up on your chest or faithful Fido follows you around the house.

This "resonance" between two (or more) nervous systems is a felt experience, a sharing of biological signals that in turn prompt chemical changes and resulting emotions, thoughts, and reactions in those around us every minute of every day. It is an endless and elegant multi-partnered dance through which we share data and create stability. We are not designed to function alone. In fact, in isolation, we do not regulate ourselves well and are far more prone to illness and death from all causes. This is why solitary confinement for prolonged periods will literally drive people out of their minds. (For more in this, see Dean Ornish, *Love and Survival: 8 Pathways to Intimacy and Health.*)

When you walk through a crowded room of strangers at a party you are receiving and sending thousands of signals. The inner life and emotions, the dreams and thoughts, the fears and darkness within each of us is broadcast by our nervous system each second of each day. People sitting around a dinner table enjoying a meal bond more deeply because of the shared experience of eating. People singing around a campfire or listening in the darkness to a storyteller are bonded by the experience of sound. Walking alone through a parking lot you may suddenly feel your scalp prickle or feel an electric sensation that triggers fear before you are fully aware that you are being observed by someone from the darkness. All of these experiences are a product of our survival-oriented brain.

We've all had the experience of being swept up in the emotions of others. Attend a sporting event surrounded by fans and it is hard not to get emotionally attached to the outcome of the game. Go see a rock band you're not all that fond of and you'll find yourself dancing and cheering with the rest of the crowd. Sherry has a friend who has a beautiful soprano voice and frequently sings in church and at weddings, but refuses to sing at funerals because, as she puts it, "It doesn't matter whether or not I know the deceased, I 'catch' the grief in the room and end up in tears."[1]

The same brain systems and functions that produce this resonance also revise our behavior. On the most fundamental biological level, whom we spend time with directly influences our nervous system. People stimulate our thoughts, trigger old unfinished business, inspire us, frustrate us, support us, wake us from our illusions, or help us stay lulled to sleep. This is the process through which we tend to adopt the beliefs, thoughts, and behaviors of those we spend a lot of time with.

Our mothers knew all about this when they warned us not to hang out with "those rotten kids." Mom was right. She knew that by being in their company you would be far more likely to do things you wouldn't otherwise do. Despite your indignation and you assertion that you simply would not do the things she feared you'd do, you also knew the truth. In the company of risk-takers, ordinarily reserved people do take more risks. We all have the desire to be accepted in a group of people, and the source of that desire lies in our brains. In the company of others our nervous systems do a very interesting dance, relaying information, synchronizing breathing patterns, decoding chemical messages, and generally attuning to each other. Thoughts and actions that might make you blush when you're alone can become a source of excitement and pleasure when you're with others who regularly enjoy those things.

Let's look at some ways that resonance and the revisions that result from your interactions with others can be used to create the life that you want.

HOW Friends Can Help Each Other With Revisions

First of all, take a second to recognize that a revision is exactly that. It's generating a (re)new Vision (images, complete with thoughts and emotions) that informs our subconscious of where we want to go.

Many thoughts and background beliefs lead us to mistakenly assume that we can't have, shouldn't have, or don't deserve something that we want. For some people, the excitement that would naturally and pleasantly come from the challenge of exploring new jobs, relationships, and other desires is replaced with the unpleasant-though equally exciting struggle we call "drama."

We all know someone who ends up in one drama after another. Maybe it's one crappy job situation after another, or someone who trusts an untrustworthy business partner over and over, or someone who constantly hires people who can't or won't do the job they are hired to do, or someone who repeatedly comes so very close to success and then finds a way to fail that just wasn't their fault. Watching these dramas unfold around you, you may be clear that your friends are simply picking the same person—with different names and faces—or the same situation and expecting that this time it will be different. This time the relationship will work, the new hire will succeed, the new business partnership will thrive, the new job will be a perfect fit. Except it isn't.

In science, this is called "experimental reproducibility"—that is, doing the same thing over and over and getting the same results. Doing the same thing over and over and expecting *different* results is one definition of insanity. Or as the folks at Despair, Inc. so eloquently put it, "Dysfunction: The only consistent feature in all of your dissatisfying relationships is you." As a strategy for getting what you say you want, well, it's never ever gonna work. The key to freedom from ever-repeating misery is to grasp what the results are telling you.

It's pretty simple, really. *If you do what you've always done, you get what you've always had.*

Your friends' and acquaintances' dramas, and the way they create them (through filters) are probably obvious to you. Their behavior may have you scratching your head in bewilderment and shaking your head in resignation. Well here's a reality check: *the odds are very good that a few of your friends look at some things you do and shake their heads too.*

It is very likely that you have a few unconscious habits that rob you of some satisfaction, stop you from going after big dreams, get you to settle for less, or prevent you from having something you want. Depending on your history and how you adapted to it, filters may help you to be successful in one area of life and fail miserably in another. How many times have you heard, "She's so smart, how can she be such an idiot with men?" or conversely, " She'd never put up with that from her own husband, why does she let the boss treat her like crap?" Of course, there are many variations on this theme.

It is likely that you do not see that your inability to have what you say you want is the product of your flawed thoughts, expectations, and actions. It is more likely that you see that failure as the product of "reality." "That's just the way _____ (men, women, the world, politicians, the economy, my parents, jobs, etc.) are."

We recognize the quirky flaws in others with a clarity that they cannot access directly. We often assume, and therefore take for granted, that people must know what they are doing. So even when we notice someone we love repeating behaviors that are self-sabotaging, we say things like "Well, that's just Jim" and ignore, or at least never mention, the behavior. What we don't realize is that the pernicious form of self-sabotage we're pretending not to notice is visible to nearly everyone *but* Jim. When we notice the same behavior in people we aren't so fond of, we may allow ourselves to sit in judgment or convince ourselves that the behavior we dislike is willful or even directed at us. In fact, for those people, just like our pal Jim, it's not about us, it's merely part of their wiring.

We tend to assume that if our friends or family members wanted to change the behaviors that cost them health, happiness, or money, they'd get on the ball and make some changes. What we don't see is that they aren't conscious of that behavior. Like a song that they learned with the wrong words, their behavior plays out unconsciously every time the melody of matching circumstances is heard.

Isn't it fascinating that a behavior we accept easily in our pal Jim—for example, that he is always running late—may be the source of ongoing fights when our coworker or mate has the same unfortunate habit? We cause ourselves an extra dose of aggravation when, after we have told that hapless clod that this behavior bugs the hell out of us and he agreed to knock it off, he keeps on doing it. No matter what he may say, there's a mighty slim chance he will be able to keep his word. Being late is a habit that has something special that the NEW habit does NOT have: repetition and emotional intensity. So don't give up, Repeat, remind, request, and then reward any on-time behavior with a big smile and a pat on the back. Really. That'll help.

Our pal's habit of lateness may be the product of a very old filter (late for school = avoid getting picked on by the bullies, therefore late = safe), or a newer one (late is a passive aggressive way to make sure that you WILL notice me) but either way, until the new behavior has enough emotional intensity (a pleasure reward—people notice and appreciate me when I am on time or early) and repetition, the old one will sometimes automatically take over.

CLUE: When someone repeatedly says they want to stop a bad habit, and you see them continuing the behavior, over and over, they could probably use some help in noticing and interrupting that thing that they do so well.

So, when you have asked a friend, intimate partner, or co-worker to change a behavior and that person has agreed to make the change, it will take time for the new behavior to become a habit. In the meantime, nagging, scolding, and shaming won't help. What works are reminders that are assertive and kind, and that support the formula: *Notice, Interrupt, Redirect, Repeat—and Reward. In the meantime you get to work on something else—your patience.*

If (and *only if*) your friend genuinely agrees ("I really want to!" not, "I know I should" or "I know you want me to") that she (or he) wants to change a behavior, then the two of you can become allies in the rewiring project—you two versus the filter. Here's how.

HOW to Be an Ally for Change

Agree that you will interrupt their behavior, or remind your pal of the agreement ahead of time when you think they are likely to repeat the old behavior. When the old behavior reoccurs, make the interruption or reminder playfully, "Hey, you're doing that thing you do that you asked me to interrupt!" Don't be mean or shaming. Don't act like a parent. This is not you facing off with your pal as if they were the subject of an intervention. You are providing the interruption—just a reality check—that gives your pal the ability to wake up and choose a new thought or behavior. The crucial part of this is that they must *want* the benefit of the new behavior. (If they are putting up with your reminders to please you, or to make it look like they are working on it when they could not care less, then they will not change the behavior.)

This works in the other direction as well. Although some of your patterns may be mostly invisible to you, the people you work, live, and hang out with undoubtedly see a few things about you that you are blind to. People who are close to you (family, long-standing friends, coworkers) see what you're doing, and they usually think you must know, too. So you can begin by asking them, "Do you see me doing/saying something over and over again that guarantees that I don't get the ____ (job, spouse, education, etc.) I say I want?"

When you can't depend on the idiot that stressed you out in the first place—that is, your own mind—it is very useful to have friends who will shake you awake when they see you've drifted off course. Pick someone to talk to who has what you want, someone who does not share in or support the excuses you may use for your repeated frustrations.

Here's what I remind my clients when they resist letting their friends help out.

Nobody can see your crap better than your friends. Even though I do this for others, I call in the troops when I get stuck, because I know it's the fastest way out of the weeds. When my mind freezes over, having someone else to wake me up is useful. I usually make a call or two and reveal how I'm making myself crazy, which may include what I'm obsessively thinking, or that I'm not taking action about something that's important to me and I don't know what's keeping me from moving forward. Often, with a good kick in the ass that may include a few solid suggestions, a blunt observation, and or an agreement to go do something specific and new, I wake up and get back into the game.

Sometimes those days take unexpected and delightful turns, leading me down forgotten paths inspiring me to create innovative ways to get things done. The reality is that we are constantly regulated by the people around us. My friends laugh with me, laugh at me, and poke me when I seem to have gone unconscious in my life. I like that. I welcome it.

In cultivating your own way to redirect your thinking and create new roads in your mind, you do two things: develop friendships with people who are pretty awake in their own lives—that is, people who are mostly at ease, pretty satisfied with life, genuinely happy, and mostly kind—and enroll them to give you a friendly whap on your noggin should you fall asleep at the wheel.

The first step is to request that they **tell you clearly in direct language** (not hint or suggest) what they observe about your beliefs and behaviors and what they think may be your glitch. Ask them to answer the question: "How do you think I contribute to having this happen over and over?" **Then shut your pie-hole and listen.** REALLY listen. Notice any urge to defend, justify, or explain your beliefs or behavior, but keep your yap shut. These thoughts are just the "used filter salesman" trying to distract you from catching on to your self-sabotage cycle. So shush. Shhhh. Tssst. Listen. Ask them to repeat if necessary. And then ask them to make a couple of suggestions and get you to agree to some kind of action, even if is just to take a break or get a second opinion before you move forward.

Here are some real life observations people have made of their friends and relatives that were both accurate and helpful:

"You want a promotion, but miss deadlines and dress like you fell out of the thrift shop discount bin."

"Every good guy you've dated has had to put up with you being late, critical, and flirting with other guys, but you treat the jerks you date like gold."

"How can you expect to be "respected" by your co-workers when you gossip about them constantly? Do you think they don't find out what you say?"

"The real reason you did not make partner is because you have a reputation for being a bully and a womanizer. In other words, you are not kind to women. We don't want that here. Two of our top partners are women. You've got to wake the hell up."

"You say you want a happy family life more than anything, and yet you are dismissive of your wife and ignore your kids. If I pulled that crap on my wife, she'd be long gone. I have watched you at company events. Flirting right in front of your wife doesn't win you any points either."

"To make you a manager, we have to see you being more assertive and making decisions without trying to please everyone. You are too careful, too hung up in being perfect, and, as a result, things rarely get done on time."

"I can't believe how much you treat your husband like a kid. I mean, he's a guy but he's not a moron. You sure sound like his mother. I feel embarrassed for him when you do that. If you sighed and rolled your eyes like that at me, I'd smack you. You say you want him to romance you, but ewww, you act like mom."

"You want more time but you don't say 'no' to anybody, then you get annoyed and act overwhelmed and put out. Nobody has a gun to your head. Just say 'no' or say, 'I'm overextended,' or even 'I'm tired.' Really, no one will think less of you. Quit being the victim. It's not appealing."

"Mom, when you jump in to do things for me that I can and want to do for myself it just pisses me off. I don't feel grateful, I just feel annoyed. When I do want your help, I promise I will ask. You do that with Dad too. Then you are always tired and you come off as a martyr. Nobody likes that about you. Relax. Have more fun. Let everybody fix their own lives."

Each of these comments may have been hard for the recipient to hear, but they in every case were exactly the wake up call that helped each of them to get a grip on how to get what they said they wanted. Now, here's what to do with the information you got.

If you get this kind of feedback and become aware of what you have been doing, ask your friends for reminders to help you interrupt the old noise. Yep, tell people that you are aware (and maybe even appalled) at how you've been doing whatever it is that you're doing. Be simple and clear. Remember, that a habitual behavior takes over quickly, like the way words of a song come to mind when a melody evokes them. At first, you may have to make the correction after the fact, or in midstream, and that's OK. You may have to say yes, then go back and say "no." Most people will acknowledge and appreciate you for your efforts. Of course, some will not. Take that as a sign of your progress, too.

The Paradox of Change

You can't change anyone but yourself. For your own sanity (and frankly, to be in touch with reality) you have got to give up hoping, wishing, manipulating, teaching, leading, and convincing other people to change. In fact, when you really accept that managing your OWN life is a full time job, and you consistently put your attention on your own thoughts, reactions, and behaviors, you find that you automatically lay off the people around you. The more you notice and interrupt your knee jerk reactions to people and events, the more relaxed you become with who you are and the more understanding and accepting of others. That doesn't mean that you have to put up with or tolerate behavior you don't want. It does mean that you can come to a realization that allows you to make choices without taking the behavior of others so damned personally!

Hello? Did you hear that? *You can make choices without taking the behavior of others so personally.* This one shift in awareness is worth the cost of this book alone.

Here's an example:

I once witnessed an argument in which a woman (we'll call her Flora) who believed that "all men cheat, period" tried desperately to convince her best friend, Frieda, that Frieda's husband of eight years would eventually cheat on her (if he hadn't already). Flora cited eleven cases in which women she knew "trusted their rat bastard husbands" and then the rat bastards were found out to be "doing the nasty"—even though they came to this conclusion based mostly on their suspicions rather than real evidence. Flora neglected to mention that she'd met most of these women at a support group for newly divorced women — these were women who shared and reinforced her beliefs and stories. Three months later all hell broke loose and Frieda threw Flora out of her house for trying (trying hard, I was told) to seduce Frieda's husband during a weekend barbeque. Flora said she was just trying to save her pal from a big letdown. Apparently she thought that the experience of having your best friend attempt to play tonsil hockey with your husband would be a smaller letdown. Not coincidentally, Flora had a history of dating married men. Frieda and her husband (whom she trusted) had a conversation about the incident, concluded that they felt bad about Flora, told Flora that they forgave her, and had the good sense not to invite her to barbeques, though they did invite her to spend Thanksgiving with them when they knew she had no place else to go. Flora declined.

Imagine being able to realize that somebody you are often upset with is absolutely not being "mean" or "disrespectful" to you, she is simply repeating unpleasant behavior that is unconsciously running her life. It isn't about you, and it isn't personal. You are then free to make a choice to accept the behavior as part of the package or to steer clear of the person and what they do, *without going through the drama that goes with trying to force people to meet your expectations.* You can come to accept the behavior or let him or her go without gossip and ridicule. What a relief!

The paradox is, when you make these kinds of changes in your own life, as you revise the way you think and react, the people around you shift. You can't change them, but when you transform your own understanding, when you change how you dance the resonance dance, every single person in your life will change. Oh yeah. Has to happen. Happy day! Every person you dance with will adjust to who you are today, some effortlessly and subconsciously, some with a knowing smile, others feeling something's "wrong" and resisting every new step of the way.

As you wake up to yourself, you offer a subconscious invitation to everyone you know to wake a little bit. Some will welcome the shift in you. Others will get mad. A few may vanish. New people will appear. Some of the behaviors of others that used to upset you begin to lose that power over you. The people around you who are accustomed to being able to manipulate your behavior may feel confused and threatened. Some of your old crowd, the ones you picked because they also had beliefs and filters that limited the possibilities for success, will not be able to understand what has happened to you. They will be easy to spot. Instead of celebrating your success, they will see you as a traitor, a sellout, or become jealous. Or they will smile and say, "Good for you" then try to sabotage your progress any which way they can.

The ones who prefer to hang on to the past, and those who count on you to commiserate or to help perpetuate their own delusions through your agreement or your silence, will get cranky and resistant and they will wonder—possibly out loud—what the hell is wrong with you. In fact some people will resist so much they'll try really hard to get you to think and react the Old Way and will pull out all the stops to piss you off. That's OK. With practice, you'll see through their bluster and dramatics to the fear underneath. They fear that their own paper dragons are clearly visible and that in your presence, their usual old complaints and blame games will fall on deaf ears. They can't keep up the pretense in their lives without co-conspirators to help hold the grand illusion in place.

If you've been doing a familiar (dysfunctional) dance with someone and over a few weeks or months you change your steps, your partner will find it unsettling at best, and if he doesn't like change or is very attached to the old dance, there may come a time when you need to make the choice to just stop dancing. Sometimes letting people go without a fuss, and without making them wrong, is simply the best way to take care of yourself.

Becoming happier, more grounded, self-aware, calmer, and more honest essentially triggers an automatic sorting system that effortlessly allows you to become closer to the people who are open to those qualities, and simultaneously release relationships in which suffering, blame, and limitation are requirements. Really, who needs that crap? Not you, or you wouldn't be reading this book.

Wendy's Story: Awareness in Action

Wendy's husband, Fred, although not very attentive to her, worked hard to keep up their house, came home on time, did manly chores like taking out the trash and mowing the lawn, and fell asleep by nine every night. Sure, he loved her cooking and appreciated how clean the house was, how smart she was, complimented her on doing their taxes, he liked how she researched things for the house and he was complimentary about the articles she wrote as a freelance reporter for the local paper. But Wendy wanted more. Wendy wanted more sex, more attention, and most of all, she wanted Fred to tell her she was beautiful, to want her.

She became aware of the way she played small, held herself back at work, and put up with the bare minimum of what she wanted from others, Fred included. She became conscious of the way she'd used being fat as an excuse her whole life to avoid doing things she was afraid to do. Those things included having a more exciting relationship with her husband. She took action. She found a mentor at the newspaper and hired a personal trainer. She decided to save money and pay for a great vacation, the honeymoon they never had.

Wendy asked for and got a full-time job at the paper and stared losing weight. She expected Fred to be thrilled. She expected romance and celebration. What she got instead first annoyed and then terrified her. After the first 40 pounds came off, Fred started calling her several times a day to ask her what she was doing and who she was with. At first Wendy liked the calls, but when they became more frequent and started to include digs about her co-workers, and "playful" accusations about being interested in other men, she told him to quit calling her when she was working. Another 10 pounds came off, and he started showing up unexpectedly at her workplace. When she was out of the office working on a story when he showed up, that evening at home he grilled her, asking accusatory questions and not believing her answers. Wendy was afraid he was going to get violent. She begged him to go to a therapist. He flatly refused.

Finally, after the final 10 pounds came off and Wendy in fact had a brief affair with a guy at work, she and Fred ended up in couples therapy. Fred revealed that he "knew" she would dump him as soon as she started losing weight. He admitted he'd been afraid that he couldn't "keep up with her" or measure up to her new image. He called her ungrateful. Manipulative. A liar. Wendy was flabbergasted. And furious. She asked him at the first session if they could try again, (he'd said no) and by the fifth session, she recognized how well he had played into her resigned, "making do" filter. *Wendy then realized that she had picked him because his fears—of being left behind, of not being good enough—and his expectation that just by being a "good boy" he deserved a reward— matched her own fears and expectations all too well.*

She admitted the part she played in her own misery by not communicating with Fred more clearly about what she wanted. He blamed her. He said she changed. He wanted things back the way they were. She said that wasn't possible. She asked for a divorce and then she did a remarkable thing. Wendy told Fred that she loved him, would always love him, and she thanked him for the part he played in helping her wake up to what she was doing to herself.

She said, "I do think I would have sold myself out for a few kind words and a little more sex. I wouldn't have come this far, felt this secure about who I am, and what I can do. I appreciate you for what you did, and I'm sorry you are pissed off and sad." Although at the time her words never made it past Fred's need to be right and stay angry, they became the foundation on which they built a friendship three years later. By then they were both remarried; Wendy to a doctor and Fred to an overweight cocktail waitress.

Do You Suffer From "Birds of a Feather Syndrome?"

When you dump jigsaw puzzle pieces out on a table, the easiest thing to do is to find all the pieces with a flat side or two and build the frame, or outer edge of the picture. The people that "frame" your life influence you and sometimes reinforce the very beliefs and habits you would be better off without. When we become unconscious slaves to this "Birds of a Feather syndrome," the people we surround ourselves with can help us stay stuck in the beliefs and behaviors that prevent us from having what we want.

We tend to surround ourselves with people who agree with us. At first glance this seems both obvious and reasonable. Why would we hang around with people with whom we did not agree? Problems arise when the people we surround ourselves with actually help us stay stuck in the mental muck that prevents us from having what we say we want.

What would you think about a woman who struggled to get sober then went right back to hanging out in the bar with her former drinking buddies, and going to the same parties with her boozy family members? You'd think her chances of staying sober were about zero, and you'd be right. What about the person who struggles to lose weight, reaches his goal, and then joins a gourmet baking club. Smart choice? Hardly. There's no difference between the alcoholic working as a bartender and the recently divorced woman who is convinced that all men are scum and who regularly has lunch with a cluster of single women who repeat and reinforce the same demeaning stories about men.

CLUE: Check to see if you have a bad case of Birds of a Feather Syndrome keeping you stuck in the same old unhappy re-runs. If the people you hang with are ALL "victims," or hate women, or think men are idiots, or blame their parents, or have low esteem, then get out there and meet new people NOW!

We tend to hang out with people who agree with *our interpretation of events*—like those birds of a feather who flock together. *We then use this agreement to reinforce our filters and actions no matter how illogical or insane they may be.*

If you look for evidence to support your beliefs so that you can be right and feel the security of your rightness, you will always find it. Think not? There are people who still believe that we never landed on the moon. People who believe despite all evidence to the contrary that the world is flat, others that think that people and dinosaurs lived together, as if "The Flintstones" were a freakin' documentary. Where would these people be if they didn't hang around each other in tight little groups that rigorously protect and defend their delusions?

You will attract, and be attracted by, people who share your beliefs, have similar stories of How Things Are, and interpret their experiences the same way you have. You'll all get to believe you are right, but none of you will get what you say you want. Begin to pay attention to the overlapping beliefs and behaviors in the people you like to gossip with, complain to, or get comfort from. Chances are you'll find some clues to how you generate or sustain the illogical beliefs, stories, and filters that have you stuck somewhere on a flat world with a pet named "Dino."

When we hang out with people who hold the same inaccurate view of reality, the same prejudices, and the same fears, we get the wrong kind of support. We get support in believing that we are blameless and that the object of our ridicule or contempt is at fault for our misery. We get support in believing that our version of things is fact, that people, the world, women, men, or some other group really ARE "that way." We continue to be right, resigned, and rigid as well as unhappy. It doesn't help so much to be convinced that you are right if it costs you all possibility of a satisfying relationship, or work, or health now, does it?

Madeline Hecks, in *Blind Spots: Why Smart People Do Dumb Things*, observes that "[o]ur knee jerk dismissal of people whose views seem stupid to us prevents us from having the conversations we most need to have." ***Just because you get people to agree with you doesn't mean your interpretation, your version of reality, is accurate.*** When it comes to having what we say we want, often it is the people who don't agree with our opinions, beliefs, and stories about How Things Are who have the most to offer us.

HOW to Make "Birds of a Feather Syndrome" Work for You

The good news is that we can use this resonance with others consciously to loosen up our thinking and expand our lives in the right direction. We entrain more easily to the healthy, useful, supportive experiences like gratitude, compassion, and altruism than we do to the slide into depression, anger, and sadness. This is why we can be miserably unhappy and find ourselves feeling great relief after a visit from an upbeat and compassionate friend. We revise each other for the better.

All of us have the power and ability (even without this book!) to recognize and revise the filters and patterns that are in our way. Some people figure out how to revise their limiting patterns when, by trial and error, something new and pleasant happens—and they notice what they did differently, and repeat it. Some people even completely revise their unwelcome patterns just by hanging around with the right people. Nope. Not kidding. It's as if you had a magic hat that prevented you from seeing dogs, and you therefore have no of evidence that dogs exist, and might go to great lengths to prove to your dog-loving friend that what he's really got is a big funny-looking cat. Ridiculous as this may seem, filters and convictions do work that way. The good news is, your friend—who loves dogs and wants you to love them, too—may be able to convince you to take off that hat, and suddenly you're seeing dogs.

In the same way that the changes you make for the better invite your friends to change, too, the simple act of hanging out with people who are successful, happy, and have the kind of life that you want changes you. You start thinking the way they think, believing what they believe, and then you begin repeating their behaviors until at some point, you realize that you have shifted, and that having what you want is easier and more fun than you thought it could be.

CLUE: When you meet people who have something you want, do you feel bitter and start making assumptions about how they got it to excuse or justify your inability to get it? One of the best and easiest ways to shift your perspective is to hang out with people who easily get and effortlessly keep whatever it is that you want and that eludes you.

Friends can reinforce what you have going for you, too. If you are genuinely happy in your marriage and your friends are happy in theirs, great. You can, just by hanging out together, support each other and reinforce the ideas and behaviors that keep relationships happy and vibrant. Ditto for your work, health, weight, overall satisfaction or any other issue that runs through your mind and body daily. *Stay near the people who disagree with your views, make you think, help you grow, and have what you say you want.*

You will find that as you stop believing everything you think is reality, and begin revising your filters, you will be more inclined to be around people whose beliefs and expectations are more "tuned" to the experiences and the life that you want. As your perspective broadens, your old, narrow view and the people who are still stuck in it lose their appeal. The poor kid who becomes wealthy, the fat girl who loses weight, the drug addict who gets clean, all have something in common. To keep what they have created day after day, they stopped hanging out with people who commiserate about how hard it is to change and who do little to improve their lives.

CHAPTER *7*

Emotions, Honesty, and Authenticity

*"Be who you are and say what you feel, because those who
mind don't matter and those who matter don't mind."*
—Dr. Seuss

E-Motions Are Energy-In-Motion

When you were very young, you knew what to do with emotions: cry and sob when hurt or sad, giggle and laugh and squeal when happy, yell and stomp when angry. You were aware that emotions run through you, taking you for a ride then leave you feeling subdued, relaxed, or at least back to neutral. Many of us learned that out-loud and full expression of intense emotions was frowned upon, and we learned to fear emotional intensity because reprimand or punishment often followed.

Repression of emotions under limited circumstances can be a useful survival tool. It helps to be able to ignore fear, anger, or despair when your life is at stake, when you are being chased by a predator, or are trying to survive on a battlefield. As our brains develop and our minds mature, we naturally become less "all or nothing" in our emotional reactivity. Beyond that, actively repressing the expression of emotion has a physiological cost, as we get "all stressed

93

up" without release to reduce or neutralize that chemistry. And, most certainly, extreme repression and denial of emotion does not work in human relationships.

Sensations and Emotions Inform Your Awareness

Emotions are names or categories that we attach to certain sets of sensory experience, or sensations. They originate as feelings in your body that include warmth, tingling, tightness, how deeply you are breathing, how fast your heart is beating, how much you are sweating. Conversely, the sensations in your body are the weathervane of your emotions, and the more you pay attention to them the easier it becomes to recognize each emotion as it arises, acknowledge it, experience it completely, and let it go. That doesn't mean you have to run around shouting like your hair is on fire, but if it IS, then definitely don't keep yourself from shouting! With a little noticing, you'll also become aware of how rapidly emotions may arise and dissipate once you are willing to acknowledge and express them. The sensations we have in our bodies are the signals and road signs that our subconscious consistently delivers. Too often, we ignore them. When noticed and interpreted correctly, these signs and signals can get us onto the off ramp, and headed down the right road.

Many of the sensations that make up emotions such as anger, sadness, joy, or embarrassment are constant across age, culture, nationality, or race. The strength of each experience of emotion—for example, whether you are merely irritated or really angry—and how you deal with it will determine how much "emotional juice" gets dumped into your system. How you experience the emotion, whether you express and clear it or suppress and hold onto it, will determine how long the chemical signals that are part of the emotions remain switched on.

Do this experiment, right now. Remember the last time you were really angry. Hoppin' mad. Ready to blow. OK, bring up that memory fully, right down to the details if you can. Go on, we'll wait...

OK, now what sensations do you notice in your body? Chest tight? Jaw clenched? Belly tight? Feel any heat? Any sensations in your hands? Lips? Brow? Breath faster and shallow? Holding your breath?

That was the sensation set called "anger," and although each of us may feel it in different ways, we all share similar sensations that carry the name of "anger."

Now let's change the channel.

Remember or imagine a great vacation. You are relaxing and feel completely at ease. You sigh, content. Remember (or invent) the details and be there. Breathe. There's no place you need to be but in this happy space. Take a few breaths and let those thoughts and images flood through you ... that's it. Ahh.

How do you feel now? What sensations do you notice in your body right now? Breathing slow and relaxed? Belly soft? Jaw relaxed? Shoulders at ease? Lips soft or turned up, maybe? Head tilted slightly back? Good for you. Be in that happy place.

The sensations you feel in your body after noticing that a friend is in the car driving behind you will be vastly different than the sensations you feel after noticing the flashing lights of a police car behind you. If the police car rushes past you and doesn't pull you over, another sudden rush of sensations (called "relief") and chemicals may warm your chest and cause you to take a deep breath.

Your body experiences a burst of chemicals whether you are watching a fire or remembering a fire. Whether you are at a party or remembering a party. Whether you are on vacation or imagining a vacation you're never been on. You can choose to bathe your body in feel-good juice or in acid simply by redirecting your thoughts. Thoughts will rise unbidden, and we're not suggesting that you can (or should try to) control your thoughts. Not gonna happen. But you can learn to experience and release emotion, revise the story you're creating and reduce the emotion, rather than repress and deny it, cooking yourself in the process.

In short, the meanings you make out of the events that happen around you ultimately change your chemistry. Minute by minute, day by day. While there are some thoughts that are more emotionally neutral than others, there are no completely neutral thoughts. Even seemingly neutral thoughts like "Oh look, there is a red car!" may evoke longing in one person, irritation in another, excitement in a third, a memory of a red bike in a fourth, memory of a bloody fight, an apple orchard, a red fire truck, and so on. Different changes in chemistry will occur in each person that looks at the red car and even among people with similar thoughts, the strength of the corresponding emotion will vary.

If you repress or deny emotions, they do not "go away." They stay, unacknowledged, in your body, causing tension in your muscles until your teeth grind or your back aches or you can't take a deep breath. Intensive, repetitive withholding of emotion causes "armoring," when hardened, constricted muscles affect posture, breathing, organ function, and cause plenty of pain. You know of at least one person that looks stiff and awkward, who grinds his teeth at night, or has chronic back or neck pain. Most likely these are the result of unexpressed, unresolved emotions. (For more on the link between emotion and illness, see *Back Sense: A Revolutionary Approach to Halting the Cycle of Chronic Back Pain* by Ronald. D. Siegel, Michael H. Urdang, and Douglas R. Johnson.)

Each day, thousands of times a day, your habitual thoughts change the chemistry of your body, producing a symphony of emotional nuances. Over time, we generate a certain tone, an emotional theme, a way of being and relating that becomes our personality. The tone we set is the pattern and rhythm of largely predictable thoughts about and reactions to experiences. Remember the radio station analogy? That tone we set up in our lives can easily be compared to the preset buttons on a car radio. If your way of being is preset to the Country station, you will have a different life than if you are tuned into the Rock station, the Classical station and so on.

We often fail to recognize that, while we may be saying that we want a life, a mate, and a career that is the Jazz station, we may, unconsciously, have our thoughts and emotions consistently tuned into the Country station. As a result, our experiences in life (figuratively, or maybe even literally) are full of cheatin' hearts, loners, drunks in bars, out-of-work cowboys, and broken down trucks. Our filters, expectations, repetitive thoughts, and subsequent search for evidence that we're right about life determine the kind of broadcast we put out and the broadcast we draw in. What can we do to fix the tuner and change the station?

The more we are able to be present in our experiences, the more skill we develop in being able to respond consciously rather than react in the same old predictable ways. When emotions are churning up the mental waters, you can trust your body to provide clear information in the form of sensations. If you learn to recognize your body's signals and express and release the emotion while it is still merely a twinge, you can nip serious upset in the bud much of the time. You will not become an out-of-control maniac if you fully express your emotions. You may feel like one at first, especially if you have repressed your authentic emotions for a long time. Like beans in a pressure cooker, taking the lid off a storehouse of withheld anger, sadness, or fear can make a mess. Emotions are messy. They evoke tears, snot, and other bodily fluids. It's OK. That's what handkerchiefs, tissues, and towels are for.

Emotions are energy-in-motion throughout the body. When emotions move through us, which is their most natural course, we are restored to our balance point. When we hang onto emotions, leaving them unspoken and unresolved to build and twist and stagnate, we poison ourselves. Even unspoken gratitude and appreciation will turn like a bad apple as we build unrealistic ideals and expectations around the object of our admiration, sentimentalizing and romanticizing the person. We put that person on a pedestal. When the day comes that he or she does something human like get mad, make a mistake, or do something stupid, instead of recognizing and relating to the real person in front of us (kind AND mean, smart AND stupid, calm AND reactive) our idealized version of the object of our affection is shattered and it is likely that the relationship goes crashing to bits as well.

The good news is that as you observe and interrupt your reactions, you not only provide yourself with opportunities to be clear and direct with people, you also develop more compassion for yourself and others. You soon recognize how much of your interactions are reactions, how much you act out of beliefs and habits rather than out of the reality of what is happening right here, right now. You discover that there is nothing that is "just the way you are," that you certainly can teach an old dog new tricks, and that those new tricks can really improve the quality of your life and your relationships. You can have more fun; less stress; take things in stride; and have more energy, power, and skill in decision making; all by identifying and revising those things that keep you in a trance.

The power to have a truly satisfying life begins when you accept that blame and buck-passing are futile—if you want to be confident and happy, accept the truth that the buck stops with you. It's not anyone else's job to make you happy, and it is not your job to make anyone else happy. When you at last give up trying to change others, you become more accepting of flaws in yourself and them, and you can then take responsibility for the life you have left to live.

You don't have to wait for a crisis, mid-life or otherwise, to revise your thinking. You can be free starting right now. You have the ability and you can choose to notice your judgments, recognize that this is not The Whole Truth, and get over your reaction before you cause yourself more stress and damage. You can cultivate a style of communication that is **simple, clear, and direct**. Both of these are tools, ways to get off the road to nowhere at the right exit.

When Pretense Becomes a Lifestyle

As children we were excellent interpreters of our parents' moods, even subtle ones. We were able to know both through our senses and our subconscious understanding of tonal and gestural clues what was going on. At times we got confused by mixed messages from the adults around us. Being told repeatedly that "nothing is wrong!" when our eyes, ears, and bodies are telling us Mom and Dad are angry was extremely confusing. Eventually, we began to distrust and/or suppress our awareness of what we knew was real, so that we could go along with our parent's version, avoid punishment, and gain approval. This is how we learned to pretend that we are not pretending, when we know damn straight we are.

For most of us, our early training—at home and school—turns us into chronic pretenders and liars. As adults, we lie. A lot. To ourselves, and to each other. Then we believe our own lies and make believe other people can't see through our pretense. As children, we're taught to be nice, to pretend we like people even when we don't, to eat what's put in front of us even if we don't like it or aren't hungry, to be interested in conversation when we're really bored, to pretend nothing's wrong when our parents are clearly pissed off, to pretend daddy's not drunk when he obviously is, and so on. We're taught by experience to be liars to avoid punishment and ridicule in school; because truth and honesty has gotten us into such hot water at home, lying becomes an automatic defense.

We were trained to be quiet and follow instructions so that our teachers could keep order in a classroom and keep schoolyard disagreements from turning physical. That was useful, because our brains were still developing and we hadn't yet mastered impulse control. However, we were not taught how to recognize, express, and resolve our emotions. Quite the opposite, in fact. We were taught to repress our emotions and the thoughts that accompany them. Without having the opportunity to see adults experience, express, and resolve strong emotions in a healthy way, we continue to suppress and even lie to ourselves rather than actually admit we are angry, afraid, or sad.

As adults, we often have translation problems that keep us from recognizing and acknowledging the information presented to us through body sensations, emotions and gut feelings. Simply put, we usually ignore our sensations and "run upstairs" into our thoughts to "decide" what we SHOULD feel and think, rather than just notice what we DO feel and think. As children we were intimately in touch with the shadow world of our subconscious and with the feelings and awareness that rise from our subconscious to our conscious minds. We trusted those signals and knew they were accurate. Most of us never learned how to accept, read, and use the information coming in from the world and from our inner awareness, because the adults around us didn't know and so, couldn't teach us. Instead, we, like the adults around us, suppressed what we knew and didn't act on. We learned to lie.

I was one of the children who learned that telling the neighbors, "Daddy drank a bottle of wine and is sleeping it off" rather than saying, "Daddy is taking a nap" meant I'd end up in very hot water. Sherry learned that no matter how verbally abusive someone was, the most appropriate response was not to get angry, but to get quiet and just take it.

These are obvious examples, and there are many very complex ways we are taught to say things and twist the truth in a misguided attempt to manage what people think or how they react. We say "Oh how ARE you?" when we mean "I can't STAND you." We say, "I'm FINE with that", when we mean "I resent you for asking me to do that." We say " Let's get together SOON" when we mean, "As soon as pigs fly." And in those complex layers of pretense that we agree to out of old childhood training, we set ourselves up for plenty of stress and dissatisfaction. It's an exhausting and impossible way to live. We're not saying that it's desirable or even possible to tell 100% of the truth—what we're saying is that the average LEVEL of pretense in our everyday lives is toxic to body and mind and can squeeze the pleasure and enjoyment out of life and render it little more than hell on earth. Being careful and lying to protect the feelings of others is a guaranteed way of preventing those close to you from knowing who the hell you really are.

CLUE: When you catch yourself being careful or pretending to manage someone's impression of you, there's an old fear driving you towards the cliff. Hit the brakes, take a breath, and allow yourself to speak truthfully.

The work of psychologist Paul Ekman on facial expressions (which was the basis of the TV show "Lie to Me") reveals that we don't really get away with hiding the truth. Ekman, a pioneer in the field of body language, especially facial expressions, has demonstrated that facial expressions are universal among all humans, and that even micro-expressions that flash across our features are picked up, registered, and "read" by our subconscious. In other words, when you talk to someone and they pretend to be calm when they are angry, pretend to be pleased when they are sad and so on, you know, at least subconsciously, that something is just not right. You may not believe the speaker or just have a little twinge in your gut that makes you doubt what you are being told. (For more on this see Paul Ekman, *Telling Lies: Clues to Deceit in the Marketplace, Politics, and Marriage.*)

Sometimes, you may even know beyond a doubt, through an expression or gesture, exactly what a friend or family member is keeping under wraps. People often have "tells"—gestures or expressions that they are unaware of, but give away the truth they are trying to hide. Think of the kid that nervously shifts from foot to foot or rubs his nose when he tells a fib. He'll swear that Mom is psychic, yet his tell is totally obvious. Well, it's no different for you. Your facial expression, body language, scent, gestures, and even the pitch and tone of your voice tell one story even as your words may tell another. People KNOW when you are bullshitting, even though they may go along with it for their own reasons. We are far more transparent to each other than we pretend to be. You may recognize a "tell" easily in a friend or register one as a feeling of unease when talking to a stranger. We can even get ourselves into dangerous situations by ignoring that unease.

The ability to sense when others are being deceitful is part of the inner assessment tool we mentioned earlier when we were talking about "thin slice" judgments. When we listen and obey those fleeting inner signals before we can override them with our habitual beliefs and rationalizations, we can and often do have a clear understanding of what's going on around us and inside us, even if we can't fully describe HOW we know.

Taking Responsibility Leads to Honesty and Authenticity

Ease and confidence with being honest occurs as we face the irrational fear of telling the truth, acknowledge it, move past it, and fully express what we really feel and what we really think. When we stop hiding and keeping secrets and tell the truth of our experiences, our lives have more flow and grace. Relating stops being a chess game as we become more genuine. As we get better at saying what we really mean, we have more energy available for healthy excitement and pleasure.

At first our authentic behavior makes us feel reckless, like throwing fate to the wind. Saying what you think, expressing what you feel, asking for what you want, and letting the chips fall where they may—that is the start of living in authentic contact with other human beings. It's exciting, and a little scary, but the payoff comes in knowing that the world will not end, you will not get fired, your friends will not vanish, your mother will not have that heart attack, and your spouse will not file for divorce because you told the truth.

Being honest and authentic leads you to be kind rather than nice. As a kid we were repeatedly told to "be nice." Many of us were never taught how to distinguish between genuine kindness and the dishonest manipulative ass-kissing strategy called being "nice". When we become adults these rules become self-enforced silence, repression, and inhibition, and we take on the obligation to "be nice" (and dishonest) even with (sometimes especially with) people we don't like. This stops us from clearing the air, expressing ourselves, and getting over our judgments.

"Being nice" and "following the rules" at the cost of healthy self-expression are among the greatest sources of dissatisfaction in our lives, at work and at home. This ongoing suppression and repression is the source of great stress, stress-induced illnesses, sleep disorders, and sexual dysfunction. Being nice ultimately costs us years off our lives and sucks happiness out of the years we do have.

Moving from being "nice" to being kind doesn't mean you're going to like everyone. There will still be people who rub you the wrong way although, occasionally, after telling them the truth about how you feel about them and getting over your judgments about them, you may decide they aren't so bad after all. It does mean that you can get pretty good at not carrying them around in your head or gossiping behind their backs. Holding grudges and gossiping are oh-so-middle-school. Really, it's time to graduate.

At the same time, don't confuse being honest with being hostile and aggressive or passive-aggressive. We are **not** telling you to let every stray irritation and passing judgment fly out of your mouth. The opposite of being silent and repressed is not being an out-of-control jerk who pours years of pent up emotions over everyone. We are not advocating that you spew your judgments and delusions like an opinionated volcano. Telling the truth is exciting because it's associated with breaking the taboo of silence and pretense. The first few times you speak up, you may feel like you're out of control and going too fast down a steep hill. That's ok.

If you have been repressed and squelched your emotions for a long time, gritting your teeth to hold back what you want to say while saying what you think you should to appear "nice," you may feel an urge just to say everything you've never said to the first few people that get under your skin. Unloading your years of frustration and pent-up emotion on the first few people who annoy you is neither nice, nor is it kind. Kindness may take practice, especially if you have been silent and angry for a long time. So if your choice is clam up like you always have or vent, go ahead and vent. You'll find the balance with practice. Those stored up thoughts and emotions are like an overstuffed closet. The first few times you open the door, all the junk falls out on your head. If you go overboard, say "I'm sorry about how long I went on" or " about how loud I got" or "about the names I called you." Do not apologize for speaking up.

Getting from repressed to real is a process, and it will take you some practice to clear the emotional clutter and take out the psychic trash before you can express yourself cleanly and authentically, without that volcanic quality. Gotta start somewhere.

We ARE advocating that you admit and reveal when you are not happy, and when you truly are happy, even when that doesn't seem "appropriate." You can begin simply by revealing that you don't like something you think you should like, or something you have pretended to like. Tell your mother that you are sick of feeling obligated to visit aunt Millie every other Tuesday and you much prefer going to the Tuesday bargain matinee at the movie theater, so you are going to do that instead, and maybe Millie would like to come along. Tell your wife that you appreciate her for cooking dinner and reveal that you really don't much like that meatloaf with the mushrooms on top. Tell the guy who keeps asking you out that you'd be more likely to go if he did something about his bad breath. Tell your boss what you really hate about your job and what you would rather be doing.

The results of these revelations may surprise you—you might find out that Aunt Millie loves to go to matinees and has an encyclopedic knowledge of movie trivia, that your wife really hates making meatloaf, that the guy has a phobia about going to the dentist and is relieved to know you think he's handsome, and you may discover that your boss loves your idea and gives you a raise to go with the new job description.

Look, here's the deal: Even if they are not happy about what you tell them, you'll find out that they knew it (or at least suspected it) all along. On some level, conscious or not, they could see past your "niceness." In our own experiences and those of clients, the positive results of being honest about what we feel, think, and want outweigh any possible negative consequences many times over.

The opposite of being silent and repressed is to become authentic and self aware—to become conscious and responsible for yourself, for what you think and for what you want. When you reveal your authentic self you open up a space for other people to respond in kind, and you start to build relationships based on who you are rather the who you are pretending to be.

HOW to Start Telling the Truth

Feel what you feel and start talking. Feel that clench in your gut and take a breath, notice the tension in your body, get in touch with what you really think or feel or want (that will take about three seconds) and allow that to come out of your mouth. Don't use a lot of words. Go for simple, clear, and direct.

Lying is the starting point for many mind games that end badly, costing us pleasure, relationships, and even our health. Lying is one of the biggest ways that we shoot ourselves in the foot.

When you put up with things you can barely tolerate while pretending everything is "just fine, really," you become resigned to misery and highly stressed. When you deny yourself the experiences you desire because you think you shouldn't, or because someone might think badly of you if you do, you limit your capacity for joy. Worse yet is denying yourself what you really want just to prove a point or out of spite. Living a life based on reactivity to others' demands and expectations (real or imagined) is just as limiting and constricted as a life lived in full compliance with the demands of others.

The truth really does set us free. We become freed from the jail of our own minds. Becoming aware of the truth within us so we can stop lying and pretending—both to ourselves and others—requires that you first notice, in the moment, whether or not what's coming out of your mouth is congruent with what you feel in your gut. Sometimes clients tell me that they "hear themselves lying" and then don't know how to pull themselves out of the lie. Well, when you hear yourself saying something like: "Sure I'll be there on Sunday . . ." or " No, really, I'm OK with that . . ." or " Yes I'd love to spend the holidays with your family . . ." while your gut is churning, your eye is twitching, your jaw is clenched, or your feet are tap-tap-tapping their way outta there, the best thing to do is take a breath or two, and say something like, " I know I just said yes, and what I really mean is . . ." or, " Ok wait, what I'm afraid to tell you is . . ." or "That's honestly not my first choice; my preference is . . ."

We're not going to lie to you (ha!), this takes practice. You will screw it up, a lot at first and then less and less often until telling the truth becomes pretty automatic. When you do screw it up, face up to it, admit it, apologize if necessary, and try again next time.

Sometimes the light bulb will not come on for a few hours, or maybe you notice your gut churning a whole day or two after you agree to something you don't want to do. Go back to the person and admit what you did. "Remember when you asked me to finish that report for you and I said 'Yes?' Well, I was being polite. (Or "I said yes before I realized I meant . . .") I don't want to finish the report for you and I wish I had told you that when you asked."

Sometimes, just because you're so accustomed to saying "yes" or "no" without checking in with yourself, the truth may shoot out of your mouth explosively. You might hear yourself say, "Report? How many times have you asked me to bail you out by helping you at the last minute? No! I will **NOT** help you with that report!"

So, the screw-up may be an overreaction—usually one that uncovers long held resentments that would be good to clean up anyway. In that case, go back to the person and own your reaction, but don't say yes to them out of feeling guilty. That would be a step backwards. "When you asked me to finish that report for you, I now realize I really went off on you. I dumped a lot of my frustration on you. I'm frustrated at how often I say 'yes' without thinking it through. I'm sorry I overreacted."

Once you get the hang of being honest, the freedom you gain is worth the fear you have to pass through to get there. You can start peeling away some of those layers of deception today. Check in with yourself before you answer—or before you swallow an answer in favor of silence. ***Don't assume that people know what you want, how you feel, or what you're thinking.*** Remember that, like you, they will typically buy into a story rather than explore the knot in their own gut that tells them you're lying to their faces. Don't leave them guessing about you.

Don't confuse this with any kind of absolute moralism about lying and deceit. In other words we're not advocating stupidity about honesty. If you are hiding gypsies in the attic, lie to the Nazis about what's up there. Don't narc on your neighbor because he smokes pot every Saturday night. What we are calling "honesty" is authenticity and self-expression used to create community, build relationships, and have more trust and ease in your life. Our insistence that you become more honest with yourself and others is a necessity for being free from the obligations, the "shoulds," and other constrictions that we keep us from true friendship, intimacy, and ease. We are recommending honesty as an essential tool to free yourself from the jail of your past and to create the life that you want.

Begin a practice today of noticing the difference between what is true and what isn't in every interaction you have. Go have lunch or an after-work beer with a friend and practice. Make an agreement with that friend to "play a truth game" and reveal all the little lies you catch yourself in while you're together and any others you may have remembered from earlier in the day. It will be a real eye opener.

HOW to Stop People-Pleasing

The habit of being "nice" is so deeply ingrained that people often become chronic people pleasers. If your thoughts often go to what the **Other Person** thinks-wants-feels-needs, and you act on that before you even check in with yourself to discover your own thoughts and desires, you've got People-Pleasing Syndrome.

We were taught to mistake people-pleasing for kindness and compassion. It is neither. What we learned as "appropriate behavior" (Don't point at Mr. D's hairy facial mole and yell "Eeeeewwww!") became no more than a sanctioned form of lying. Long after we have learned the impulse control that keeps us from shouting out the creepy, the odd, or the obvious we go on lying under the heading "appropriate behavior." We made the leap from not bleating out what we think and see to pretending we don't think and see what we goddamned well know we think and see!

This is often a large part of the public image we work so hard to maintain. And it's exhausting. Even if you last heard the words "appropriate behavior" spoken by your Great Aunt Maude or by Sister Mary Paininmyass in third grade, the notion of "appropriate" and "inappropriate" behavior is probably pretty ingrained.

People-pleasing started as our way to manage the moods of adults, whose reactions (often loud and punishing) to our truthful but impulsive behavior made us choose compliance to avoid the rejection that our little brains were hardwired to interpret as a threat to survival. The problem of over-attachment to "appropriate behavior" arises from being rewarded for controlling our impulses, while never being encouraged to speak the truth. The confusion arises between knowing not to blurt stuff out and believing that we must pretend in order not to upset anyone, especially The Authorities. People-pleasing did you some good at least some of the time. Yeah, it might have kept you out of the principal's office when you were a kid **but it'll put you in the doctor's office when you're an adult.** It's a recipe for anxiety.

If you are a chronic people pleaser you have systematically trained those around you to expect that you will do anything to please and that you will also overlook their behaviors that, in fact, drive you nuts. At the same time, you most likely feel guilty if the people around you are upset or angry and you are likely to put up with criticism, demands, and domineering behavior. To become a doormat, first you have to lie down, and people pleasers find plenty of ways to encourage others to flatten them.

One symptom of People-Pleasing Syndrome is attempting to make others happy by sacrificing something you want in order to give them what you think they want or need. Then, when they're not grateful, you become the resentful victim because you gave up something you wanted to make someone else happy. Attempting to gain others' approval (or manipulate them into doing stuff for you) at the expense of your own desires is an exhausting and futile way to live.

People-pleasing is not real generosity. Generosity has an internal payoff (pleasure) and doesn't replace taking responsibility for your own happiness with doing for others. If you get enjoyment from asking (not guessing) those close to you what their dreams, desires, and favorite meals and movies are, and then pleasantly surprising them, great! But if you do things for others to obligate them, to make yourself look good, to "make" them happy so they won't yell or drink, or to keep them from getting upset, to gain approval or avoid gossip, there's definitely something rotten smelling up that relationship.

Often, we make ourselves miserable and resent the people we try to please yet we still fail to win the approval we seek. Approval, even when we do get it, is usually chump change, since there are generally only a few people whose opinions mean anything to us as adults, and those people are usually the ones who approve of us whether or not we do what we think they think we should do. Dr. Seuss spoke the truth when he wrote "People who mind don't matter and people who matter don't mind."

Another symptom of People-Pleasing Syndrome is emotional insatiability. You may find yourself compulsively keeping score, focused on making sure that you get what you think you deserve, unable to give your time and attention to others freely because you starve yourself emotionally so much of the time. When you manipulate others to give you what you want (or think you should want), you come across as needy, a bottomless pit, an emotional black hole. Do you find yourself voicing questions and statements like: "Why doesn't anyone call me back? How come nobody wants to be my friend? Friends don't last." Danger! Warning! Pleaser Alert!

Symptoms of the People-Pleasing Syndrome include striving to be liked by everyone and to avoid rejection by being "nice." If you are a chronic people pleaser you probably deny yourself even the most basic awareness of what you own real preferences are, and so you cannot avoid an ever-present feeling of invisibility, of being overlooked and denied. As a result, you are not only needy, guilty, and anxious, you are also very angry under that fake pleasantry. When you allow yourself to say no, to ask for what you want, and reveal what is going on with you, then the approval games begin to lose their hold over you.

Most of us have operated in people-pleasing mode for so long (most of our lives, in fact) that the gap between an event and recognizing our body's reaction to the event—the difference between what comes out of your mouth and how you really feel—can be as long as a day or two. Keep up with the practice of checking in with your body, and you can reduce that to a few hours, then a few minutes, then a few seconds until that body-check is the first place you go.

Dawn's Story: The Opposite of "Nice" is Not "Nasty"

My supervisor and I have had a turbulent working relationship for more than twenty years. I went to work every day with knots in my stomach, feeling like I had to walk on eggshells. I avoided her whenever possible. I didn't speak up and was sure she'd fire me if I told her how I felt. In short, I was turning her into my parents and consequently she was treating me like a child. She yelled. She criticized. I worked overtime. Made plenty of mistakes. Sometimes I forgot to do an important thing but spent hours on the details. Frankly, I often acted like a child and didn't ask for clarity when I didn't understand what she was asking of me. I guessed. I got things wrong and defended myself and sulked when she corrected me. I was unproductive and obsessed with pleasing her. It wasn't working. The "nicer" I was, the worse she got. The "nicer" I tried to be, the worse I felt. I wasn't sleeping well. I felt anxious all the time. I wasn't taking care of myself and my home looked like a war was fought in every room.

Raven told me to tell her what was going on for me. I was terrified, but asked to speak to her. Much to my surprise, she sat down while I was having lunch. My fear was so great that I wanted to bolt. I thought of asking her to see me at another time. I took a breath. I took another. Then I told her how my experience of her had been stopping me from speaking, and that this was so hard for me, that my words seemed stuck in my throat. She was looking at me and smiling.

I took a breath. My fear quieted. My words began to flow effortlessly and clearly, as if I rehearsed for years! Once I uncorked myself, the words just came. In just a few minutes, I revealed what was going on for me with the people pleasing, fear of her criticism, avoiding asking for clarification and the rest of it. I told her I related to her as if she was my controlling father. She told me that she hates weakness and that the little girl act I was doing triggered her, too. She said she wanted me to be an adult . . . after all, we are both women over 50 years old.

We then said what we wanted from each other. We even agreed on a way to interrupt each other if we forgot. We have both been pretty good about sticking to those agreements. We have a new and healthier relationship. I never thought that would be possible. Ever since we had this conversation, I have been going to work a lot more calm and happy. I am also much more productive. I never dreamed that such a brief conversation would have such a powerful impact on my life. I now have more confidence in taking on other conversations where fear once stopped me from speaking.

Yes, she has occasionally reverted to her yelling critical "parent" behavior, but I can now interrupt her, or take it less personally, or ask for what I want instead of just cringing and trying to please. That genuine contact made a big difference for me. Now I am much more able to separate what she does from my old business with my parents. Yes, it has taken me 50 years of living and 20+ years on this job to realize what was going on here, but finally I am living a more authentic life and I am much happier. I have continued to catch myself people-pleasing and making myself the victim with my parents, boyfriends, and even with the way I hired people to do work around my home. I realized that this was like a virus that infected everything.

I am happy to say that my way of relating to both of my parents has changed and improved dramatically, my home has had major work done and is now a lovely and welcoming place, and I am calmer and more at ease than I have ever been in my life. I never would have guessed that telling the plain and simple truth in my relationships would have changed everything in my life to such a degree. Finally, I am happy with myself, and my life.

Life gets easier, and you judge others less harshly when you are no longer trying to make them happy so they will take care of you. Cut out the middleman (or woman) and take care of yourself. When that happens, people tend to become more interested in support- ing and nurturing you. This is vastly different from manipulating, complaining, and badgering someone to treat you a certain way. Take care of yourself, be honest about what is going on with you, and then you can accept—or reject—the situation or individual without the level of drama and struggle you are accustomed to creating.

Here are the steps for HOW to do this as illustrated in Dawn's story:

- Notice what you're thinking and feeling, and
- Have an honest conversation (not a blame-making one)
- Reveal what you are imagining and thinking, and
- Include clear direct requests, plus
- Make agreements for relating with more awareness for here on out.

It doesn't have to take all day, just cough it up like a hairball and get on with your life.

Your Image Is Your Imaginary Self

To create the life that you want, you have to recognize the gap be- tween the image of yourself that you present to others and the au- thentic person that you are. Your image consists of everything that goes along with what you think you should do, what you think others think you should do, and all the differences between what you actually think and what you or others think you should think.

Your image was crafted from the traits and behaviors that kept you looking like a "good girl" or "good boy," and that drew attention, praise, and rewards while avoiding shame, ridicule, and punishment. Your adult image is composed of the masks you wear to manipulate others into seeing only your good qualities while you excuse, ignore, downplay, hide, or blame others for your real or imagined shortcomings.

We learn to keep our real and authentic preferences, our real and authentic judgments, and our strong emotions carefully managed, dimmed, or hidden from the outside world. This is an exhausting and crazy-making process and it requires that we use a large amount of our ability to be present (our awareness, life force, psychological energy, spiritual juice, Genius) to hold this "Good Girl" or "Good Boy" illusion in place. Meanwhile, underneath the mask, we seethe, cry, and long for a real life.

Some part of your life is most likely a sham, a pretense based on what you want others to think of you in order to maintain the illusion that you are in control and that you can control what others think of you. So you may go through much of life with a fake smile painted on your face while you whine and gossip with other repressed, powerless people, until a brick to the head wakes you from this trancelike state. When things do go wrong, these behaviors actually serve to make the emotion and the story and upset even BIG-GER—with no relief in sight.

If you think for a New York minute that you are fooling anyone but yourself, you are deluded. Yes, of course there are people who pretend that they are fooled by your performance, and some may even lie to your face if you ask them what they really think of you, but hey, they deal with their emotions the same way you do and they just want you to return the favor. Consider the people around whom you say to yourself, "How could they possibly think I buy that load of crap? I see what's going on!" At least one, right? And yet that person may be clueless that his or her pretense is so transparent.

Remember, we are designed to share information constantly—and our smell, body language, pupil dilation, and other subtle and subconscious communications may clearly say one thing while our mouth says something else. To anyone in proximity, this just feels wrong, wrong, wrong. Of course, many people (we'd call them posers, inauthentic, phony, or just plain full of shit) make maintaining their image a full time job. Is there a place in your life where you do this? Around your parents? With your boss? Take a look at your life and, bearing in mind that people already have a clue about how full of crap you are, do yourself a favor and knock it off.

As you get better at paying attention to yourself, you are going to be more aware of other people's authentic moods and real feelings. You may quickly and unconsciously decode tone of voice, gestures, and facial expressions that reveal what others try to conceal with their words. Your body knows what is real, even when you lie to yourself. When what people say is not congruent with the rest of their communication, your body gets a "ping" of recognition. Trust me when I tell you that your inner world may be more obvious to those who know you well than you are willing to admit to yourself. A large portion of our communication is non-verbal, and while we may be in collusion to hold the pretense of our "perfect images" in place, we are simply not that unaware. We often know something is off, even when we don't know how or why we know. We may dismiss, deny, ignore, overrule, or cover up what we know, but most of us, much of the time DO know when somebody is yankin' our chain.

The Real You may be forgiving one day and petty the next, kind on Tuesday and feeling cranky on Friday. If you keep the people around you informed about your own emotions and the events, thoughts, and imaginings that accompany your emotions, then they don't have to make stuff up to explain your behavior and reactions.

Left to their own devices, they might imagine that they are the cause of your mood, or think that they have to walk on eggshells around you to avoid triggering you. Tell them the truth about how you are the source of your emotions, and they'll register that you are—gasp—less than perfect.

Their reaction to this revelation may surprise you. Sure, there may be some who think less of you for revealing your less-than-perfect Authentic Self, and there will be many others who will respond in kind and show you their less-than-perfect selves (as if you didn't already know). The less seriousness you place on the temporary nature of moods and emotions (yours and that of others), the easier it is to build relationships based on true intimacy. It is so much more juicy, powerful, and rewarding to relate Authentic Self to Authentic Self than it is to relate as your Image to others' Images.

Now, we're NOT suggesting that you deliver a litany of your worst flaws from a soapbox. Confessing every flaw and secret to every available person in the interest of "honesty" is masochism. Practice dropping your mask around the people you care about and want to be in daily close relationship with. Start there.

Living a life of pretense in order to manipulate other people's opinions of you requires a tremendous amount of time and energy to maintain. That's not to say that inflating our good qualities and downplaying our flaws isn't human. Of course it is. There is a grave difference between slight exaggeration of our strong points, and the careful plotting, planning, lying, and pretending that we convince ourselves we must engage in to maintain our relationships, our jobs, and our families.

You may make yourself sick to prevent Aunt Martha from knowing you hate her meatloaf, while telling your boss you love the music he pipes in to the break room when you secretly loathe it, while pretending you'd "love" to help your manager with that extra project, while lying to your wife to prevent her from knowing that you volunteered to stay late to get it done, while pretending that you'll hurry right home to help out with the kids, while the whole time calculating how many drinks you can have on the way home before your wife is able to tell you've been drinking.

Pretense like this makes you sick and crazy. Literally. When you are at ease and relaxed in your interactions with others, this energy is freed to be better spent maintaining your health and creating the life you want. You can almost hear your brain frying when you say stressssss.

Most people maintain an image, a mask, for each role they play—employee, boss, spouse, parent, sibling, child, lover. When you are "acting" a role for others most of the time, you feel that stress as pressure and obligation. Your belief that this deception is a requirement or a need is largely mistaken. It is mostly a product of your imagination based on what you think people should see and hear from you. *You are spending your energy to convince them to think what you think they should think about you.* Wow. I know you followed that, and it's craaazy making!

Your authentic personality comes complete with talents, flaws, strengths, weaknesses, and fears. In other words, the real you is a human being that has far more in common with other human beings than you may suspect. If people know you as your image but have never been made privy to your real desires, judgments, dreams, and ideas, then who the hell are they relating to? They don't know *you*, they know the invented version of yourself that's on display to gain approval.

Telling the truth about what you think; your fears, flaws, and judgments; and your deep desires will create far more opportunities, relationships, and good stuff than you can imagine. To reveal yourself doesn't mean advertising a list of your crappy decisions and irritating traits. It means relaxing, putting an end to *most* of the pretending that you do. It means saying more about what you think and feel rather than shoving your words through the filters of carefulness or appropriateness or political correctness.

HOW to Find Your Authentic Preferences Buried Under the "Shoulds"

Sometimes if you've spent the majority of your time and energy creating and protecting your "ideal version" of yourself, it might become difficult to even know what to order from a menu or to choose a movie without thinking about what other people might think about your choices. Creepy, right?

And what happens to the "real you," the person with authentic likes and dislikes, opinions, and desires? That real you stays hidden under the weight of unexpressed emotions, lies, secrets, withheld information, putting up with things, saying "yes" when you mean "no," and all the rest. The belief that it is better to look good than to feel good is poison. This toxic carefulness costs you at the most fundamental biological levels. Feeling and wanting and thinking one thing while saying and doing something else naturally increases stress chemicals, causes muscle tension, and robs you of energy and enthusiasm. Burying your real beliefs, thoughts, emotions, and desires will ultimately bury your health, bury your relationships, and may even bury you.

You may be at a loss to even know what you really want, as the quest to preserve image and please others drowns out the small still voice of true preference. Asking "What should I want?" "What is the best choice?" "What if I make a mistake?" "What will they think?" "Is this the appropriate thing to do?" becomes a noisy, intrusive mental habit that takes the place of noticing and responding to your genuine thoughts and desires.

Once again, the place to start is by noticing the sensations in your body. Everything you need to know is in your body. Your body is the medium of communication between your subconscious and your conscious mind. It is the vehicle of translation between your authentic self and the outer world. Your sensations and the emotions they describe are the key to finding the hidden world of your authentic self.

Notice the tension, how you hold your breath or breathe shallowly, the way you brace yourself when you talk to certain people. Notice the way your jaw and chest tighten when you are annoyed as you hold back your thoughts. Notice how tired you feel after spending a day with people you think you *have to* be careful around. Begin by noticing, slowing down your words, and taking a breath. Check in with your body. The Truth is *In* There.

Remember that sensations are clues to your emotional state. Certain sensations are good indicators of particular emotions. Tightness in your belly or your jaw are pretty consistent indicators that you're angry. Warmth in your chest and you're pleased, even happy, and so on.

You can rediscover your genuine preferences by noticing your thoughts, taking a few deep breaths, switching your attention to your body, noticing your sensations, and then following through as you uncover that you like, desire, dislike, or loathe whatever you're trying to make a decision about. This will work well for getting back in touch (literally) with everyday choices.

Strong emotions are a different story.

HOW to Spot Emotional Leaks In Yourself and Others

Many people feel edgy and fearful when experiencing strong emotions and use food, alcohol, and other substances to distract themselves from those strong sensations, much less—God forbid—expressing them. After all, expressing a strong emotion might let the people around you know for sure what they already suspect—that you are angry, sad, and dissatisfied under that happy and content smiley face. Lies committed to preserve one's image appear as false notes in your conversations, gestures, and facial expressions. Your subconscious cannot be fully suppressed, so yes, people know you're bullshitting them. Of course they are probably pretending not to notice, at least until they can talk about you later.

Ultimately, the efforts made to suppress what you are feeling will not work. Emotions are energy in motion in our bodies, and when we do not give the e-motion a way out, so that our system can go back to balance, something, somewhere has to give. Even if you succeed in co-creating a level of denial with those around you there will eventually be hell to pay. Suppressed emotion commonly emerges as chronic pain, or a heart attack, or a head-on collision. Often at first, it emerges as increasing conflict and drama. Soap operas at work and at home. Delightful.

Creating drama allows people to justify releasing those stuffed-down emotions by blowing things out of proportion and creating others as "bad guys". You naturally are cast as the "good guy," all the while maintaining the illusion that you are not responsible; you're the victim. "After all," you may say, "ANYONE would be upset about what she (or he) did."

At its worst, the drama might eventually develop like this: "I'll pretend I don't notice how much you hate being married and you pretend not to notice how sad I am most of the time. I'll pretend I love the job I hate so I can have money to gamble and you pretend you hate the job you love because you know I'd rather you didn't work. Then, next quarter when I get fired and come back with a gun; or next summer, when you get fired and commit suicide, everyone can pretend that they are SO SURPRISED because we were such a happy-go-lucky couple."

In less dramatic examples, we can still catch ourselves (and others) when barely contained emotions ooze out despite what we imagine is our carefully controlled front. Strong emotions leak out sideways through the cracks in our awareness and become visible as side comments, unconscious frownie faces, eye rolling, misplaced anger, headaches, heartburn, the dog acting up, restless legs, anxiety, and many other symptoms and signs.

If you see your spouse flirting with a neighbor and then pretend that you aren't jealous when you are, that emotion may leak out sideways. You may get a headache when your partner cuddles up to you, feel anxious and cranky for no apparent reason, go holler at your kids for not cleaning their room, or decide to take the dog for a walk while dinner is cooking, so it burns. Even though a stuffed monkey could see through your behavior, you can go on pretending that nothing is wrong. Of course you're not punishing your spouse for chatting up that hottie down the street. Yeah, right. You may also be punishing yourself for not being "good enough" to keep his eyes from wandering. Now there's a miserable way to employ your brilliant imagination!

There's a much, much better way to employ your genius. Give it a real job. Employ your amazing and powerful mind to create the life you want rather than resist the one you have. Contrary to popular belief (and um, remember how long we foolish earthlings though the world was flat) it is simply NOT TRUE that once we start expressing emotions we become out of control nut-jobs. It's when we wait and wait and pretend and deny and repress that the energy of our emotions takes on tidal wave proportions. Even then, all you can do is ride out the wave rather than generating even more energy by creating stories and justifications to make yourself right about the size of your emotional log-jam. Chill. Relax. Take a nice, deep breath. If you're going to terminate your Halloween costume of an image, might as well do it in one fell swoop.

If you want a gentler way, then don't wait. Open your mouth as soon as the first body sensations get your attention. Right then, when you would typically clam up rather than say what you think, just go ahead and say what you think. Really, we're serious. Go ahead. Forget about your Image, just be yourself.

There is a proverb that applies to this conversation perfectly. "Act while the thing is small, before the drops of rain become the raging river."

When you become skilled at noticing the signs of an emerging emotion as the sensations in your body, and then express that emotion immediately (or as soon as possible) and directly to the person whose behavior triggered the emotion, you will be able to resolve and release and shake off the drops before they can even form a creek. Do this consistently, and your relationships won't end up going out with the raging current!

HOW to Let Your Authentic Self Out of the Box

Start simply, by noticing your body tense or clench when you have something to say but won't let yourself speak up. Then breathe and, quick, before you talk yourself out of it, say something.

Start by expressing opinions in situations where you would usually keep your thoughts to yourself. You get extra points if you speak up when you think you shouldn't, and especially if you get excited when you express yourself. Although nobody but *you* can give you permission to express yourself, you might use the trick of telling yourself that it is better to ask for forgiveness than ask permission to speak.

If you get stuck (especially with a boss, spouse, or parent) try one of these lead-in phrases.

"I imagine you won't like my opinion and ... (then spit it out without justification or explanation)"

"What I'm afraid to say is ... "

"What I'd rather you didn't know about me is ... "

"What I didn't say yesterday is ..."

"I know I said yes and now I realize ..."

"What I make myself anxious about telling you is ..."

When someone is speaking to you, if you find that your attention has wandered because you've had a reaction, or you're bored, or you get triggered and feel irritated, don't just pretend that you are still paying attention. Speak up. This might sound like: "I haven't heard a thing you've said since you mentioned my sister. In fact my gut is clenched. I guess I'm not over what she said last week."

As you speak, notice your body. Feel whatever you feel. ***Let it be there.*** Tension, tightness, tingling, heat, cold, clammy hands, breathlessness, whatever. Notice it. Let it be. Breathe. Let it go.

This reporting strategy works as well in the bedroom as the boardroom. It's simple, clear, and direct, and allows those in your life to know and understand what is important (and not so important) to you. That's a good thing.

If your mind starts sputtering and you start getting even more distracted thinking about the "validity" or "appropriateness" of your reaction or emotion, take a breath and speak over that voice. You can't make yourself not have emotions, they just show up, like the tide. The question is, what are you doing with them? Are you storing them up? Building a case out of them? Making yourself sick pretending you don't have them? Or are you feeling them, letting them move through you, and speaking your mind when necessary, to get over yourself?

How much energy do you currently spend suppressing yourself by being careful, watching what you say, and pretending you are fine when you're not? Imagine what your life might be like if you redirected all of that energy to create strong reliable relationships and a deeply satisfying life.

- What would happen if you simultaneously stopped pretending and said what you wanted in clear, simple, drama-free language?
- Imagine the depth of your friendships if you let people know your real preferences and desires. Imagine how much easier it would be to ask what someone wants rather than guessing.
- Imagine the ability to create strong intimate relationships unfettered by "carefulness," relationships grounded in honesty and kindness rather than pretense, secrecy, and manipulation.

Remember, these instructions are not license for you to be an intentionally irritating, judgmental jerk. But hey, if that's who you are under that nice guy facade, by all means let him out. After he has had a few good rants, you may discover he was just frustrated about being bottled up for so long. You will also discover that you don't have to get pissed off to express yourself, although at first, since you've been holding back, you may feel a rush of emotion—a combination of fear and anger—that you can use to get your mouth working. It's ok. Better loud than not at all. Then relax. Breathe. Forgiveness is still easier to acquire than permission.

Even great people have some rotten traits and rotten people have some great traits. If you are not a complete asshole, revealing your flaws just makes you more accessible and lovable, more reachable, more human. People feel that you are just like they are. They relax. And, *if you really are* a complete jerk, then no amount of manipulation will make your cover story stick, so either way you're stressing for nothing.

CHAPTER 8

How Self-Reference Builds Roads to Our Preferences and Desires

"So many of us are not in our bodies, really at home and vibrantly present there. Nor are we in touch with the basic rhythms that constitute our bodily life. We live outside ourselves—in our heads, our memories, our longing—absentee landlords of our own estate." —Gabrielle Roth

What healthy well-balanced adults who create satisfying lives and harmonious relationships have in common is that they are able to identify and motivated to act on their needs, preferences, and desires while staying in contact with others. In other words, functional authentic people are self-referent. They check in with themselves, know what they prefer, and set out to get it.

You have to be able to refer to your self—your own desires and preferences—as your bottom line when making choices, rather than habitually doing (or not doing) something because you think you SHOULD, or someone else thinks you should, or because you THINK someone else thinks you should. Being self-referent requires telling the truth about what we feel and what makes us happy or miserable. Self-reference means learning that we can have, and are responsible for having, whatever we desire. So, if we desire happy relationships, then kindness and empathy (rather than fake niceness) are factored into our behaviors. Self-referent does not mean isolated and/or selfish—on the contrary, when we're fully aware that our happiness is our own responsibility, we don't waste time trying to make others "be" a certain way, which frees us to choose people who already have the traits we want in a friend, boss, or mate.

The path to becoming self-referent generally begins in young adulthood when we find that to be true to our own desires, intuitions, passions, and interests, we must of necessity reject some of what we have been told will or should make us happy. We may still take into consideration what we are told by those in authority, but we no longer merely obey an authority without doing an internal reality check. For example, as toddlers we had to be told, probably more than once, that hitting and biting were not acceptable ways to interact with our peers. As we grew up, most of us reached a point at which we realized there was more benefit in using our verbal abilities to have an argument or negotiate an agreement, rather than just hauling off and smacking someone we disagreed with. We develop a preference for maintaining relationships with people with whom we don't always agree. We prefer to stay out of jail, so we opt not to rob the corner store. We prefer to have an income, so we do what it takes to get and keep a job. We learn that we can trust our preferences. They will lead us towards what we desire.

Really, you can trust your preferences. If you stop pretending you are happy when you're not, and seek out what brings you happiness, you are not going to become a fist-fighting, lazy, unemployed, bon-bon eating loafer, or turn into some kind of vigilante or loose cannon. In fact, acting on the basis of preferences is what will prevent you from showing up at work (or the dinner table, or the schoolyard) with your shotgun when the stress becomes unbearable!

Your preferences will lead you forward and will urge you to use your talents, make lasting relationships, contribute to others, have fun, try new things, create lasting traditions, and change the world for the better. In short, act on your preferences and you will live up to your potential as a unique and powerful human being.

Finding your preferences is a primary step in self-discovery. Follow-ing your preferences will lead you to being, having, and doing what you desire.

Let's take a look at how to get in touch with what you need, want, and prefer to have.

HOW to Know What You Want and Get It

Need help KNOWING what you want because you're out of prac-tice? No problem. Having what we want can sometimes seem hard-er than putting together a thousand-piece jigsaw puzzle in the dark by the light of six fireflies. Some of us are so out of touch with our own bodies and our own desires that when asked the question "What do you want?" a series of painful emotional contortions takes place. We approach each decision as if we will have to live with this choice forever, as if we could *never change our minds* or have something else. Then we bypass the information (the sensa-tions in our body) that tells us what we truly want as we desperately try to figure out what we *should* want, what o*ther people* think we should want and what *we think* other people think we should want. This is an exhausting loop to be stuck in and it will make you feel tired, sick, and crazy.

This loop can happen so fast that even making a selection from a menu is exhausting or paralyzing. Sometimes fear of criticism is behind this one, or fear of punishment or fear of ridicule. Whatever the cause, the effect can make us unwilling to even know our pref-erences, and so cause a kind of pervasive numbing that blocks the pleasurable sensations which inform us of our likes and dislikes. First of all, add the words "right now" to the question. "What do I want *right now*?" not for the rest of my life or even the rest of the day ... just right now.

Wants and preferences are related. Let's say I want pizza and I've had two decent meals and I prefer to reach my weight loss goal for the month, so I order the grilled chicken salad. But If I want pizza and all I've had today is a salad and an apple and I prefer to feel energized rather than cranky during the movie I'm about to see, I eat pizza. Preference is not rocket science, is not based on "should," and is not difficult to discover.

Sometimes, even when we do know what we want, we don't act on it. We talk ourselves out of having what we want for all kinds of invented and ridiculous reasons. Does any of this resemble your behavior? Knowing what to do doesn't count for much if you don't do what you know. Here's where to start.

HOW to Tell a Want from a Need

To survive we need food, water, air, touch, shelter, and sleep. Remember those basics from infancy? OK, that's IT. That's what you need for survival. Period.

Everything else is a want and we all have wants and desires. It's our job to sort out what we do by recognizing our preferences based on those wants and desires. They can enrich our lives, inspire us to action, call us forth to do things we never thought we were capable of and help us forge bonds with others to co-create, and even pro-create. We don't have to earn the "right" to want what we want.

If we reject, ignore, or deny what we want too often or for too long, we get angry and demanding. Maybe even self righteous and entitled. We convince ourselves that our want is a NEED and then start telling other people what we NEED.

I need more space!

I need you to call me every day when you are away!

I need you to help me!

I need you to tell me you love me!

I need you to spend more time with me!

I need you to treat me with respect!

I need a bigger office!

128

AI-YI-YI!! Let's face it, nobody enjoys being around a "needy" person.

Pretending your wants are needs turns you into a powerless, needy, and unappealing person—a victim looking for a place to happen. *When you don't ask directly for what you want and then turn your wants into needs, your behavior creates the self-fulfilling prophesy that you fear most: disapproval and rejection.* And then you can play victim and martyr and whine about how much you do for others. All because you don't get what you want.

CLUE: When you turn a simple want into a need, a rule, a must, a should, or a condition (give me this or else!), you will drive yourself crazy with blame games and victim stories and you will drive others crazy, too. Oh yeah, and you also drive them AWAY.

The solution? ASK for what you want, make the asking a request (not a demand) and be willing to take "no" for an answer. This will take practice, but will free you to get what you want far more frequently and will also help you recognize that if you're not getting what you want from a person, you have two clear equally valuable choices: accept that that person will not give you what you want and get over yourself, or get over the person and get what you want from somebody else.

Do Try This at Home

What if you could have anything your heart desires? What would that be? First, right now, give yourself permission to imagine having exactly what you want. I mean ANYTHING. Put your "Needy Nelly" to work making an absolutely unlimited list of stuff you want to have, to do, and to experience. Yes, all of it. Take off the restrictions and limits that may inhibit you from putting some things down because they do not seem reasonable or possible. Right now, just put it all down.

Do you want a new career? Open a coffee house? Be an astronaut? Have kids? A world tour? A house in the woods? A body makeover?

A divorce? A business, cello lessons, time to write a book? Want to sing in a band, dance the tango, fly to the moon, get a Ph.D., become a painter, a doctor, a psychic? Be on TV? No limits! You have permission to want whatever you want. Feel the juice flowing in your veins as those desires spark to life and the pleasure and satisfaction that just imagining those things brings you!

In reality, many of the desires you have are reachable, if you are willing to stay in the creative process. As you persist in this your subconscious often delivers a version of what you desire. It may not look exactly like what you had in mind, but definitely fits the description. It's useful to accept that what you end up with may differ somewhat from the version you had in mind.

Here's an example. You want to perform music in front of an audience. So maybe you are too old to audition for "American Idol" and won't be "discovered" and offered a recording contract, but you can still go to open mic nights, or play in a band, or join a choir, and let your love of music have an outlet. From the time you were a kid you wanted to be an airline pilot. Maybe you won't make that career change, but you can still take flying lessons and have a great time, maybe even find ways to make your living flying a plane other than piloting for an airline. A friend of mine did just that a few years ago. You want to live near a large body of water, and you want to see that water from your home. Maybe you can't afford a lake front mansion, but could you find a great condo or apartment overlooking the lake? That's what I did! Sherry said she wanted a relationship with a man who could dance and cook, and now she's married to him. The catch? He has two cats, and she's allergic to cats. The solution? Put a HEPA filter on the air handler, run the vacuum, and dust a lot. So, there ya go.

The old ways you stop yourself will show up as you think about giving some time and energy to creating the life that you desire. I know someone who is a good artist and is a veritable Martha Stewart with crafts but after the initial excitement at the inception of a project and the purchase of supplies, she constantly denied herself the pleasure of doing it. She even retired early thinking she'd then have the time and money to "play" and instead found herself up to her eyeballs in art supplies. What she discovered was that she'd make time to paint or work on a project, then at the last minute decide to do something more important, useful, or necessary around the house. So she hired a maid to manage that. Six months later, projects still not begun, she finally said. "It's me. I am so creeped out. I finally realized that I avoid playing and do some kind of 'work' because I get anxious thinking about the way my parents would always have me focus on work and chores before play, so that finally when I did get to play I felt rushed and tense. Now, when I start to paint or lay out supplies that anxiety comes back and so I do something else."

Well, she had an honest conversation with her parents and also started engaging friends (playmates) to do things with her, and within a few months she was able to relax, have fun, and even share the results with her parents (who were thrilled for her). She started imagining what it would feel like (good, happy, fun) to be fully engaged in a project and was able to successfully get beyond that moment of anxiety or unpleasant thought and enjoy that preference.

HOW to Deal with Dueling Desires: What is Your Preference?

You want to eat ice cream on a daily basis, and you want to lose 10 pounds. You want to sleep until noon and you want to keep your job with the steady paycheck. To choose among conflicting wants and desires, ask the question "Which do I want more in the Big Picture? What do I prefer?"

We all have preferences. You may like green better than pink, chocolate better than vanilla, tall men better than short men, round women better than skinny women. Many of our preferences change with age and experience. Our preferences may overlap with those of our parents, at least early on, since both our genetics and environment have something to do with our likes and dislikes. As we move beyond the lives our parents lived and expand beyond their ideals, we evolve. How do we know what we prefer? For some people this is an absurd question. For many of us, it is of critical importance.

You may have desires that you decide to leave unfulfilled, based on your preferences—the BIGGER desire. You may be attracted to your neighbor, but prefer not to risk upsetting your spouse or getting a divorce (or being beat to a pulp by your neighbor's boyfriend). You do get what you want, because your preference, the BIGGER want, is to stay married, and sleeping with your neighbor would be a deal breaker, so you let that want go. (Of course, you could always ask your spouse about a threesome, but that's a whole other kettle of fish.)

Determining your wants and your preferences is not always simple. You may want a steady income. You may also want to quit your job and tell your boss to kiss your ass. Which do you want more? You may decide that this job isn't worth the headache, and start looking for a new job. Or you may decide that you love the job, the people and/or the location enough to risk an honest conversation with your boss, tell her the truth about how you are feeling and what you want, and see what happens. What you can't do is change your boss, although you might be surprised at how much an honest conversation may improve your way of relating to the boss. It's all about preference.

You may want to be well taken care of, to have less stress and to quit working and stay home and be a full-time homemaker. To do that you would have to win the lottery, inherit a fortune, or (more likely) marry a man who wants to support you and will not resent you for staying home while he works. But your boyfriend, at age 35, is still living with his mother and living off his unemployment benefits. Is your desire to be taken care of a bigger desire than to stay with your boyfriend?

What is your preference? How STRONG is that preference? Is it a simple desire or is it a deal breaker? How can you support yourself to live a life based on preference?

When we hold our desires lightly, as preferences rather than needs or must-haves, wants serve us. If you prefer black olives on your pizza but your friend prefers it plain, you can give up the olives and you'll still eat pizza. You can get olives the next time. Life goes on. Or you can make your friend bad and wrong for ordering a plain pizza, or refuse to eat because you didn't get what you wanted, so that you're just left hungry and less likely to be included in the next pizza outing.

Keep in mind that many of our wants come and go like breath. Some days you want to wear blue, other days, red. Some days you want to quit your job, other days you love your job. Some days you are happily sharing your living space with someone else, other days you want a month alone in a cabin in the deep woods.

Here's the flip side: sometimes, day after day after day after day we do want to quit the job, or get that divorce, or to move to another city, but we won't let ourselves.

Do your wants own you? Do you make yourself miserable if you don't get EXACTLY what you want? Do you make your happiness depend upon whether or not you get what you want EXACTLY the way you want it from the ONE person who really should live up to your expectations?

Well now, there's another opportunity for *notice, interrupt, revise, and repeat* until you grow up. Really. I mean that in the kindest possible way. The paradox is that to grow up, you have to take your wants as seriously as a child at play. In other words, give your wants your complete attention with an equal willingness to drop them in the mud and run in to have dinner.

We talked earlier about the ways that filters that once protected you may now be keeping you from having what you say you want. To revise those filters, you'll have to become more aware of HOW you keep that rerun playing. You may not want to do what it would take to revise some of your filters. And that's OK too. That doesn't make you a bad person. Even if you decide *not* to do something, it's better than wishing and hoping and unconsciously repeating frustrating habits over and over. There's still some conscious choice in the mix.

A guy once told me, "I haven't had a date in 10 years. I was always miserable in relationships. I knew I either had to stop sleeping with people or get therapy, and I don't want therapy. So I just quit being in relationships. I don't mind being alone." It's not a crime to be a picky judgmental recluse, though frankly, it's not very good for health or longevity. But hey, it's your life. If you admit how you are and are willing to live with the results, good for you.

To get the life you want, you have to give up the one you've got. Yes. That's what it costs. Sometimes that's easy to see and understand. The guy who's unemployed and stays up until two in the morning watching TV and drinking beer with his buddies, mooches dinners from his Mom, and picks up waitresses for all-night sex marathons will have to give all (or most) of that up to work a day job and make some money. Not rocket science, right?

Recurring Patterns of Unfulfilled Desires are Memos from Ourselves

Do you wake up day after day after day dreading going to work, or leave work dreading going home to your mate, or spend the weeks before the holidays dreading visiting your in-laws? Do you often spend time daydreaming about moving to Alaska, or living alone, or wishing you had become a doctor, or gone to law school, or married that Indian Chief? These recurring thoughts are clear memos from yourself that you'd do well to pay attention to.

One way we stop ourselves from moving in a new direction is that haunting phrase "What if I'm wrooong???" So what? It's not as if all of our decisions are 100% irreversible. Unless of course you're about to step off the bridge, but aside from a leap into oblivion (and frankly, I know of a few people who even survived those), you can nearly always make a new choice.

I know of people who got divorced and remarried to the same partner (one couple did it twice!), others who quit and then got their jobs back (a few of them with higher pay and better conditions), others who have moved away and then moved back (because no matter where you go, there you are). I know people who ditched wedding plans the day before the wedding, others who bought and sold a house within a few months. *In the end, there is no way to know for sure how much you will enjoy having what you want until you get it.* And even if you don't like it much, you've had an adventure, learned a few things along the way, know yourself better, and at least you quit whining about not having what you said you wanted. When it comes to going for what we want, most of us aren't even playing with particularly big stakes. We're worried about pissing off the boss or the spouse or we can't say "no" to something we dislike doing. Sheeeesh. Get bigger and better problems. Honestly, that's the best solution *ever* to resolving petty, imaginary, and self-generated problems. Tackle a real one. Create a challenging and enjoyable project that will get you something that you want. Your mind and body crave this kind of challenge and excitement because it is how we grow and evolve. We live longer, happier lives when we create meaty challenges to lean into.

HOW to Build the Road From Here to Your Desire

Create a strong vision of something you want to have or to experience. Clip out some pictures,
    talk about it, Google it, write a few sentences about having/experiencing your desire as if it has already happened. Vividly imagine it as if you have it, and revel in the surge of pleasure and satisfaction having it brings. Do a few of these activities every day for a week or so and something very interesting happens: you will notice what's in the way. It will stick out like a fork in the spoon drawer. You will notice those pesky thoughts about why you can't, shouldn't, or

just won't get it, and you will feel the irritating tension that throws a wrench into your pleasure ride. You know what to do next: interrupt those thoughts, bring your attention back to your desire, and, if needed, you can go back and clean up lingering issues. Your ideas will then bloom; you will be inspired! That's the time to plan, to ask for help, and to create a time line that will get from your current experience to the one you keep imagining. To do this will require that you lay your desired vision right on top of the old reality, make it vibrant and attractive. That's how to start laying down that new blacktop road to satisfaction.

This goes far beyond simple "setting an intention." This process brings your thoughts, emotions, expectations and actions into congruency. To make anything happen, even to go get a glass of water, you need congruency among your intention, your imagination of the outcome, your attachment to having what you want (will it be worth the effort?), and the behavior required to obtain it. You notice you're thirsty, you imagine what it would be like to have a drink of water, you remember where you keep glasses, you walk to the cupboard and get a glass, walk to the tap, hold the glass under it, decide when you have enough water in the glass, turn off the tap, drink the water. Congruency in intent, imagination, and behavior gets you what you want.

It also gets you what you don't want. You (unfortunately) have that congruency firmly in place when your old limiting thoughts produce unpleasant emotions, expectations of "not having" and resignation, followed by self-defeating behaviors. The system works PERFECTLY. When you understand that, you can get it to work for you to bring you what you want. That's the beauty of knowing HOW.

Asking For It

The easiest way to get what you want is to ask for it, simply, clearly, and directly. Makes sense, right? Do we usually do that? Hell, no. We tell ourselves that we that we are making a clear and direct request when really we're suggesting, hinting, implying, applying guilt-trips—almost anything other than just freakin' asking for it.

If you notice yourself doing everything but asking directly for what you want, stop. Take a breath. Ask yourself, "What do I lose by just asking for it? How am I scaring myself around this?" You may be afraid of looking foolish or stupid. Yeah, that old preserve-the-image-at-all-costs game again. Go ahead, dare to be foolish, just ask. In fact, you are less likely to look foolish if you ask directly than if you hint, imply, or otherwise try to manipulate the situation to get what you want. If you ask, and they say no, you can ask somebody else, or ask again later, ask differently, or accept that no and get on with your life, rather than suffering in anticipation, or sitting in judgment, or wallowing in self-pity.

My clients often call me "Captain Obvious" or "Master of the Obvious" and employ my services as an English-to-English translator to straighten out the tangled murky conversations they have tried to pass off as clear requests. To be honest, it's one of the things I like best about doing what I do. It's often funny and people leave pretty happy about what they've learned about their filters and how they jury-rig communication.

Sherry has seen this happen over and over again in the workplace. There's the employee who tells the boss all the details about her sick mother, but never quite gets around to asking for some time off and then complains to her coworkers about how cold and unfeeling the boss is. Then there's the boss who wants everyone to like her, so she drops a lot of hints about the report that's due next week but never quite gets around to asking you to work on it because you might get irritated, then waits until your annual performance review to tell you that you need to "show more initiative." There's the staff member who waits until he has signed on to take a job elsewhere to tell the boss directly how unhappy he's been and what she could do to improve things. For the sake of your coworkers' sanity, not to mention your workplace productivity, just ask for what you want when you want it, will ya?

Too often our focus is on simultaneously trying to maintain an image, not piss people off, avoid rejection, make other people happy, and manipulate them into giving us what we want. You might as well get a job as a sideshow juggler—one of those guys that'll juggle a raw egg, a chainsaw, and an umbrella all at the same time. Hell, that's easier, because at least it's possible to be a success at doing that!

Communicating About Wants: A Review

Our ability to ask clearly, simply, and directly for what we want is key to long-term happiness. Do you want to have a good shot at getting what you want? Yes? All righty then, use this approach.

1. Call wants what they are, and drop the "I need" story. ("I want more time with you.")

2. Ask directly for what you want. ("Will you go to a movie with me on Saturday?")

3. Tell the truth. ("When you work Saturday I imagine you are avoiding me, I scare myself. And I really do miss you and want to be with you more.")

4. Ask what he/she thinks. Shut up and listen. Really.

5. See if there's a way you can BOTH get what you want.

Remember, changing old habits requires repetition. That's OK. Don't throw up your hands if you don't get what you want and say, "See? I knew that honesty thing wouldn't work!" It takes time to revise the old way you think, feel, and relate.

Persist playfully. Make requests, not demands. Be willing to accept "no" as an answer. Take responsibility for getting what you want. If you don't get what you want, the way you want it, decide if you want to keep doing what you're doing or seek out others who are more inclined to give you want you want.

Let your partner (or your sibling or your boss) off the hook either by accepting what is so, or by finding a new partner (or boss. Not much you can do about the sibling). *You cannot MAKE someone else do something just because you want them to want to.* If you make yourself depressed over this kind of thinking, call your coach or therapist. Yes, right now. It's crazy thinking.

By the way, plenty of what we want has nothing to do with the behavior of or participation with someone else. We just stop ourselves from asking for it before the words can even come out of our mouths. Remember that you don't need permission from anyone else to want what you want. Give yourself permission, then let the other person know what you're up to *without* creating a drama, justification, explanation or defense about why you want what you want.

Tell the people in your life what you're doing to create what you want (taking Saturday afternoons to myself, not cooking on Friday nights, quitting my second job, going to the movies with my pals on Sunday, taking a class, going skiing for the weekend), and then work out logistics, and balance what you want with what they want so you can both have a good shot at relaxation and satisfaction. This isn't about asking permission to want what you want or to have what you want—*it's about finding a mutually agreeable way for both of you to have what you want.* These are the key steps to having and keeping good relationships.

The stronger the desire, the more you may need to negotiate to ensure you get it. Although wants are not needs, and aren't necessary for your survival, they certainly may be deal-breakers. A key step is to prioritize your wants—decide which wants take precedence over others. The wants that rise up your priority lists are your preferences. Some of them may be non-negotiable.

Here's how a negotiable set of wants can work out:

You work with people all day long and go to the gym after work every day. Your idea of a great weekend is lying around in your PJ's reading, making love, and ordering takeout for dinner. Your brain wants quiet. You want to relax. Your fiancée, who works in his home office on the computer all day, has a different way to relax and blow off steam. He wants to go out Friday night, go to clubs or big restaurants, have people over on Saturday, or go skiing all weekend. He wants to watch football in the living room with his buddies and have you make delicious man-treats for them all.

Um . . . do you think that after the wedding either of you will change what you want? That'd be NO. You may each waste lots of energy trying to change the other. Or you could spend it negotiating the territory without making it a requirement that either of you participate in each other's method of rest and relaxation. Maybe you agree to a leisurely bike ride or hike on Sunday or to occasionally going out with a small group of friends for dinner. Maybe he goes on ski trips with his buddies, and limits the football parties to Super Bowl Sunday. Maybe you take the occasional Friday afternoon off so you have the energy to go out to a club. *Think both/and rather than either/or.*

In any relationship—intimate partner, family, workplace—it may not be possible for both of you to have all that you want. Instead of making demands and issuing ultimatums, ask yourself: How can we cooperate and support each other so we EACH get a lot of what we want?

Getting what you want is often possible if you look for it in the right place. You won't find apples on a lemon tree, so start by finding the right orchard. Rather than expecting other people to deliver all of what you want, look for ways to satisfy your wants that rely primarily on your taking the initiative and creating satisfaction for yourself.

Anything that you want is fine to want AND hooking your happiness to changing the behavior of others is a set-up for misery. If you make your happiness dependent upon convincing your alcoholic spouse to sober up and pledge his undying love for you, or if your hang your happiness on the expectation your checked-out and unreliable "best friend" is going to suddenly see the light and start returning calls and showing up on time for things, you're setting yourself up for disillusionment and disappointment. You can become an astronaut and fly to the moon faster than you can get another person to "be" a certain way because you want them to. That just ain't gonna happen, in this or any other lifetime. You can't turn an elephant into a giraffe no matter how hard you try.

You may want the person you are dating to be honest. That's a fine thing to desire. But if the one you are with lies repeatedly, then, rather than trying to make that person over according to your wants and driving yourself nuts in the process, find your common sense and use it. Break up with that person and move on to another partner who tells the truth. In other words, you can look for and get what you want elsewhere. That's how to get what you want. You want apples? Find an apple tree. You want honesty? Exactly.

HOW to Have What You Want: A Summary

- Check in with your body and observe how you feel
- Notice what you think—truly, under whatever static and noise you may have.
- Be honest with yourself and others. You can be honest AND kind.
- Know your preferences. (What makes you happy?)
- As you learn, adjust accordingly. Many preferences change with time.
- Ask for what you want.
- Use language that us simple, clear, and direct.
- When in doubt, don't assume. Ask a question.
- And relax. Really. Do stuff that you find relaxing. It will help. A lot.

Shoulds + Pretense + Mind Reading: A Recipe for Poison

The original "shoulds" were rules that helped us avoid punishment and learn to self-regulate. As adults, "shoulds" and "shouldn'ts" create resistance, resentment, and unnecessary fears.

The ghosts of childhood punishment and ridicule linger in the hallways of our minds and scare us. We will avoid feeling the discomfort generated by thinking of possible rejection, so we put off asking for that raise or that date or anything else we want but believe we can't have or might not get. We end up frustrated and confused. We become pretenders who pretend we are not pretending. We pretend we don't want help, or touch, or praise, or acceptance, or that we don't want anything at all. We may even believe that we shouldn't want anything, or that wanting things is selfish or that if we get something we want that means somebody else can't have what they want. It's a sure recipe for dissatisfaction and unhappiness. And it's crazy thinking.

For a little taste of freedom, take a moment right now and imagine how your life would be if there were nothing you should do or say and nothing you shouldn't do or say.

What would you do that you don't let yourself do? What would you stop doing that you do out of obligation? Take just one minute, right now, to feel, see, imagine your life without "shoulds."

Now, how do you feel? Free? Happy? Eager to follow your preferences? Feel terrified? Wonder how you'll get through the day without that inner critic pushing you around? Relax. Tell the Shouldistic Critic to get outta town and replace the jerk with a better kinder Preference Reminder. You'll stay on the right road—just minus the potholes.

When you get stuck habitually *doing what you think you should do* you can't figure out why your life isn't working since, for Pete's sake, you are doing what you were taught to and you expect your reward! Why hasn't the boss seen my over-the-top super-duper performance and given me a raise? Why hasn't my husband figured out that I want him to want to spend the weekend with me instead of his golf buddies?

For one thing, mind-reading is not a reliable skill, and furthermore it's not anyone else's job to anticipate your desires and make sure they are fulfilled.

"Whaddya mean?" you cry, "That's what I do for them!" Well, knock it off. Even if you are a really good people-pleasing mind-reader who anticipates and fulfills desires without being asked, who the hell ever said that this was your job, your obligation, or your destiny?

Put your skills to better use than doing for others what they are perfectly capable of doing for themselves. We don't mean for you to turn into a self-absorbed creep that does nothing for anyone. Do something you WANT to. Or wait until they ASK. Then you can choose whom you want to help, how much help you want to give and when you want to give it. That's right, you can say "no" as well as "yes" and the world will not end.

Our constant unspoken and unmet expectations lead to relentless judgment and blame which in turn poisons our ability to continue relating with compassion, honesty and openness. Pretending that you don't have to ask others what they think, feel, and want puts you on the road to misunderstanding, resentment, and relationship breakdown. But hey, if you want to be alone, that's one way to go about it.

For those who are perpetually compliant People Pleasers, (remember that virus?) life goes something like this. Instead of doing what you want to do, or saying what you want to say, or asking for what you want, you do one of these three progressively wacky things:

1. You do what *you think you should do*, or

2. You do what *other people think you should do*, or

3. You do what *you think other people think you should do*.

It's bad enough when you do *what you think you should do* instead of *what you want to do*. Now you may be thinking, well, if I did what I wanted to do, I'd sit home, lose my job, have sex with the mailman, ruin my marriage, eat ten pounds of chocolate and get fat! No, most likely you would not. Why? Remember those preferences? There are things you might feel a momentary impulse to do, and you won't because you have a preference for having an income and a place to live, being in a happy marriage, and staying in good health. Based on those preferences you would not quit your job and sit at home, drag the hot postman into the bedroom, or eat the entire contents of your kid's Halloween treat bag.

When you start doing what you actually want to do, your preferences will surface to guide how you behave. You might, for example, take a nice vacation or a "mental health day" from work, or even find a new job that you enjoy. You might flirt with the mailman, have hot sex with your husband and eat two bites of really good chocolate and feel satisfied. You're looking to have more pleasure, fun, and satisfaction in life and gaining weight, getting divorced, and being penniless will definitely NOT create that!

Of course, it's no mystery that ***doing what other people think you should do*** means that you can abdicate responsibility for your misery since you have "Them" to blame when things don't work out. It is also a way to justify procrastination. Either you think that you need to confer with several people to get their opinions on the "right" thing to do and the one and only way to do it that will be perfect, deliver results, and won't be a mistake. Or you simply refuse to do anything because you don't like doing what others think you should do and yet you won't let yourself do what you want to do. Oy, what misery.

But oh, let's look at that third and most useless plan—***doing what you think other people think you should do.*** Here, the inevitable outcome is bleak. In this scenario, you first have to delude yourself that you know (without asking, of course, because that would be too direct and "not nice" and possibly even impolite) what others are thinking. Then you imagine that your actions will please and satisfy the unfortunate soul who is the object of your delusion. Why is this person unfortunate? Because when you (usually grudgingly) do what you think someone else wants you to do instead of what you want to do, you imagine that there will be a payoff. That payoff will be their approval or recognition, at the very least, because they should be pleased that you did what you thought they thought you should do. Sound like a convoluted and childish set-up for failure? It is.

This level of wacky behavior often ends up sounding like this:

Jim: I sure wish I hadn't told my boss I'd work every Saturday in May.

Jan: I can't imagine why you did. I thought you wanted to take a class on Saturdays.

Jim: What do you mean? You wanted me to work! You said we needed extra income.

Jan: Yeah, but I never said I wanted you to give up your class. I said I could work more.

Jim: Yeah, right. You wanted me to work and you don't even appreciate my effort.

Jan: You're nuts. I never said I wanted you to work Saturdays. You didn't even ask me!

Jim: Oh, I know how you are. I know you don't want to add another shift on your job!

Jan: No I don't but—

Jim: There, you see, I was right! I knew it!

Jan: Bullshit! I just mean there are other options besides you working Saturdays.

Jim: Ungrateful cow!

Jan: Stupid jerk!

There, wasn't that productive, enlightening, and, perhaps, familiar? Doing something that you don't want to do because you think it will please someone else, *and doing it without even asking them if it will please them*, is not only dumb, it is a core pattern that causes plenty of hard feelings and irrational fights. How can you get any satisfaction or get over a fight that's based on something that you completely made up? Leave the mind reading to the Psychic Friends Network.

The biggest mistake we make in relating to others is to believe that we know what someone else thinks of us or wants from us. The

ONLY way to avoid that mistake is to ask, ask, ask, then believe what they tell you. If they're playing it safe, saying what they think you want to hear or simply lying, it's not your problem, you ASKED. Honestly, most people most of the time will give you a pretty straight answer if you ask them in a clear, direct way. In fact, they'll probably be relieved that you're not making something up instead of asking. So if you think someone wants something, or doesn't want something, if you think they are avoiding an issue, or avoiding you, or that someone's angry at you—ASK.

HOW to Know if They Are Thinking What You Think They're Thinking

ASK THEM. PERIOD. Really. That's it. (Master of the Obvious strikes again.)

Examples of Clear Direct Questions

"I was going to work this Saturday; did you have something else in mind?"

"Are you hinting that you don't want to have sex, or am I making that up?"

"You've been so quiet, I imagine that you're mad at me. Are you?"

"When you stay out so late I convince myself that you are bored with me. Are you?"

"I've been avoiding asking for your help. I think you're too busy and I shouldn't ask you. And I would like your help."

"When you complimented Sally I started to wonder if you were trying to tell me to lose weight Were you?"

"I really want to golf on Saturday and I figure you don't want me to go, and that if I do, you'll be pissed off. So, is there any truth to that or am I being paranoid?"

"You keep sighing and complaining about how hard this is. Do you want help?"

"Did you forget to do the dishes? I think you're hoping I'll do them if you stall long enough. Are ya?"

"Do you want me to pay for dinner?"

"I worry that you want to date other people. Do you?"

Try your own. You'll be glad you did. Then really listen, paying full attention to the answer.

CHAPTER 9

Communicating with Yourself

"Hundreds of thousands of impressions from the invisible world are eagerly wanting to come through you. I get dizzy with the abundance." —Rumi

We have two minds: the Deep Mind, which is our subconscious and the Surface Mind, which can become confused and think it's running the show. When we listen to the messages from our bodies, and support each of our minds to do what they're designed to do, we experience harmony. (Cue up the angel choir!) Congruence, which is another word for harmony, is the foundation for effective communication between people and within us. When our thoughts, emotions and actions are congruent, we often get what we set out to accomplish, and when we don't, we learn from the experience without feeling the need for a pity party. When we have dueling beliefs, or shoulds battling with preferences, then we need to know how to create harmony out of that chaos.

To do this, you have to learn to quiet your mind long enough to notice what your senses and sensations are telling you. If you can quiet the noise of your mind for a few moments, you can separate what only seems to be real from what actually is. Then you can make clear observations, interrupt old patterns, and create new behaviors.

Make the effort to establish a regular practice of meditation, yoga, or other kinds of mindfulness practices. Doing this will help you to integrate the intelligence that comes to you as sensations and sudden flashes of insight, allowing you to make better, more conscious choices—choices that are not simply a repeated product of your filters and expectations. This is what it means to "lose your mind and come to your senses."

Our marvelous minds are pretty quick to sort what we see and hear and feel into categories so that we can quickly grasp what is coming at us and going on around us. As we've said, those rapid recognition "thin slicing" programs can be useful tools in many situations. We subconsciously process thousands of incoming pieces of data and receive powerful impulses that might urge us not to trust a stranger, or to change lanes, or to get back into the building microseconds before something life threatening occurs. When we listen and obey those signals, we can, with ease and grace, move out of harm's way as if by magic. There is a deeper intelligence at work here. Real intelligence is not just our intellect. Without modification from our emotion-processing limbic system and without being informed by our unconscious, our intellect can (and sometimes does) get us harmed or even killed in pretty short order. Just visit The Darwin Awards website (http://www.darwinawards.com) for a humorous look-see at how our "reasoning" mind can kill us off.

Even if you're not a candidate for a Darwin award, ignoring your deeper, sensate intelligence will still create a mess in your life. When it comes to everyday human interaction, the information we receive as sensations and impulses are often ignored or misinterpreted, leaving us with only a filtered take on events that we then confuse with what actually happened. Remember "dueling beliefs"—where what you say you want opposes what you actually do? Often that duel gets set up when we habitually dismiss and ignore the messages in our bodies and the sudden impulses that arise seemingly out of nowhere ("Don't go with him." "Something's wrong here." "That's a lie"). That conflict is real trouble.

For example, a woman may ignore warning signs (obvious to others) that a potential boyfriend may be violent, or may be a liar or a cheat, even when she's had those experiences before. With practice, she could learn to identify and recognize that the feeling of "familiarity combined with tension and anxiety" when she meets a potential mate is a clear memo to be heeded rather than dismissed. She can then correctly interpret this as a warning, and make a conscious choice rather than blindly repeat the past.

When you are able to question your conclusions and assumptions you can arrive at an interpretation that is based more in concrete (observable) reality. It is especially important not to believe everything you think. Learning to be attentive to sensations helps, because one way your subconscious speaks to you is through your body's sensations and impulses. When you notice your thoughts, notice what you feel (as sensations) in your body and notice what is going on around you, and then consider what you want and what your options are, you stand a better chance of acting based on what's possible rather than on delusion (what's impossible).

When we insert "social filters" to override our gut feelings, we can put ourselves at real risk of harm. When you have a surge of fear for example, rather than act on it you might damp it down with "What would people think?" or "I should give everyone the benefit of the doubt." or "He's just had a hard life" or "He's just trying to be nice, I shouldn't be so suspicious." or " I shouldn't tell people what to do." In fact, your subconscious, having picked up on clues that your conscious mind hasn't registered, is clearly screaming for you to get outta there! I have heard these kinds of overrides used in situations where obvious danger signs were noted and registered not only by the person at risk but by friends, relatives, and even strangers who observed the interaction.

Gavin DeBecker, a world-renowned expert on evaluating risky situations, says that, "A gut feeling is in fact a cognitive process, far different from the step-by-step thinking we rely on willingly. We think that conscious thought is somehow better, when in fact, intuition is soaring flight compared to the plodding of logic. The human brain is never more efficient or invested than when its host is at risk. At the moment when our intuition is most basic, people tend to consider its function supernatural." (from Gavin DeBecker, *The Gift of Fear*).

Learn how to communicate well within your own mind by becoming the Observer of your own thoughts. This is one of the most useful practices you can teach yourself.

Here is one way to get this practice started: *when you hear yourself say "it", remember that YOU are "it"—there is no "it."*

When you say, "It makes me angry" turn that into "I make me angry"

"It's comforting to think . . ." becomes "I'm comforted by thinking . . ."

"It drives me crazy" is "I drive myself crazy"

Practice this long enough and it will become part of how you speak about your experiences—and that will have many subtle (and probably a few not-so-subtle) effects on how you create your experiences.

Communication Glitches and the Conflicts They Spawn

Most of us were taught a whole boatload of inaccurate and useless things about relating with other human beings. Never in our education were we taught a clear model of how to deal with strong emotions, communicate honestly, relate effectively, or cultivate intimacy. This leaves us with a great deal of trial and error, bad advice, heartache, confusion, incorrect assumptions, and unhappiness littering our relationship roads.

The first challenge in clear communication is to know what to do when you feel angry, hurt, and disappointed. You knew once, but you have forgotten how to express and get over your emotions moment by moment. Remember when you could yell at your friend to "Cut that out!" then go right on playing with her and loving her?

Another challenge is to overcome the false belief that you are responsible for causing the emotions and reactions of others. We often blame ourselves for, take personally, or overreact to other peoples' anger and hurt. When someone takes what you say or do and attaches an interpretation to it, then gets all bent out of shape about that interpretation, this is not your fault and, really, there is not much you can do to control it.

Annoying habits you may have acquired include:

- You hold it all in until you reach overwhelm, then blow up irrationally
- You take your frustration out on the bank teller, the kids, employees or spouse, instead of whomever you're actually upset with
- You do the act-irritated-but-swear-you're-fine routine
- You mope and say "I'm just tired" when even a sock monkey puppet would know you are just playing the role of The Victim.

We are each the source of our own thoughts, judgments, and emotions. They aren't implanted in our brains from a spaceship, nor do they infect us like the flu. We generate them. It is each individual's assumptions and expectations that cause one person to laugh something off, and another to react defensively or angrily to the same event. No one but you can make you happy *or* miserable (although certainly people can help you get wherever you're headed).

This isn't to suggest that you abandon compassion and never take others' feelings into consideration—we're all about being kind (not nice), remember? So don't try to justify acting like a jerk by deliberately baiting someone, then saying, "I can't 'make' you angry, only you can make you angry, so there!"

Typically we are so busy constantly and habitually judging our own performance or passing judgment on others that we barely experience moment-to-moment reality and rarely check in to see what our bodies are telling us. This is a big part of how we make wrong assessments, add meaning or motive, create drama, say dumb things, walk off in a huff, pick fights, and generally cause ourselves unnecessary irritation and suffering. Cut yourself, and those around you, some slack. Use the tried and true formula—Notice, Interrupt, Revise, Repeat—to help you STOP believing the motive you assign to others' words or actions, and to stop assigning motives, period. Cultivate a sense of humor about the nutty things you and the people you love do.

As you become a better observer and learn to notice your interpretations and become less quick to believe them, you will be better able to see and understand the sensate information that's always available to you. You will develop a calmer, more assertive, and less judgmental attitude. You will feel more secure, and will trust your larger intelligence to make better decisions.

Start to notice your most common complaints about people. Constant complaints tell us far more about our expectations and filters than about "how things are." When you have a complaint that repeats from one relationship to the next, your mind may be altering events, blinding you to what's really happening in order to conform reality to your expectations.

A Tale Of Two Interpretations: A True Story

I went to lunch with a couple, we'll call them Mark and Lydia, who had been having communication problems. One of Lydia's usual complaints was: "He hardly ever touches me. He's not affectionate." Mark's usual complaint was: "She doesn't appreciate me. I can't do anything right for her."

During lunch I paid attention to their interaction. Mark put his arm around Lydia twice, and both times she leaned away. He then moved away from her on the bench seat. He patted her leg once while he was telling me something interesting that she did. He stroked her arm when he mentioned a trip they were going to take. He kissed her before he left us to our coffee and went back to work.

During the conversation, Lydia mentioned an idea of Mark's that she thought was "brilliant", and she talked about the work he was doing around the house. Looking right at him, she said that he'd done a great job with a particular project. She also reported something she wanted him to work on that weekend, and why she felt it was a priority.

What do you think they each remembered about the lunch conversation?

Lydia remembered that he moved away from her. She did remember that he kissed her goodbye, and dismissed it as "habit." She did not remember the arm stroke or thigh touch and said she "might" remember him putting his arm up behind her once when they first sat down because it snagged her hair. "See," she said, "He just doesn't seem interested in me."

"Oh brother," I thought, "Here we go." When I spoke to Mark later that day, he remembered Lydia's "complaint" about what she "expected" of him over the coming weekend, but not the two compliments, and not the "brilliant" remark.

As Mark and Lydia's interaction and interpretations show, when we have cultivated a story about someone, as long as we insist that our version and interpretation of events is right, we won't have clear communication, and thus an improved relationship, with that person. We're too busy relating to the person our filters show us, instead of the person who is actually there. When a filter is dragging you around by your hair, you will only remember what fits within the parameters of the judgments you have established. *Most importantly, when you are fully convinced you are right before you stop and observe, and before you even ask a question, you will think backwards from your reaction to supply the evidence.* Take a breath, quiet your mind, and become present as the objective witness to help you pick your way through the minefield of your filtered experience.

HOW to Correct a Communication that is Blowing Off-Course

- Observe (notice)
- Question (interrupt)
- Reveal or Request (redirect) and
- Repeat

As soon as you recognize you're "off to the races," about to get caught up in some interpretation of events that's beginning to make you feel annoyed, hurt, outraged, righteous, judgmental—as soon as you realize you're heading down another tense, unpleasant road—before you go over the cliff, see if you can interrupt yourself just long enough to observe and notice information you may have overlooked.

Notice: Acting from self-reference becomes possible when you can notice your automatic reactions that usually run the show. Take just a second or two to simply notice—what you are seeing and hearing, then what you are thinking, and then what you are feeling in your body. After noticing your thoughts and sensations, ask yourself, "Ok, is this the only possible interpretation? No. What else could he or she have meant? How are these thoughts making me feel?"

Question: Next, identify what you actually want, or want to know, and ask. And we do mean ask, not accuse, suggest, imply, berate, or assume.

Reveal or Request: Reveal what you were thinking and how you were taking yourself off course, and if you have one, make a request for what it is you want.

Yes, this is another version of notice, interrupt, and redirect; however, when there's another person involved, whose words or actions are triggering strong judgments and emotions in you, then taking a step back before you confuse your reactive judgments for reality is a good plan.

Five Communication Corrections

Here are some additional ways to practice simple, clear, direct communication.

Enlist a Communication Correction Coach. No one knows your quirks like a good friend. Get a friend to tell you when you sound like an idiot. This is not only a great way to interrupt self-sabotage, it's fun to return the favor. It'll make you closer. We promise. This practice covers ALL communication glitches.

Get down off that soapbox. Nobody enjoys being talked at as if you were a cop, their third grade teacher, a priest or—worst of all—their parent. This is a quick way to lose friends, lovers, and jobs. If you find yourself in a "should"-laden, finger wagging, moralistic, self-righteous mood, or if you just generally feel superior, zip it. The practice is this—repeat after me: "I am the only adult whose beliefs and behaviors I have the authority to correct." Repeat as necessary. You might consider a tattoo.

Learn to stop while you're ahead. If you have a bad case of going on-and-on-and-on, join On and On Anon! The meeting starts at seven but no one knows when it will end. Really, you know who you are. The practice is this: think before you speak for an entire inhale. Then make your point with as few words as possible and shut up. If you can't seem to stop yourself, pay attention to your listener! When his eyes dart to the door or glaze over you are to stop speaking immediately.

Don't ask, do tell. All you interrogators who control the conversation with your endless questions while artfully avoiding having to answer any about yourself might effectively run the presidential debates, but in ordinary life you are on the fast track to having people run away when they see you coming. This conversational strategy will start to validate your insecurity because people will react to you the way they react to the thought of a colonoscopy. They cringe. For you, the practice is this: Invite the five people you are most insecure around to ask you anything they want to know about you. Then tell them the truth *in one sentence* and say no more.

Let someone else have the last word. If you have last-word-itis, you will make any of your communication blunders worse by justifying, defending, and explaining the what, why, and how you said the first thing that led to a misunderstanding. Put a sock in it. This one is especially likely to spiral out of control when communicating by email, which lacks the 93% or more of communication that is nonverbal, so more words are just more gasoline on the brightly burning blaze. Your practice is this: When your words or intent are misunderstood, rather than defend, explain or justify your position say, "I'm sorry you feel that way. It was not my intention for you to feel hurt or angry." Then you can agree to disagree rather than bludgeon the other person with your desire to be understood (by which you really mean "agreed with"). Just get over yourself.

The Red Dress: A Fable

A couple is out for dinner and as they walk to their table they both notice a beautiful woman in a red dress sitting alone at a table close to theirs. As they are seated, the husband glances over the wife's shoulder and he smiles. The wife, sure that he's smiling at the woman, finds herself thinking about her age, her first husband's infidelities, the birthday the current husband forgot, and before long she is furious. She eats in stony silence despite her husband's attempts to draw her out, and when he asks her the obvious question, " What's wrong?", she answers " Nothing!" which of course means, "You idiot! I'm pissed at you for looking at that woman and smiling."

By the time the check arrives, her looks can fry a chicken. Hubby is confused. She's gearing up for a battle in the car and has called to mind several items that annoyed her earlier in the week that she was overlooking (and stockpiling) until now.

As they get up to leave, she makes a dramatic pivot on her spike heels to give the Other Woman an evil glare, only to catch her shoe on the rug, and while she tumbles to the carpet she notices that where the Other Woman had been seated, her husband's business partner is now chowing down a steak. Hubby helps her up, and in passing the partner she finds out that the Other Woman, apparently now in the restroom, is the partner's fiancée. In the car she bursts into tears. What a waste of an evening and a perfectly good dinner!

The moral: When you feel the wind-up starting, stop. Observe, ask, reveal, request, repeat.

Let's rewind this drama. What if she noticed what she saw and felt, and revealed what was going on? What if she, after observing her husband smile over her shoulder said, "Hey, did you just smile at that woman we passed when we came in? I'm feeling pretty bland compared to her. I'm feeling kinda jealous." He might reply, "Whoa, honey. My partner just sat down with her. I smiled at him. She's his fiancée. And sure she's pretty but I'm plenty happy with you."

Notice that she revealed, not accused, and asked a question rather than made a statement.

This is NOT permission to turn your insecurities into accusations and spit them all over the place as though they are facts. Here's an example of what NOT to do. She might have said, with a higher pitch and louder voice: "I saw you smile at that woman! What do you think I am, blind? I know I'm no beauty queen, but do you have to disrespect me?" We repeat: This is what NOT to do.

One of our biggest communication mistakes comes from assuming that things we imagine are facts. We pretend that we know what other people think and want and that our interpretation and the meanings we attach are the truth. We also assume that we know their motives. What we have learned in many years of listening to people talk about their problem is that many of our so-called problems are a direct result of people convincing themselves that their thoughts and beliefs are objective reality. Big mistake.

If you have repetitive thoughts that torment you, your mind will look for evidence as certainly as the minds of the two guys in NY with that $20 on the sidewalk. If you don't teach yourself to question your knee-jerk reactions, most available reality will be filtered out of your awareness. What you are left with is a story in your imagination, plus what you are driven to notice by the filters in your mind.

The Problem with Gossip

It's been said that gossip is the most efficient way to move information through an organization. Pretty much everyone gossips, and the conversations at the coffee pot or the printer or the water cooler often are a great source of information on what is happening in the workplace—except when it comes with a layer of resentment, judgment, jealousy, imagined motive, or poor memory from the tale teller. The same is true for gossip that goes on at the family reunion or among a group of friends.

Some gossip is relatively benign—expressing an opinion or judgment about some celebrity's choice of eveningwear isn't going to do much damage to relationships or reputations among your friends, family, or coworkers, and if you're funny it may even add some entertainment value.

Gossip is toxic and destructive any time you are "venting," playing victim, or in any way reporting your critical opinion to anyone other than the person you are actually talking about. This is true whether you are passing judgment on workmates, family members, or anyone else you know. We use toxic gossip is to manipulate, control, or attempt to damage the reputations of other people.

Unfortunately, gossip is often the glue that holds people together. By sharing juicy bits of gossip, the gossipers get to believe that they are better than the poor slob they are gossiping about, at least at the moment. We all love that feeling of righteousness, often combined with indignation, that comes with pointing out one person's shortcomings to someone else. We feel bigger, better, smarter, and right when we make someone else smaller, less than, and wrong. It's petty. It's ugly. It's social cannibalism. And despite that momentary feeling of superiority, gossip is a game played by those who lack true personal power.

All of that self-righteous, indignant, need-to-be-right belief that "I would NEVER do that," is a front. Behind all that bluster, there is a fear of being found out, a fear that we might be a little too close to having our own shortcomings revealed. This is especially true when the judgments we have of others also apply to us, as is often the case. Control freaks are the first to criticize other control freaks, and liars gossip about other liars for a good reason: it takes one to know one. We get ourselves in trouble when we forget that our judgments about the motives or morality of others isn't fact, *and our opinion about others says more about our own intolerance, self-righteousness, and shortcomings than it says about them.*

Gossip is fueled by our mind's capacity and inclination to judge others. As we've talked about earlier, our capacity for judgment, especially "snap" judgments, evolved as a useful tool to help us steer clear of danger and hopefully avoid objects, predators, and situations that were, for our hunter-gatherer ancestors, potential threats to our literal survival. Trouble comes when we forget that our judgments aren't fact, and our opinions aren't always accurate. When we guess about a person's issues, actions, and motives and then share that information as if it is fact (we may even label it "our truth") we are adding to stress and resulting stress-related illnesses—for ourselves, and potentially for those about whom we gossip.

We often forget that gossip has a long shelf life. What we know about seeing incorrect news in the media applies to gossip. A sensational inflammatory story about someone, even if it is completely fabricated, is remembered, and we often continue to suspect that there may be something to it even after a correction, retraction, or verdict of "not guilty" has been issued.

Gossip is a way we avoid "confrontation," by talking about, rather than to, the person or persons in question. If you have an assessment that is derogatory, a complaint, or a resentment, gossip will not help you get over it. If you take it to the person directly, and present your opinion as an inquiry (not an inquest), you create a way to get over your judgment. This isn't a confrontation, it's just a conversation. The point of the conversation is not to confront or accuse based on assumptions, but to recognize the distinction between what is actually so, and what are unfounded assumptions, beliefs, or imaginings.

It takes discipline and effort to break the gossip habit and to step back from the drama it evokes. If you spend time with people that engage in complaining and gossiping, refuse to be dragged into the ugly game. Here's how.

HOW to End Gossip in Two Easy Steps

1. Talk directly TO people that you are upset with rather than about them. The only possible exception is if you are talking to a friend about *how* to talk to the person you are feeling irritated by, hurt by, or judgmental about.

2. Refuse to participate in gossip. Nothing stops a gossip-monger faster than a clear, simple, and direct refusal to participate. Just. Say. No.

Whether you are at work, with your in-laws, at church, or at a party, it is possible to refuse gossip and drama by interrupting the gossip-monger. Keep your language simple, clear and direct. State the obvious, such as:

"I am honestly not interested in hearing about Janet's alleged affair-unless Janet decides to confide in me."

"I've got my own issues, so discussing Bob's inadequacies isn't what I want to do."

"If you are angry at Bill, then please go talk to him, not to me."

"I'm here to have a good time and this conversation isn't working for me."

"I'm not willing to keep secrets, so don't tell me about Joe's problems."

"Did you ask Beth what she meant by that remark? Could you be wrong? Please talk to her instead of me."

"I understand that your feelings are hurt. Please go talk to him about that."

"I'd rather count the floor tile than listen to you gossip!" (That always stops 'em.)

Refusing to participate in gossip helps to remind you to take your own complaints to the person you have complaints about. Clear, direct language gets your point across and gives the other person an opportunity to redirect his or her own behavior. Not that they will take your suggestion, but at least you won't be pulled into the story.

Yes it will most likely make you a little twitchy and anxious to have a conversation about yourself instead of a blame fest about the other person the first ten times you do it. That's OK. Feel the fear and do it anyway.

HOW Being Authentic Works at Work

Honesty combined with clear communication can work wonders at work. Dropping your Image in favor of revealing your Authentic Self can be a powerful, positive step in the workplace. As mentioned earlier, we spend entirely too much time and energy painstakingly attempting to manipulate the opinions of others to project and protect an image of ourselves that we think is required for us to be accepted. Our image doesn't reflect an accurate version of who we really are, since we shift masks depending on whom we are in front of. Protecting an image is a waste of time and energy. Even at work.

Taking responsibility for consciously creating better relationships with your boss, your coworkers, and those you supervise is a huge step toward a more cooperative, happier place to spend the majority of your waking hours. Asking for what you want in simple, clear, direct language is a great negotiating tool. How can I get what I want and do so in a way that you can have what you want, too? The most effective businesses and organizations incorporated this into their cultures. Their employees are mostly happy, feel that they are part of a team, and are taken care of pretty well. Clear, direct communication is an excellent way of relating at work and elsewhere in your daily life.

CHAPTER 10

Your "Get Out of Jail Free Card"

"Life isn't about finding yourself. Life is about creating yourself." —George Bernard Shaw

Happiness isn't a life without upset, but a life in which you have the power to get out of your own way, effectively resolve stress, and consciously self-regulate. To create pleasurable, satisfying lives, we have to figure out how to grow up and get over the worst of the useless crap we carry around that keeps us locked into patterns of belief and behavior that just don't work. Although this may seem either impossible or obvious to you, we do, each of us, unconsciously play out family issues in our jobs and relationships. We keep on looking for, and generating, that comfortable, familiar emotional context, that special mix of pleasure and tension that feels like "home."

You are the only one who can take on the job of doing over or making up for what your parents did or did not do, or for what you imagine they did or did not do. So the short course in getting beyond any left-over family "viruses" begins with deciding consciously to take on the job of parenting yourself.

You get to create new permissions, break old taboos, create new traditions, and revise your habits by using rewards and self-discipline. You get to rebel against authority in a constructive useful way, and challenge the assumptions you have been living with, and the assumptions others try to sell you on.

It's fun. It's powerful, and it works.

Please Note: If you are dealing with serious issues resulting from childhood abuse or sexual trauma, seek the help of a professional therapist, counselor, or clergy.

Even though most of us had upbringings that did not involve serious physical or psychological abuse, few of us emerge from a "normal" childhood without some areas where we never quite finished the process of becoming a fully functional adult. Look around you and you'll begin to see how many adolescents in adult bodies there are.

It takes self-awareness and discipline to complete our development into autonomous, self-referent beings. In our teen years, we reach a point in brain development that, to those in authority, looks like constant rebellion. Teenagers are risk-takers, questioners, taking little at face value, and craving excitement and new experiences. We are designed to rebel, to become independent thinkers and to move into the next phase of adulthood and maturity. Ideally, we do this by keeping what was useful from our childhood experiences and our parents' lessons, and revising or rejecting things we do not wish to replicate.

Some people never let themselves rebel (or their rebellion is so effectively squelched when they are teens that they never complete it) and enter adulthood in age only, still feeling like children waiting to be recognized or taken care of. They fear stepping into their own authority and power. They complain about authority figures (managers, bosses, presidents, celebrities, spouses) to each other like kids talking under the covers with their siblings, but never get beyond the blame game. Unaware of how they got stuck there, they are still tethered to parents—they still live according to their parents' expectations, rather than their own preferences, and they don't develop adult peer relationships with their parents. Nor can they feel like real adults when in their parents' company. They eagerly put others, especially authority figures and spouses, in the "parent" role and find themselves limited and paralyzed by the very same emotions that dominated their childhoods.

Some people go the other way and reject authority completely, reacting so strongly to their past that they strive to become the opposite of whatever their parents stood for or wanted for them. Their constant knee-jerk rejection of authority isn't freedom either, because they still base their choices on what their parents don't want, rather than following their own adult preferences. It's just a mind-jail with a different view.

The walls of that jail—whether blind acceptance of authority, reactionary rejection of authority, or something in between—keep us from seeing Reality as it is, and our lives are based on inaccurate and irrational childish fears and assumptions.

CLUE: When you notice that you have the urge to make a request, express anger, ask for clarification, or express a want or desire and then suddenly have an irrational thought like "My spouse will leave me if I ask for that," "Mom will drop dead if I say that," "I'll never hear the end of it if I reveal that," "I'll get fired if I . . . ," "They'll stop being my friend if I . . .," or "They'll get mad at me if I . . ." that's the time to take a breath, and prepare to rebel against the false voice of fake authority that has you thinking and acting like a teenager instead of an adult.

Rebellion doesn't require that we hate our parents, dismiss our bosses, or think that those in authority are stupid, mean, or oppressive. ***Rebellion is the rejection of the assumption that we must accept what we are told by An Authority.*** It may include an exploration of opposing views. Checking in with your own experiences and desires, you can then make a more conscious choice about the issue or course of action. Don't believe everything you think. Experiment to see what thoughts, beliefs, and habits work for you and which ones work against you.

If you are really honest with yourself, you might realize that in some ways you expect (or hope) that your spouse or job will give you something that you think your parents didn't provide enough of: praise, acknowledgement, support, permission, trust, freedom, honesty, clear guidelines, and so on.

As we rebel and test assumptions, we cultivate a more accurate method of decision making. We move from the world of rules and blind acceptance of authority to a world in which direct experience shows us how much gray there is between the two extremes of black and white answers. We become aware that right and wrong, and good and bad, are relative and complex, and moral decisions are complicated and are rarely absolute.

We each inherit a "family virus"—that special blend of habitually unspoken resentments and requests, secrets, ways of manipulating, wacky communication, childish stubbornness, fed by our judgments and channeled through our individual family roles. It makes 40-year-olds feel like naughty grade school kids or tongue-tied teens. It makes you, or a maybe your sibling, listen to your mother's complaining or criticizing in jaw clenching silence, then whine to you or take that frustration out on the kids, hubby, or a pint of Ben and Jerry's. It's that urge at work to see what you can get away with when your manager (who sounds so much like your father) points out a mistake you made. And it's that underhanded communication that goes on in families, keeping the same old fights and same old complaints and same old stories alive year, after year, after year.

Do you prefer to feel like a capable adult, have more down time, speak your mind, ask for what you want clearly without playing guessing games, speak up honestly, get over hurt and resentment quickly, not get hooked when your family "starts in?" Sure you do.

First, just take a look at your reactions and, if you don't let your rationalizations, defenses, and excuses distract you, you will see pretty clearly with whom and in what situations you stop thinking and feeling like an adult. If you like to write, when you catch on to them write them down. If not, write them down anyway.

Next, make a conscious choice to free your bosses, friends, and family from the impossible task of parenting you, and take steps to create the feelings and experiences you wanted but didn't get, or get enough of, in childhood. Be an investigative reporter for your own life. Note the energy that you currently waste on family virus-inspired head games, playing victim and/or blaming yourself and others and begin to give it back to yourself as kindness. Then, give yourself permission.

HOW to Give Yourself Permission to Grow Up

Identify how you get triggered to feel young and insecure, and then deliberately create a few "permissions" that will give you a specific way to redirect your thoughts when you feel the Family Virus coming on. Keep doing this, and you'll be able to create some freedom for yourself, set healthy limits, and break old worn-out family taboos. Here are some examples:

I give myself permission to ask for what I want even at work.

I give myself permission to step in and parent myself when I feel threatened.

I give myself permission to ask for clarification before I believe my own interpretations and hurt my feelings.

I give myself permission to express and get over anger.

I give myself permission to tell my mother how crazy I make myself when she carries on about Aunt Mary, and Dad, and my sister.

I give myself permission to interrupt my mother.

I give myself permission to give myself time to rest and have fun.

I give myself permission to feel and speak up like the grown-up that I am.

I give myself permission to tell my spouse what I like during sex.

Tim's Story: New Permissions as a Power Tool

Tim, at 59 years old, found himself increasingly anxious around his wife's family, especially his brother-in-law, Ted, who talked constantly. He would suddenly realize he was angry, then he would have a few beers and either pick a fight or leave the house. After his wife sent him to anger management classes, he just stayed in the other room away from his brother-in-law when the family visited, feeling tense and miserable until they left. Then he'd drink himself to sleep. Tim had plenty of old "be a good boy" taboos operating, so we used permissions to override them.

I give myself permission to have fun at family gatherings.

I give myself permission to notice as soon I start getting irritated at Ted.

I give myself permission to take a breath when I get tense.

I give myself permission to ask Ted to change the subject or to interrupt him.

I give myself permission to accept Ted as is.

I give myself permission not to like Ted.

I give myself permission to leave the room and have fun.

I give myself permission to sooth myself without drinking or eating.

I give myself permission to have adult-to-adult conversations with any family member and reveal what I think and what I want.

I give myself permission to be seen and heard.

I give myself permission to know I'm a good person and still say what I think.

I give myself permission to do what makes me happy.

We created the above permissions and Tim used them in three ways. He read them after he woke up but before he went down to have his coffee, wrote them once every day, usually during a break at work, and he also used them mentally to interrupt his old habits and to remind himself to speak up.

Within four months (and five family get-togethers) Tim was able to completely transform his stress reaction and old behavioral patterns. He interrupted Ted and asked him to change the subject (politics) and later took Ted aside and asked him to give up trying to start debates at family events. Tim revealed how long (12 years) he'd been holding onto resentment about Ted's political ideas, and said he wanted to shake hands and agree to disagree. Much to Tim's surprise, Ted agreed. Tim then asked his wife stop handing Ted drinks as an attempt to shut him up. She quit doing that. Then Tim bought a basketball hoop, and a horseshoe set. What started out as a way for Tim to go out and have fun on his own became a new and satisfying way for Ted and Tim to play together, literally. They even now occasionally give each other good-natured political jabs.

You can really generate some energy and excitement in your life by deliberately breaking family-enforced taboos and worn-out traditions. Neither your life nor your relatives' lives depend on your continuing to keep old family secrets, overlooking abusive or just chronically annoying behaviors, or playing endless rounds of "Let's Pretend" to keep your image (or other family members' images) intact. When your reasoning mind starts to cough up all the reasons why you *should* keep doing the crazy thing, or why you *shouldn't* tell mom you're done listening to her relentlessly criticize her own sister, remember that *those thoughts are what keeps you feeling like a frightened or naughty child. Then give yourself permission to ignore them!*

Giving yourself new permissions is one way to effectively boost repetition and emotion when you want to create something new in any area of your life, not just with your family. It works well even when you're not completely sure what's under the surface.

Cathy's Story: The Rewards of Saying "No."

Cathy was miserable at work. She had been at the same job ten years. She didn't have an assistant, even though other managers at her level did. She regularly stayed late and came in early to get everything done, and done perfectly. She never said "no" to a request from a coworker. She hadn't had a raise in three years. Then she was reprimanded for gossiping. She felt like a victim. She was having trouble sleeping.

Her permissions were:

I give myself permission to leave on time even if everything isn't done.

I give myself permission to feel afraid to leave, and to leave anyway.

I give myself permission to ask for help and/or an assistant.

I give myself permission to tell my manager how stressed out I am.

I give myself permission to do yoga before work rather than go in early.

I give myself permission to ask for a raise.

I give myself permission to learn how to work smarter.

I give myself permission to say "no" when I don't have time to help out.

I give myself permission to say "no" to Linda who goofs off then asks for my help.

I give myself permission to look for a new job.

I give myself permission to say what I think and let the chips fall where they may.

It took Cathy five weeks and three conversations, (and saying one "no" so loud her manager came running from his office to see what was wrong) to retrain her co-workers and her manager to stop asking for her help late in the day. She did yoga in the morning and left work on time even when she came home and worried that she was going to be fired for not completing every project on her desk before she left. Nobody noticed. She was astounded. At week four she sat down with her manager and spilled the beans, telling him that she had been hating work but now she was leaving on time, that she hadn't been finishing every project, that she wanted help if he expected her to do so, and that she felt underappreciated.

"Look, I know that you may just fire me for what I'm doing, and that's OK. I can't go back to having sleepless nights and not having a life," Cathy said. Her manager was shocked. He had no idea that she'd been working herself up and thought she just enjoyed her job. He said, "So how much of that smiling and staying late and saying "yes" was going on because you thought you had to do those things?" "A lot" she said.

He was very quiet and Cathy was sure the axe was about to fall. But this is what the manager said: "OK, so from now on you will share Mark's assistant on Wednesdays and Fridays and by the way, it was never a requirement to complete every project that landed on your desk before you left for the day. I had no idea you were trying to do that. No wonder it seemed like you lived here." At the first of the year, Cathy got a raise.

Once you have some new permissions in place and working for you, you know how to be your own parent—the adult who will now step in when you have one of those spontaneous age regressions.

I had a client, Harry, whose mother was brutally critical. He is very smart and very capable. He is in charge of overseeing the operation of a large, elite country club. He's great at communicating and feeling at ease with employees and peers but quickly turns into a child, complete with downcast eyes and ass-kissing manner when a member of the board asks a question or makes a suggestion. He was killing himself with overtime doing things that were neither productive nor necessary. Here's what he did: He decided how much he needed to work to keep the place running well and created a few new permissions about speaking honestly and letting Big Harry step in when Little Harry cringed in fear. At the next Board of Directors meeting, the first time a request from a Board member triggered the Family Virus, Harry literally lifted his head, squared his shoulders towards that board member and said: "I have in the past spent lots of extra time and effort doing things you asked to please you, though often they were things that did not improve the quality or efficiency of the service we offer. I imagine that by now you trust me to know what works and what doesn't to keep things running well. If I have time and I think your idea has merit, I may look into it; otherwise, I will stick to my original plan." Then he braced for impact, sure that a storm of ego and demand would follow. The Board Member said, " OK, great, Harry, you're the best at what you do. If it ain't broke, don't fix it." Harry just said, "Thank you." Inside, he told me, Little Harry yelled, "Wow!" and was dancing a jig.

That's what it is to parent yourself. Quick course corrections, compassionate criticism, and consistent positive reinforcement are the ingredients that help people of all ages feel competent, capable, and able to take risks and correct mistakes quickly. In other words, act like an adult. Notice and replace your internal parent voice with the voice of Grown-Up You and you will become responsible in the true sense of the word: one who is able to respond, rather than react to life and all the change it brings.

Some people are blind to the limitations that unchallenged family rules and assumptions can have, blind to the tangled threats that keep them trying to please and be accepted by their parents at all costs. Sometimes, they may not know how imprisoned they were until their parents are gone. Here is one example.

A Tale of Two Siblings

Two siblings, who are in their 40s, led lives that were strongly and negatively influenced by their controlling, manipulative mother. For those outside the family, and for herself, Mom generated and maintained the illusion of that she was a kind, devoted, and long-suffering parent. She certainly demonstrated an appearance of concern and contact with her kids that to the untrained eye might exclusively look like familial devotion. And yet her over-the-top behavior put her at the center of the action in an attention-getting, grandiose way, as if she were looking for votes to become the next Mother of the Year.

In private she was aloof and internally critical of her children, speaking to them as if they were ten years old, and alternately heaping false praise on them and giving them the cold shoulder if they declined to do her bidding, holding them hostage to a rigid code of behavior.

The fear of rejection and the silent treatment combined with the nasty, backbiting gossip she doled out as punishment for any infraction left them both tense and on guard most of the time. Being careful of what they said and did to be sure Mother did not get upset (and reveal the viscous gossip she really was) was a full-time job.

Then each of them (with my encouragement) began to rebel. One child announced that Mother could no longer dictate whether or not he cursed. As an adult he could say whatever he wanted. He also realized that she insisted on coming to all of his birthday parties, and that her presence made being playful and free with his guy friends impossible. He told her that this year he would celebrate with her separately, having a party on his own. The other child, a daughter, told her mother to stop calling her baby names—it made her skin crawl.

The outrage, wailing, drama, and gossip that Mother created for many weeks thereafter woke both siblings up to the deeper, darker tentacles that were affecting other areas of their lives. They had been raised on judgment and criticism, the need to look good at all costs, and the belief that they never had enough—despite the fact that they were well off and money not even remotely an issue for any of them. The cost of staying tethered to Mother in this childish way was staggering. Marriages, health, and friendships had suffered under the relentless stress, constant self-doubt, fear of ridicule, and more.

Within two years of these initial acts of rebellion, Mother died suddenly and unexpectedly. Much to their surprise, both children reported that the feeling of relief far outweighed the feeling of grief. They were surprised and a little disturbed by that realization. In the weeks following her death, each child became more at ease, more relaxed, and more able to act on preferences without wondering what Mother was going to think or do. In other words, they started to grow up. Did they love Mother? Yes, definitely. They had simply never challenged the family dynamic and did not realize how poisonous her influence had been. They are now finding their own way and discovering what makes them happy, with speed and ease.

It is never too late to grow up and enjoy many of the benefits of adulthood we dreamed about when we were kids. As we test the assumptions and revise the rules we learned from our parents and other authority figures, we develop the capacity to relate to them (and others) without fearing their disapproval. As we grow up emotionally, the fears and rules that once kept us prisoners no longer stop us. Our parents may become our friends in the process, and we may have a new sense of ease with our spouses and bosses. As we assert our adult decision-making power and make our own mistakes, we can ask for their advice without taking their word as law. When that happens, the relationships we have become more honest and cooperative.

As we do this, we are more able to set aside what we think others expect of us and want from us, and create alliances with people who accept us as we are, warts and all. In this process we also awaken to the simple truth that all people are good and bad, kind and inconsiderate, tolerant and judgmental, smart and dumb, including ourselves. Compassion is a key trait shared by self-aware individuals.

Parenting yourself well is a radical act. Now, before you scare yourself with terrifying visions of cashing in your 401-K and moving to the islands or getting arrested protesting for a political cause, remember that the word "radical" means "root," that is, the source, the core, the nutritious nugget at the center of things. When you allow yourself to act from the center of yourself, from your true emotions, desires, talents, and drives; when you are then "in the flow" and no longer swimming against the tide, you have accomplished something radical, a change at the root of your life.

At the core of the being that you are is the authentic and childlike presence of your real thoughts and desires. The Hero of Your Life Story is right there, tucked away under the pretense, pressure, and demands you place on yourself. The Hero of your tale is willing to take a chance, ask for and accept help, face fears, and act in radical ways. You will, like every Hero, receive help, clues, and inspiration along the way. This book is one of your allies.

As you finish growing up, you may find yourself inspired to strip away the excess in your life, spend more time by yourself, start a relationship, end a relationship, and above all, give yourself permission to take time to laugh, and to do that which fills you up, gives your life meaning. Sure, you may find, at the root of your personal truth, that you want to sell the house and move to Alaska, or drive to DC to protest social injustice, though you may be just as likely to discover a potent though repressed desire to play the piano, fly a kite, adopt a child, tell the truth about something that's keeping you at odds with a sibling, express a hidden desire, dare to fall in love, dance naked in the moonlight, color with crayons, buy yourself a new laptop, write a book, or create another inspiring project.

Strip away what you think you should be, strip away what other people think you should be and there you are. Give up whatever in your life no longer serves your conscious efforts to create what you want, and you will discover what is at the root of your own authentic self. Below the surface, your sense of yourself operates like a gyroscope keeping you mostly on course despite self-sabotage. The signs, signals, and impulses that radiate through to your conscious awareness, when interpreted correctly, can give you that ability to alter course quickly and with seeming effortlessness. As you let go of how you think things are, how you "should be"—and instead, notice then accept yourself as you are, warts and all, this is the point at which life just gets easier.

Once, when my girls were little I took them to a park and while they were playing, I sat on a park bench within earshot of two elderly folks sitting in silence. After about ten minutes, the man said to the woman, "Do you know what a pain in the ass you are?!" and after a good three second pause, she said "Yep." Then after another few minutes of silence, she said, "Do you know what an irritating bastard you are?" and he responded with a chuckle, "Sure I do." After another minute or two he said, "Well, I'm glad we got that settled. You ready for lunch?" and she said, "Yeah, been ready." Then they stood up, and hand in hand they made their way over to their car, smiling the whole way. At the time I thought this exchange was odd, uncomfortable, and yet heartwarming. I repeated the tale to several people, and thought about it for a long time. I realized that what I had witnessed was real honest mature love and acceptance in all its glory.

HOW to Upgrade Your Past and Alter the Present

Here is another way to uncover and alter filters and self-sabotaging behaviors that originated in your childhood.

1. Write a succinct paragraph describing your childhood as if it happened the way you wanted it to be, and about the adult you have become because of that new childhood. Write it as if it were true. Start with the parent you feel the least close to.

2. After you do this, list the top five things that you would do be doing differently in your life today, had this really been your experience.

3. Now put these five things on a time line and do them. If you need help to do them, get it.

Linda's Story: A Childhood Revised

Here is what Linda wrote as per the instructions above:

"My mother and I were close. Even though there were five of us, she always made time for me and noticed little things I did that were special. She often asked me how I was doing and even if lots of other things were going on, she made time to listen. There were lots of us so her advice was pretty short and to the point. Even in my teen years, when I left home to go to college—even though I know she wanted me to stay home and help out with the little ones after my Dad died—she encouraged me to go. I went home a lot the first two years and she was really grateful to me for visiting and helping out. I wanted to, though. I didn't feel obligated. Today I have a great job with a team of people working under me and a solid marriage to a man I really love. My mom laid the groundwork for me to make good choices and have what I want."

Here is Linda's original story about and experience of her mom:

Linda said her mom was actually a harsh taskmaster. She played the victim, locked herself in her room, made Linda feed and watch the other kids and was probably suffering from postpartum depression. After her dad died, her mom started drinking and Linda fled to college, guilty about abandoning her siblings, but sure she did the right thing. When she went home to help out, mom would cry and throw temper tantrums and threaten suicide if Linda went back to college. Eventually, mom went into rehabilitation and then therapy, the kids went to Aunt Arlene's and mom did a pretty good job of taking back her life. Linda was still furious with her mom though, and now at 43 was still abandoning herself by working in jobs with no future, lending and giving money she couldn't afford to people perfectly capable of taking care of themselves, eating poorly and sleeping badly. This kept her feeling like a victim, still waiting for her mother to notice her suffering and rescue her from herself.

After writing that first paragraph in which she consciously revised her childhood, Linda considered how this childhood might have instilled thoughts and behaviors and she listed these five things:

1. I look and feel great because I cook at home and work out every day.

2. I refuse to work at dead-end jobs and now have a great job that I love.

3. I never lend or give money to others unless I have my bills paid and basics handled first. I no longer obligate myself to make others more important than me.

4. I do not make excuses and instead accept help and advice from my friends.

5. I have a roommate and share expenses so I can save money and finish my degree.

Over the course of the next 18 months, Linda got serious about making good on every one of these five items and as a result, completely transformed her life. She got a roommate, saved money, joined a gym, bought a bike, shared cooking duties, learned how to create a great resume, changed jobs, let her friends do a mini-makeover for her birthday, and in the process, forgave her mother and created a new relationship with her.

Wow. Growing up. It's a beautiful thing. It's a decision followed by actions. You can do it, too. Even if you're pretty damn happy, there are probably still cobwebs in your thinking than can be cleared out with this little practice. Sure, the re-creation phase may take a while and require that you enlist some help from your friends. So what? Becoming the person you might have been is not unattainable. You can rewire many of the habits and beliefs you have mistaken for "how things are." You have the power to free yourself from those filters.

HOW to Talk to Your Parents

Talking directly with your parents, whenever possible, is the best way to go about getting over whatever "hangovers" may be still gumming up your life. Revealing your thoughts and observations isn't just useful for "confronting" parents, it's useful for clearing out debris left over from what our minds constructed as our loving and imperfect parents raised us. Here's a good example of how to do that:

Sherry's Story: What Are You Waiting For?

By the time I got around to doing this work with Raven, my father had been dead for nearly 20 years. My mom was still alive, and I had the chance to talk with her and clear up a lot of old stuff from childhood and adolescence. I spent a weekend with her, and over the course of two days we had several conversations, each of which lasted a couple of hours. At the start, I told her that this wasn't about my blaming her or my dad for anything. I told her (and, to my great fortune, this is completely true) that I had never, ever doubted that she and my dad loved me completely and unconditionally. I told her that I wasn't going to allow her to say "I should have.... "

I put off having these conversations with her for YEARS. The stories I had that held me back were utter bullshit—she was too old, she wouldn't understand, she'd get too upset, she'd be too hurt. My mother was raised on a farm with her older brother and male cousins. She trapped and skinned muskrats and sold the pelts to make money when she was in high school. She played field hockey and basketball in high school and college, and she spent 20 years teaching English in a public high school in New Jersey. Her nickname among students was "Mighty Mrs. Mini-Marts" (she was all of five feet tall) because of her penchant for wading in to break up hallway fights and her general intolerance of nonsense in her classroom. In retirement, she played golf several times a week and traveled the world. Yeah, too old and fragile my Aunt Fanny.

When I finally did talk with her, I told her that throughout my life I experienced my place in our family as on the outside looking in—I saw myself as always different, excluded from things that my parents and siblings did together. I also had the impression that we never had enough money, and that worries about how to pay for things colored everything we did as a family. As a teenager I wove this into a story that I was in the way, a burden on her and my dad, and that the sooner I was out on my own the better it would be. The choices I made about college and career were rooted in that belief. I distanced myself from my family as quickly as I could and stayed emotionally and geographically distant for years, all the while playing the role of happy family member at holidays and vacation visits. At the same time, I was always a "good girl"—my biggest adolescent rebellion was to become a devout Christian and join a church.

From her, I learned about the challenges she faced as a young mother in the 1950's with a colicky baby (me) and little social or family support. She told me how, when I was an infant, she sometimes felt like a failure as a mother. I saw my child self through her eyes—this little girl who could read before her fourth birthday, who loved school, and was always so well-behaved. She said

"Looking back, I think that you were so good at taking care of yourself we probably neglected you because your sisters were never that easy."

We talked about her relationship with my dad, which was based on a lot of indirect and manipulative communication, and on my mother capitulating to him on pretty much everything in order to make sure he was happy—but (from my observations) he ever really was all that happy. I asked her if they ever fought about anything and she said, "No, and we probably should have." I told her that my reaction to their relationship was to decide that I didn't want to get married or have children, because that would mean giving up on myself.

We talked about all of this and a whole lot more. I expressed resentments and appreciations; we laughed and cried and rejoiced and regretted; and after that weekend our connection was both stronger and more relaxed than it had ever been.

Shortly after I spent that weekend with her, I began a relationship with the man I eventually married. And shortly after I got married, mom died suddenly of a heart attack. I am forever grateful that I did this work with her.

The work/play of becoming free and more engaged, intimate, spontaneous, happy, intelligent, wealthy, satisfied, and self-aware never ever ends. We can approach the "work" as an exciting and interesting adventure—our personal journey—one that continues to deepen and enrich every aspect of our life on earth, for as long as we are alive.

And, if you are making yourself feel overwhelmed about all this parenting and growing up stuff, take a break. Go play.

There's no requirement, no "have to" about how much work to do or how self-aware to become. We are not saying that you "should" or "must" do all or any of this stuff we're suggesting. We are saying that you *can*, and we thought you might want to have a "get out of jail card" so we're clearly telling you some tested formulas for doing that.

One thing we can guarantee it this. When you begin to have success in making significant changes in your life, you will feel fear. You are taking steps away from the comfortable and familiar and into the unknown. Do it anyway. The more you notice but refuse to be stopped by fear, the easier taking new actions will become.

Sherry's Story: Feel the Fear and Do It Anyway

I've been plagued by a fear of heights, something I probably learned from my dad. In my mid-30s I took up rock-climbing. It was fun, challenging, and brought me right up against that fear. I learned that FEAR does not always equal DANGER. Sometimes fear is just a bunch of brain signals and hormonal reactions and that's all there is. Here is my story.

I begin each climb with a mixture of dread and desire. I want to do this; I love how it feels when I'm doing it well, when my movements are smooth and my mind is clear of everything but the moment. But in nearly every climb there comes this moment of panic, when I can hear that voice so clearly, "You're fat, you're weak, you're clumsy, you're too old, you can't trust your belayer, you're going to fall and get hurt, you can't, you can't, YOU CAN'T!" The voice is loud and I'm stuck listening to her. I'm 20 feet off the ground and I can't move, that voice won't let me go up and my pride won't let me go down. My feet are planted on quartz flakes that stick out about a half-inch from the rock face. I can't believe I'm standing on them and I am certain that if I move **anything** I'll fall and fall and never stop falling. I'm clutching the rock so tightly that the tendons in my fingers are screaming and the muscles in my forearms are beginning to burn. My face is so close to the rock I can smell it, earthy and dusty and chalky. The voice is still yelling. Fear is making my heart race and my breath is coming in short pants.

I realize I need to breathe; I take a long, deep breath. In that instant the voice is gone and I'm standing on these footholds and it's so easy; they seem so big. I'm still afraid, but I make my hands and arms relax. I breathe deep, put my right foot up on an even smaller flake, shift my weight, stand up on it, reach for the next hold, my left foot finds a nearly invisible nub and sticks—shift, stand, reach, hold—sweat drips in my eyes and runs down my back, I'm at the crux, the rock looks so smooth but my feet find the nubs, my fingers wedge into tiny cracks, moving up, breathe, find a perfect finger jam, one more toe-hold and I'm at the crack, lay-back to the top, the muscles in my forearms are knotting as I reach the anchor, mantle up and over and I'm standing on the cliff looking down 50 feet at my belayer on the other end of the rope. She's got this grin on her face because she knows exactly how it feels, and I say "Give me a minute up here, then I think I'll climb down."

CHAPTER 11

The Power of Forgiveness

"If you want others to be happy, practice compassion. If you want to be happy, practice compassion."
—The Dalai Lama

Forgiveness—What's In It for You?

All of us have probably had experiences that brought us deep emotional pain. Betrayals, affairs, addictions, deaths, the discovery that your father wasn't your mother's first husband, that you have a half-sibling who was the result of your father's "youthful indiscretion," assaults, even things as serious as the murder of a family member of friend. How can we forgive acts that trigger immense pain? What difference does forgiveness make anyway?

First of all, we hold grudges like the feudin' Hatfields and McCoys for offenses far less significant than the ones listed above. Just read the letters in your local paper's advice column to get the "flavor of the day" in chronic resentment. It's what keeps Dear Abby, Ask Amy, and Carolyn Hax in business—heck, even Miss Manners gets them. We hold on to feelings of anger and frustration with friends or family members who fail to invite us to an event, neighbors who let their lawn get too long, co-workers who perpetrate slights (real or imagined), parents who don't bail us out of our mistakes, spouses who don't live up to our expectations, and on and on we go.

Getting over resentment and hurt is a requirement for well-being. Studies show that people who learn not to hold grudges and are able to forgive transgressions (real or imagined) are literally happier, healthier, and even wealthier than their unforgiving counterparts.[1]

PLEASE NOTE: If you have experienced severe trauma, a rape, an attempted murder, or anything else of that intensity, please seek counseling. This information is NOT meant to replace therapy but may be used to enhance your therapeutic experience.

Gregg Easterbrook, writing about forgiveness on beliefnet.com, summarized it this way, "Increasingly, psychological research has begun to show that being a forgiving person is essential to happiness. Even when someone wrongs you, feeling anger or hatred only causes your life to descend into misery and resentment: You are the one who suffers, not the person you're angry at. Forgiving, on the other hand, can lift the burden. When spiritual figures taught us to forgive those who sin against us, they weren't just pronouncing holy philosophy. Rather, they were giving practical down-to-earth life advice."

Easterbrook notes that forgiveness has only recently become a subject of research. He cites the pioneering work of several psychologists, including clinical psychologist Everett Worthington of Virginia Commonwealth University. Worthington found several negative health indicators that went with being unable to forgive, including:

- stress-related disorders
- lower immune-system function
- increased rates of cardiovascular disease
- more episodes of clinical depression

What Forgiveness is (and is Not)

To get over blaming someone—forgiveness—does not mean glossing over what they did or didn't do. It means deciding to stop making yourself feel bad for something that is no longer happening. Forgiveness begins with the decision to feel better, the willingness to release and get over your anger, the wisdom to admit that life isn't always fair, and the compassion to love yourself enough to stop holding a grudge. To forgive requires owning responsibility for yourself and practicing new ways of relating to others and new ways of seeing yourself in the world. Forgiveness can occur with or without reconciliation. You are not required to like the person or approve of their way of thinking or their behavior to recognize that hanging on to your judgment and rehashing what happened affects you, limits you, upsets you in an endless cycle of powerlessness. Only you can stop that cycle.

When you are angry with someone, especially a parent or partner, you assume that this person could have and should have known how their behavior would hurt you. You therefore make their actions mean that you were not loved or worse, not worthy of love. This is the awful seed that pushes you to stay enraged or become embittered. You may also believe that forgiveness, if granted, means that the person gets away with what he or she did.

CLUE: If you think that you have forgiven someone for something they did or said, pay close attention to your thoughts and notice the sensations in your body when you are with them, talk to them, or think about them. If you notice tension or tightness in your body, if your thoughts about them include blame, you are not over it.

Forgiveness cannot be attained through an act of coercion designed to make someone else understand you or to offer an apology. It is not a mental feat you accomplish through reason. Nor does it include ignoring what happened and putting yourself in danger by wiping the slate clean or starting over, only to open yourself to another incident. Forgive the thief AND keep the door locked. Reconciliation is not a requirement for forgiveness.

Forgiveness begins with one human being recognizing the frailty and flaws of a fellow human being. It is about getting over yourself, and the blame and hardness you hold within yourself. It is finding the bond that holds all of us in this world together. Along with compassion, the capacity for forgiveness is the hallmark of really being human, and an adult. Forgiveness is a deep and powerful ability that makes us stronger and healthier in many ways.

This is a recent interview with a current client.

R: Tell me about your relationship with your father.

DT: Well, "then" or "now?"

R: Both

DT: The father I grew up with was a control freak. Mean, opinionated, a yeller and a hitter. While I wasn't hit much, my brother got it pretty bad. I was terrified of my father. He controlled everything. He even threw out food my mother bought if it was something he hadn't "approved of." My mother wanted to buy turkey bacon and he said "no." I mean it was crazy. Even in restaurants he'd reach over and season my mother's food. Totally bizarre. And he'd start yelling without warning, so we all walked on eggshells all the time, trying to keep him feeling happy and of course, it didn't ever work. And it never ended. My brother eventually moved away, and had—has—his own really off-the-rails behavior. He's not mentally right even now, but that's another story.

For me, even as an adult, through my 30s and 40s I let my parents—the Victim and the Bastard—control almost every aspect of my life. I didn't fully realize that he was, and had probably always been, mentally unbalanced, until a few years ago. My parents even had keys to my house. I made no decisions without checking with my father, and lived in constant fear of criticism and disapproval until I developed paralyzing anxiety. At that point, with coaching, I realized that all of the things I thought were "normal" in my family were creepy and neurotic.

R: Did your relationship with you father impact other areas of your life?

DT: Oh man, did it ever! I hated my job, though I stayed 23 years. Hated my "critical" boss, though I admit I did countless things to drive her batty until she criticized me—often in front of others—then I got to be the Victim (like mom) and still I neither stood up for myself nor quit. And hey, I was a nurse, so I could have worked elsewhere. But I also picked really checked out, unavailable men, and put up with what I now recognize as dangerous behaviors.

R: Can you give me an example?

DT: Sure, I went on a date with a guy who pulled out a gun and rubbed it against my leg, then invited me to the neighbor's house for a beer and instead of running for the hills, I went next door, then out to dinner, and though I did make a break for it after dinner I retold the story thinking it was funny, and only when the reaction I got was one of shock did I realize what I'd done. Of course my father was always talking about violence, especially about killing himself and somehow I just made that guy's behavior OK. Now I think, "Wow. What was I thinking?"

I dated men who were either control freaks, telling me what to do, or Victims like my mother, who were weak, wimpy, and unappealing. But I thought those were my choices! Nice—a victim—like mom, or mean like dad.

R: And now?

DT: I have a great boyfriend. He's strong but sensitive. Free spirited and down to earth. And he comes from a close, connected, loving family. I'm now part of THAT family, and it's so different and wonderful to be around them. I also see how they interact without the constant drama, and it helps me be more spontaneous and relaxed to be around them.

R: And work?

DT: Oh, I retired last year, after getting things cleared up with my boss and developing a real relationship with her. Those things happened as I worked through my fear and forgave my parents, especially my father, but also my mother.

R: How did you do that?

DT: Well it took a while and it wasn't pretty at first. When I got so out of it with my anxiety, I wasn't sleeping, my heart was racing, my memory was shot, and I was constantly paranoid. The thought that my parents could (and often DID) come in my home when I was at work and move stuff around, and that my dad constantly found fault with what I did (or did not do) just finally made me realize what a truly twisted unhealthy way of relating my family had. I first took back my house keys, changed the locks and wrote my parents a letter saying that I needed a break, time off, and revealed how I felt and how I was going to live from now on, making my own decisions, even if they were bad ones. They were really pissed. REALLY pissed.

But slowly, over time, I got better and better at separating my love for my father from the fear of him that held me prisoner in my own life. I also recognized that my father was mentally off, had probably never recovered from his war experiences, and that he was often depressed, and probably anxious—like me. His memory was also starting to fail and my mother was in total denial that he had a problem. Slowly over the next 18 months, as I took charge of my health and my life, I started to wake up. I took care of myself. I got on some meds to balance my brain and learned practices that reduced my panic attacks. Though I still kept some distance from my parents, and made an effort not to go to Drama-Town, we went out to eat together and started talking regularly again.

My father actually started to become softer. Easier to accept. And I became more of a responsible adult and said more of what I felt even if I was frightened. I started getting over my fear. My father liked hearing me speak my mind! I could speak up and nobody would die. I even interrupted my father when he started going on and on about old war stories and when he started talking about killing himself (which was a favorite mealtime conversation). I even said something when he started to season my mother's food!

The more I put my attention on myself and said what I wanted and what I felt, I became less and less afraid, and forgiveness was part of that change. I swear it's like I was asleep my whole life. Then I woke up and saw—literally—I was living in a dark house with ancient ugly furniture and wearing clothes that were too big and that I was essentially depressed, repressed, and neurotic. I started spending the money I'd been too fearful to spend and made my home a pleasant place to actually live in and enjoy. This was a huge difference from the days I'd once spent hiding in the bathroom because my father was at the front door.

I started to enjoy him—both of them, really. And I quit taking my mother's victim shit so seriously, though I sure figured out where I learned my victim shit from. Her constant complaining drove me nuts. I started stopping her rants, and also got myself busy with my own life. I worked out, meditated, found a boyfriend, got a dog. The more I had a life and took care of myself, the more I forgave my parents and enjoyed their company. I had to quit waiting for them to change, be different, fix me, make me feel better, praise me, and be the parents I always wanted. As I accepted them *and* treated myself better, life got easier. And I discovered I liked my parents!

My father, as it turned out, had dementia and started having more serious problems with confusion and memory loss. Instead of becoming belligerent, like some people do, he became even more able to tell me that he loved me, and that he was proud of me. It was like a miracle. Then, just this past December 2011, his health suddenly took a dive and we discovered he had cancer. He passed within weeks, but in that time, I stayed by his side, loved him, laughed with him, and received the love, the kind looks, and the words I never ever thought I'd have from my Dad.

R: What about your mom?

DT: We're good. She actually has allowed herself to start changing the house and doing things that she'd stopped herself from doing all these years. Though I know she'll miss dad, she's also in some way relieved, I think, and free from the victim story she'd used to keep herself walking on eggs with him for decades.

R: What do you think is the most important thing you got out of forgiving your parents?

DT: I got myself back. I woke up. And now I have a real adult life that I enjoy. I also got my patents back—as real people not as characters in my drama.

HOW to Forgive Parents

Here are a few examples of conversations that you can have to start experiencing forgiveness.

If your parents are alive and not suffering from Alzheimer disease or other kinds of dementia, begin the process by having an adult-to-adult conversation, or more likely, a series of conversations, with them.

1. Do not blame them for what you are doing in your own life, but do speak plainly about what you learned from them. For example: *I learned to be careful and now I find that I have a hard time being spontaneous. I'm always on guard with people and constantly think about what they may be thinking of me.*

2. Reveal the things they said or did, and the resulting beliefs and behaviors that you have carried over into your own life. *Mom, you told us never to talk about Daddy's drinking and you lied about why he got fired from so many jobs. Now I second-guess a lot of my decisions and even wonder if my friends really like me of if they're putting up with me the way you put up with Daddy, all the while complaining about him to us, but telling us not to tell anyone else.*

3. Tell them what you're doing and what it is costing you to continue repeating the things you learned growing up. Take responsibility for the fact that only you can change your life.

I feel like I'm going crazy trying to guess what people want and what they're thinking. I have a hard time relaxing and sometimes I even wake up at night worrying about things that are meaningless.

4. Make peace with the reality that they did the best they could to parent you (even though you may think it was a crappy job). If you have been blaming them or if you resent them, say so and say you are ready to get over any judgments you may have been holding onto. *I resent you for telling us to keep secrets and for lying about daddy getting fired and for all the complaining you did. I don't want to keep holding on to any of this old stuff. I know in my heart that you did the best you could. I know you loved me. I know that only I can stop doing these things, and I will. I will tell the truth in my life. I won't keep any of your secrets anymore, so don't ask me to. I won't listen to your complaints about Daddy or intervene if you are mad at my brother. I will forgive you and I will forgive myself for how I have carried these crappy behaviors over into my life.*

5. Don't expect agreement or an apology. You may or may not get either. Neither is it necessary for you to hash over, understand, or figure out the past. Don't get caught up in debating what happened or why. Your job is to put the past where it belongs—in the past—and get it out of your daily life and keep it from screwing up how you think and act in the future. *I am not telling you that you are a bad person and I am not making you wrong. I am letting you know how I feel, and how I will be practicing a different, healthier way of relating. I am not asking you to do anything but listen to what I have to say.*

6. Do the one thing that matters—accept them as they are. You don't have to enjoy their company, and you don't even have to like them, but if you don't accept them and release the past, you will be stuck resisting all of the ways that you resemble them, and your chance for freedom will be bleak.

The formula is: Report, reveal, and request. Do this rather than regress, repress, and react like a child.

Thank your parents (in person and out loud) for the useful things you got from them. Reveal the unfavorable things you still think and do that interfere with your satisfaction in life and tell them that you are revising some of those beliefs and behaviors. This is shorthand for telling them that you are growing up. Doesn't matter how old you are, it's the same old story. If you are still angry about things they said or did, or about beliefs and self-sabotage you learned from them, reveal that. *Reveal, don't blame.* Talk about you, your experience, and your life.

Let your parents know that, rather than pretend you are not angry when you are, or instead of sulking and giving them the silent treatment, that you will speak up from now on and deal with your emotions as they arise. Then do it. Act like a grown up.

Let your parents know that you are not telling them to change to make you happy. Ask them for what you want, (recognition, more contact, less contact, money, to be appreciated, whatever comes up for you) and be grown up enough to accept not getting it from them. There are other people on the planet to rely on if you're parents aren't able to fulfill your requests.

Report, reveal, request, and stay in the conversation until you are over wanting to blame, to change, or to get an apology out of your parents.

This process could take some time, and may take several conversations. We promise you that getting unhooked from your history and becoming an adult in the presence of your parents is worth every moment of self-doubt, fear, and frustration you may experience while working things out. Most of the time—not every time, but 90+ % of the time—people who do this end up feeling closer to their parents and more competent and at ease in their own lives.

The Story of M: I'm An Adult, Mom

The process outlined above will look something like this real conversation between one of my clients, who is in her 40s and her mother, who is in her 70s:

> Mom, there are things that I do to myself that make my life harder. I play the victim, I create drama, sometimes I smile and pretend that I'm OK even when I feel very angry, and I have a really hard time asking for help. I think I have to do everything myself, then feel exhausted and put out. I judge others harshly and waste time telling myself that if they would just change my life would be great. I have lots of rules and try to manipulate people into taking care of me and make them wrong when they don't read my mind and do what I want. Of course, as I said, I don't say what I want so if you can't read my mind, you are out of luck. I'm tired all the time. I drive myself nuts. I hold myself and others up to standards guaranteed to lead to disappointment.

> I don't want to say this, but here it is: I learned these things from you.

> I am not asking you to change and I am not blaming you for how much I do these things to myself. I am telling you that I am working hard to change this behavior. You still do plenty of these things. Sometimes I get really annoyed with you and pretend not to. I want to stop doing this to myself.

> No, please just listen, I'm not done.

> I repeat, I am not asking you to change and I am also letting you know that I will no longer agree with you out of habit. I don't want to reinforce these bad habits in myself and in your company it's easy for me to fall back into them or to commiserate with you. That's going to stop. I may get mad, mom, but I'll get over it. I want to be with you, but not this way. This stinks."

Mom went on to explain, defend, and justify her behavior and to say that she's happy and that her life works. Though her daughter could have argued or challenged the defense her mother mounted, she simply repeated:

Mom, my objective is not to make you wrong or to change you. My goal is to change my life and increase my own satisfaction. To do that I will be more honest with you, and I will no longer do things I don't agree with just because I think that's what you want, or that's what I think you want. I'm an adult, Mom. I'm going my own way and will make my own mistakes, rather than repeating the old ones over and over and over.

Feeling relieved that she was not being blamed, Mom just said, "OK."

That was a good start for what will be an ongoing discovery of relating, as the daughter continues to see herself repeat and reject the behaviors until a new pattern has formed.

HOW to Forgive a Spouse, Mate, or Partner

When a mate fails to live up to expectations—they have an affair, or steal company funds, or have hidden a previous divorce—usually, the first words the offended partner utters are, "How could you DO that to me?!" followed by, "I would never, *could never* do that!" Piling self-righteous indignation and moral outrage on top of hurt and anger is like tossing gasoline on the grill—guaranteed excitement and the burgers get cooked, but they are not very tasty. The hurt and anger can be dealt with and it is possible to find relief, and even forgiveness. We'll use the example of getting to forgiveness over an affair.

Be angry. Feel the hurt. Resent your partner for the affair and for how you feel. Cry it out. Stomp around. Tell a friend.

Then accept reality. Accept that your spouse did whatever he or she did and don't waste your brainpower trying to figure out WHY.

Remember way back at the beginning of the book we talked about the uselessness of asking "why?" Well, here is exactly the kind of situation in which it is the most useless. You can choose, deliberately, to express and get over your anger, hurt, fear, and desire to cause mayhem and murder.

Then get in touch with other, more useful questions and ask those instead. Questions like: Do you still love me? How long have you been sleeping with her/him? Who ended it, you or s/he? Are you in love with her/him? Do you want to repair this marriage? Are you willing to go to couple's therapy? Is our relationship unsatisfying? Have you been holding something against me? Have you ever cheated before? How do you imagine you'd feel if I'd had an affair?

Ultimately, to make an informed decision, you must take an honest look at the quality of your relationship and whether or not you actually want to be together, or if you just think that you **should** be together. ***An affair can be a deal breaker, yes, but it can also be a warning sign, an opportunity to get to know each other more deeply, a wake-up call, a gift.***

- Many couples become closer, stronger, and more intimate as a direct result of the work they did to rebuild their relationship, including forgiveness.
- Other couples get divorced only to discover they still love each other and regret their knee-jerk decision.
- Some couples get divorced and are happy with their decision, reaching forgiveness and becoming friends, recognizing that they are not compatible or not in love.
- Some couples get divorced and never get over the upset of the affair, one living in blame and anger, the other living with resentment that the other would not forgive.
- Sometimes the partner having the affair falls in love, asks for a divorce and the spouse is completely blindsided, left wondering what the hell happened.

- Worst of all, sometimes they stay together but never deal with the issues that existed before, during, or after the affair. Life is reduced to payback and misery.

Forgiveness and full disclosure—honesty—will give you the best shot at being able to assess how to proceed. **Report, reveal, request,** and stay in the conversation. To create a foundation for the possibility of a new way of relating to your partner, or with others, first reveal and then agree to revise whatever habits and communication issues each of you contributed to co-creating the dissatisfaction. Then you can arrive at a resolution that will work whether you stay together or not. If you decide to stay together, it is also very helpful to talk with other couples who have been through a similar event and successfully stayed together.

HOW to Practice Forgiving Yourself and Others

Forgiving yourself and others is a learned skill that has enormous value. Here are a few things you can play with in your daily life to help you develop your skills in the art of forgiveness.

- Watch how you leap to judgment and irritation in a grocery line, while driving, at work, or at a party when somebody does something you don't like. Learn to say to yourself, *"Really? Am I that busy? That self-involved? That easily offended? That petty?"*
- Investigate the meaning you have assigned to the words or action, and explore other possible meanings that are neither about you nor about how "wrong" the person is. To help yourself with this, ask "What might be on their mind? Not feeling well? Argument? Car issue? Tired? Worried about bills?" Can you forgive him or her in that moment? Yes you can. Take a breath. Get over yourself.
- Honestly assess your own ability to be a jerk. Write down stupid, mean, and dishonest things that you have done. Include things others have accused you of. Ask yourself how you

would forgive a friend who had done these things. Cross them off as you forgive yourself. Make amends if necessary. If you get stuck, reveal those mistakes to a friend and ask for input. Most of the time we do stupid things because we are afraid, checked out, unaware, or distracted. When we forgive ourselves we feel more compassion for others as well. Help yourself recognize that mistakes—even big ones—are part of a learning curve, and look at your motive. You will likely realize that you did not set out to create upset. Most people don't.

- Take yourself through a story of something that happened— "something somebody did to me" -complete with imagined versions of the offender's motives, self-righteous rebuttals, and stored-up resentments fueling the tirade. First, observe your body. Feel all the unpleasant sensations *you* are generating. Notice from the observer's chair how this rant would look and sound if you were watching. Now hit the brakes. Take a breath. Ask yourself what this tirade is costing *you,* how these *thoughts* make you feel, ask how they poison your attitude, even towards innocent bystanders? Then look for any background thoughts running. Do you feel stupid because you "should" have known? Do you think you "caused" the other person's actions, or that you deserve what happened? Are you locked into self-righteousness holding onto an imagined motive that you could not know but have assigned the other person? Forgive yourself for those worthless and inaccurate thoughts. That will help you begin forgiving the other person as well.
- Reacting (speaking and acting unconsciously and without awareness of what's generating the reaction) rather than responding (noticing thoughts and being alert and present in the moment) to people and circumstances is the source of most upsets.
- Honesty, owning responsibility for your own well-being, and compassion are the keys to unlocking forgiveness.

Getting to Forgiveness: A Review

- Holding on to the hurt and anger punishes rather than protects you.
- We forgive for our own sake, to relieve our suffering, and heal.
- Forgiveness does not mean that what happened was justified.
- Accepting what happened will help you to let it move into the past.
- The more you can be present, the easier it will be to get to forgiveness.
- Hanging around with people who are outraged for you will not help you.
- Commiserating with angry people who have had similar experiences will not help you.
- Expressing emotions and allowing the love you still have will help you move on.
- Moving on can take many forms, forgiveness helps create healthy solutions.
- Ask clearly for what you want and make agreements to help to build trust.

CHAPTER 12

Romance, Friendship, Love, and Intimacy

"Love takes off masks that we fear we cannot live without and know we cannot live within." —James Baldwin

Addicted to Love

What we think of as "romantic love" starts out as a roller-coaster ride of sensations and emotions, thanks to the hormones and chemical signals that literally make us temporarily addicted to each other. Our ancestors needed to bond long enough to make babies and evolution supplied a chemical high so profound we feel sick and weak (withdrawal) when our beloved is out of sight too long. Let's face it, we are tools for reproducing our DNA. Love chemistry is certainly not limited to baby-making, though that's what developed the intensity of the initial bonding.

After the biochemical high wears off, what you have—if you were pretty good at consciously building a relationship along the way—is a combination of acceptance, kindness, mutual respect, and compatibility. To have greater ease in love relationships, examine your rules, expectations, and fairytale beliefs and then start revising the ones that are holding you back.

CLUE: Although you may not have the same kind of unhealthy, unhappy relationships other family members have, if you can't seem to stop yourself from being attracted to unsuitable types, or from becoming a jerk when you get involved with someone, your Picker needs an overhaul.

HOW to Find a Mate When You Need to Fix Your Picker

NOTE: Even if you have a mate, you'll learn a few things about yourself in this section, so read on.

Your "Picker" is the recognition program in your brain that assesses people and matches them against your criteria for what feels like "home." You can also think of this as your "attractor" pattern. If your Picker is working well, you will pick a mate with whom you are compatible, share common ground, and have a level of understanding and communication that keeps your relationship alive, healthy, and fulfilling. You will replicate the good healthy traits you experienced in your parents' relationship or the traits you worked to develop when you found a role model for relating that was better and happier than the one your parents had. In other words, when your Picker is working for you, your relationships will "feel like home" in a good, useful, and heartwarming way.

Unfortunately, many of us have been handed down Pickers that were broken generations ago.

If you repeatedly find yourself in relationships with people who end up disappointing you in the same old way, you probably have a broken Picker. It's part of the Family Virus. Instead of analyzing the layers of dysfunction that make a sick Picker tick, let's just refer back to the notion that your mind soaked up some bad data about relating and in the spirit of passing on a generations-old tradition, you are now making prickly picks. This leads some people to decide they will just have to be alone or endure marital misery. Not so. You can fix your Picker, or at least improve it enough to get you out of the relationship ditch and back on the road again.

Of all the excuses people give for repeating things that make them miserable, the words "Well, I guess that's just the way I am," trigger in me a nearly uncontrollable urge to slap the person senseless. This is the Mother (and Father) of lame excuses for staying unconsciously committed to avoiding responsibility for—and doing the work involved in—having satisfaction in life. It is the cry of the loooozzzerrr. So if you ever hear yourself saying (or thinking) "Oh, I guess that's just the way I am; I guess I'm destined to go through life alone," slap yourself awake. That resignation is NOT the road to happiness. If you enjoy going it alone, dandy. But if you are resigned to being alone and pretending it's dandy, knock it off.

If you want a satisfying, fulfilling, intimate relationship, you will need to rewire your attractor pattern—the set of beliefs and convictions and filters that contains the emotional ingredients that you have associated with love, partnership, and mating. Oh yeah. What a mess some of us are in this department.

Some people are resigned to being alone because:

"I don't believe there is a someone out there for me."

"I can't trust myself to pick an emotionally healthy partner."

"I refuse to settle for the kind of person that's always attracted to me."

"I would rather be alone than be with an asshole."

"I hate the way I act when I'm in a relationship."

"I can't take any more disappointment."

"I always think each new one is different from the others, but they never are."

Here is a clear set of practices that will help you fix your Picker. Don't get me wrong, you will always be attracted to a "type." The key is to find a healthy version, an upgrade of the favored type that gives you thrills and a challenge but not a mess and misery. The list is followed by a real life example.

HOW to Fix Your Picker

You can and will find a compatible and reasonably healthy mate if you look at the thoughts, beliefs, and behaviors that describe HOW you keep getting the same results. Asking a good (and unflinchingly honest) friend to have that conversation with you is a great idea, and using the points that follow to fuel that conversation is a place to start. In the past nine years there have been ten marriages among my friends and clients that have all done some version of the instructions below. Some of them (including one woman in her 60s) were certain that after years of awful rerun relationships they were destined to be alone. The evidence speaks for itself.

- What traits and behaviors do you find attractive at first and that, in retrospect, always spell trouble? These are your "red flags." As in, Warning! DANGER!
- What thoughts do you have and what rationalizations (the meaning you make) do you use that make you ignore or overlook those red flags?
- Think about your last relationship. Review what he/she *said* (that you believed) compared to what he/she *did* (that you overlooked) and get to the facts.
- The next time you meet a potential partner, at the first familiar "thrill" examine the evidence, interrupt your thoughts, and revise your meaning.
- Reinforce your observations. What people DO is more telling than what they SAY. What people do is reality, and words are only words.
- Let potential mates know as soon as you see a red flag. Talk about it, and instead of rationalizing it away because sex appeal is clouding your ability to think, ask yourself if this behavior is something you are willing to live with forever. If not, and you see that the red flag repeats, you can say, "No, thanks," and move on.

- Ask yourself where you may be deluding yourself and ask a friend you trust for feedback.
- Try new activities, go to new places, and meet more diverse people than those you're accustomed to. Try getting to know someone you're not immediately attracted to but recognize as someone who has qualities you'd like in a mate. Experiment. See what happens. You might be pleasantly surprised.

Diane's Story: Red Flags Revealed

Here is a real life example of this exercise as completed by a friend and former client of mine who realized that her Dream Man was actually a Nightmare—and much too much like the other high excitement lovers she'd been misled by in the past.

Diane's Delusions vs. Reality Exercise:

Delusion: I believed four years of sobriety meant he could be trusted not to cheat or lie.

Reality: His behavior included two affairs and many lies about finances.

Delusion: I believed his porn addiction meant he was an exciting, open-minded, hot lover.

Reality: His addiction to porn eventually made it impossible for him to relate to me.

Delusion: I believed because we shared a joy for creating a beautiful home he'd never lie.

Reality: His actions demonstrated that while he did share my joy, he also lied.

Delusion: I believed that his working so much out of town was OK because that time spent apart kept the spark alive.

Reality: The separation fed my insecurity about his fidelity which I ignored, until I discovered he had been unfaithful. Multiple times.

Delusion: I believed that our being business partners and selling him half of my assets would keep him committed to our relationship.

Reality: We are business partners and he is committed to protecting his assets. Period.

Delusion: I believed that spending most of his free time wrapped up in sports and golf gave me lots of space to "do my thing."

Reality: We shared very few common interests and barely connected. I was often lonely and dissatisfied.

Delusion: I thought his lying to me meant that he didn't trust me with the truth.

Reality: Lying repeatedly just meant that he lies habitually; it's not about me.

Delusion: His saying he loved me meant he was committed to me and to honesty.

Reality: His words of love had nothing to do with his ability to commit or relate honestly.

Diane's Self-Observation:

I have a core belief that I deserve to be punished for having wants and needs in a relationship, because those wants and needs make me unlovable. I'm only lovable when I make my mate's wants and needs my priority, while suppressing my own. I have attracted men who "get" this about me. Punishment equals daddy-love. Infidelity, emotional abuse/neglect, financial irresponsibility, withholding, manipulating, passive-aggression—these behaviors are the "punishments" I have been wired to believe I deserve from my addict daddy. So basically, without an addict in my life, who am I?

Consistent Red Flags Diane had Overlooked:

Addictions and "Bad Boy" behaviors including:

History of unresolved conflicts and hostility in relationships with ex, and others

Financial chaos, instability

Feared/respected by others

"Instant" intimacy—too much, too soon, feels pushy

Persistent underlying anger

Absence of close friends, male and female

Imbalance of work and play

Quick-trigger temper and defensive/offensive reactions

Poor health and health habits

No interests outside of work and sports

History of lies (yes, they'd tell me, even brag about lies they told)

Diane's Review of What He Said Compared to What He Did:

He said: I have no need to see anyone else; I'm happy with you.

He did: Have ongoing sex with at least one woman that I caught him with and had numerous sexual conversations and emails with others.

He said: I don't know who keeps calling me; I don't recognize the number

He did: Only answer his cell (when I was around) if it was one of his children.

He said: I made a mistake in my checkbook and have to pay you later.

He did: Paid someone else instead

He said: I'm too tired to have sex

He did: Turned on his computer when he thought I was asleep and masturbated.

He said: She's just a friend.

He did: Exchanged sexual emails, jokes, and porn.

He said: I want to spend the rest of my life with you

He did: Refused to discuss anything to do with our future, beyond hanging on to our assets, and wanting to buy a big house with my money.

Diane did a fine job connecting the dots. She spent the following year dating and, in her words, "I had the very best year of my life after I did that work and even forgave Ken. I am meeting calmer, funny, more honest men, taking it very slow and I am conscious of red flags and make a point of asking good questions and listening to my gut. I'm happier than I have ever been."

HOW to Create Questions that Reveal Red Flags

These questions can be easily included in conversation during a date. This is not meant to be an interrogation, but more of a shared fact-finding session. The second or third date is a good place to do this. Yes, that soon, before you become sexually intimate. Once you have sex (unless the sex is particularly awful) the hormones and brain chemical you generate make you less likely to want to probe more deeply, at least for a while. So yes, if you want a mate that's not a rerun, ask good questions, really listen to the answers, and check your gut reactions. You may even want to get yourself a good book on body language assessment, just to help you stay grounded in what you can notice. (If you like the answers, and your gut gives you a green light, then sex may be on the menu.) Give these questions a shot.

Are you friendly with your ex? If what follows is full of anger and hate, or blame, or a dodge, you have one red flag.

What interests do you have? What sort of things do you do with your friends? No friends, no interests—two more red flags.

What pisses you off most about people? If the answer is a diatribe about the opposite sex, that counts as two red flags right there. Leave before dessert. Really.

Tell me about your family. If the conversation is avoided or sounds like a soap opera, full of angry people holding grudges, you will want to ask a part B to this: How do you deal with/get along with them?

You also want to volunteer if you have an addict in your family tree and ask if there is an alcoholic or addict in theirs. If you hear a calm, levelheaded answer that includes therapy or sobriety or a pleasant childhood with close ties, you are green to go. Otherwise listen for red and orange flags. Remember that unfinished family business gets dumped into relationships.

What do you want in a relationship? Are you looking for something casual or are you looking for a mate? If what they want isn't the same as what you want, it's a big red flag.

Statements: (Trust your gut and listen carefully to the response when you reveal these or similar statements.)

I want a relationship that is relaxed and honest, so lying is a deal breaker for me. I just don't put up with it.

I want to be with someone that shares some interests with me and balances work and play. I've made mistakes in the past and I am more aware of my preferences now.

I am not interested in taking on any drama. I'm looking for a person that has already worked on his/her own "stuff."

Sherry's Story: And They Lived Honestly Ever After

I'm one of those who met and married the love of my life after doing this work with Raven. I was in my mid-40s and had a lifetime history of long-term yet unsatisfying relationships with men and women who were unable or uninterested in any kind of real intimacy or commitment. I had convinced myself that I really didn't want to get married because I was a radical feminist who had rejected the patriarchal construct of matrimony.

In truth, I was busting my ass to create committed, intimate relationships with partners who had neither the interest nor the ability to meet me halfway. When I did meet someone who wanted intimacy and commitment, I ran away as fast as I could. Then I started doing the work described in this book. I cleaned up old issues with my mother (my father had already died) and my sisters and then got to work fixing my Picker.

That exercise of looking for red flags in the first few dates? Well, my early attempts at meeting potential mates set off red flags, flares, and sirens. I kept at it, and within about two months and after about 15 or so first dates, I met the man I eventually married.

We were engaged six months later and married a year after our engagement. It is the first marriage for both if us, and we were both 48 years old when we married. Now my biggest fear in life is that he'll die before I do—because I know in my gut he is as committed to making this relationship last as I am.

How did I do it? When no sirens, flares, or red flags went up on the first date, I decided to take the risk and just tell him the truth—the truth about what I was thinking, how I was feeling, what was going on for me. I said things like, "I really like you and I don't want to mess this up. One way I mess up relationships is by having sex with the person before I'm emotionally ready for that level of intimacy. I'm not going to do that with you."

I did a lot of the usual crap, trying to live up to his expectations, trying to manipulate him into living up to mine, blah, blah, blah. I caught myself, I stopped, I reported to him what I was doing and then did it differently. And the coolest thing happened. The more honest I was, the more honest he was. As I was owning up to my own bullshit, he gave himself permission to own up to his. The more authentic I was, the more authentic he was in return.

We both still have our moments when we fall back on old habits of thinking and behaving. We get a lot of practice in catching each other (and getting better at catching ourselves), interrupting, and redirecting. We both know that this is our recipe for happiness, and we just keep on stirring and cooking.

HOW to Have and Keep Love in Your Life

Love is an available and potent force in our lives. We all want to love and be loved. We all want to experience the warm glow of an open heart and that tingle in our blood that makes us swoon with tenderness. You can have that experience regularly and profoundly as long as you remember that *you are the source* of feeling love. Here is a recipe for creating that ongoing experience with those you love.

Begin With Simple, Clear, and Direct Communication

Speak Simply. Don't complicate your communications with lots of unnecessary information, explanations, or stories.

Be Clear: Say what you mean, ask for what you want and do not hint, suggest, bargain or manipulate. Stick to reality. Do not confuse your interpretation of what happened with the facts.

Be Direct: Speak in terms of "I think, I feel" and "I'd like you to." Rather than hinting, implying, or vaguely describing what you want, and then hoping you'll get it, ask for it directly.

Love, whether it's the love of a mate, of dear friends, or of parent and child, is always frightening. The fear of loss, whether through death or someone leaving us, is always present. Loss is a part of life and it will happen. Everyone you know and love right now will either leave or die, unless you leave or die first. In the meantime, though, you can create a lot of wonderful, satisfying experiences— the things that make life worth living, and worth all the risks. Love, when you let yourself feel all the joy and terror it brings, makes you smarter, healthier, and more able to enjoy life.

Cultivate Acceptance: The Key to Lasting Love

Our tendency to polarize—good/bad, right/wrong, kind/mean, smart/stupid—and our tendency to believe that those assessments are The Whole Truth is a major source of self-deception and dissatisfaction. There are no people who are all bad or all good. Sure, a few sociopaths and saints may come close. The rest of us are mildly neurotic yet brilliant mixed bags and we are doing the best we can.

Honesty and acceptance create real intimacy and authentic contact, allowing us to get over upsets, anger, and hurt without destroying our relationships. When it comes right down to the core of it, love, real lasting love that holds over a lifetime, be it the love of mates, friends, or parents and children is really *acceptance*. That's the real deal. Acceptance. That's what intimacy is, and that's what makes forgiveness and ongoing growth and change in any relationship possible. Acceptance is love. When you accept yourself, flaws and all, and accept others, flaws and all, without hoping, wishing, and scheming to make them live up to your expectations, or make them change to make your life easier, then (and only then) have you arrived at real intimacy. You probably know how to do this already. This may resemble your relationship with your best friend or maybe even with a favorite sibling.

Acceptance does not mean you never get angry. In healthy long-term relationships, the fullness of expression is alive in all of its variations. Getting angry and expressing and getting over the anger is part of what strengthens any relationship—whether we're talking about marriage partners, business partners, family members or best friends. This is part of what sustains intimacy. Think about your longest-term and closest friend. It's likely that he or she has said or done things that have sent you into door-slamming, plate-pitching fits of frustration—whether or not you actually slammed or pitched or otherwise expressed yourself completely. *Yet you don't demand that your friend change to suit you. When the dust settles, you know you will still be friends. You know that your friend will be who they are and continue to do what they do.*

We often make the mistake of committing to someone for who they COULD be, rather than who they ARE. That is a recipe for failure.

CLUE: Ask yourself honestly whether or not you would accept a lifetime of whatever behaviors you find least attractive in your potential partner. If you start selling yourself the story that he or she will change, settle down, grow up, or otherwise reform after you move in together, get married, or have a child, you are in trouble. Your expectations and beliefs are the problem.

What if he/she wants to change anyway? How do you know if someone really wants to change a behavior? It's pretty simple. Here's the anatomy of authentic change:

The person doesn't like his/her own reaction to something, or a pesky behavior.

They recognize it's costing them something.

They tell people they're working on it.

They ask for or seek help to revise the behavior.

Then they do something new until the new thing sticks.

If you do not see those steps laid out plain as can be, and you are pretending that someone will act differently because YOU asked (coerced, manipulated) them to, you are deluding yourself. Anyone who wants to replace a self-sabotaging habit will go through these steps. It's a version of "Notice, Interrupt, Redirect, and Repeat."

We get into trouble when our idea of how we want someone to be bangs hard against the reality of who they actually are, and we won't let go of our idea of them. Marriages fall apart, businesses collapse, and parents and children stop speaking when the demands of our illusions are in conflict with reality.

HOW to Have Friendships That Last

What makes great friendships last? What creates the kind of closeness that spans decades and allows us to step back into conversation with a dear friend after a six-month, two-year or 20-year gap as if they'd been over for dinner just last night?

The recipe is: equal amounts of acceptance, honesty, and compassion. Whether shaken or stirred, it's a cocktail guaranteed to produce lasting intimacy.

True friends are those whom we allow to see and know us as we are. We let our image fall away often enough that the disowned parts of ourselves, our petty judgments, our senseless fears, family secrets, and deep longings are to some degree made known. We can relax in the company of true friends because we are real and transparent instead of pretentious, and mutual acceptance overrides the background of fear we may experience in much of the rest of our lives.

We cut our friends slack. Regardless of their eccentricities, deficiencies, or quirks, we say, "Oh, that's just Joe." We sometimes say it with a combination of affection and frustration, but the idea that we should or even COULD change them isn't part of the package.

We might confront a friend in anger if we think they are being an ass or putting their marriage or health at risk, but in the friendships that last, we don't ditch them, hold it against them, or preach to them when they screw up. We say our piece and then love them, maybe even shake our head and offer up an "I told you so" when the shit hits the proverbial fan. *But even then, we say it with an open heart and a helping hand, never even thinking that we might write them off because they didn't shape up.* Such friendships speak to the reality of compassion, an ability to speak our mind while simultaneously accepting the person regardless of their ability to get a better grip on what their behavior may be costing them. This is intimacy. This is love. And it's a far cry from the way most of us relate to our parents, siblings, children, lovers, or spouses.

HOW to Fight and Get Over It

One key to relating in a way that keeps love alive is by learning how to fight and get over it—the "it" in this case being your judgment and hard feelings. The ability to fight and get over it makes or breaks relationships of all kinds—partners, friends, and even coworkers.

If you can argue, forgive each other, and make up without holding a grudge or forcing your partner to agree with you then you have intimacy. This is reality. You take care of yourself by being honest, angry, and clear with your partner and by getting over the anger (or frustration, or other emotion) and back to neutral after a fight without clinging to lingering judgments. If you can do this you have found a way to maintain clear and direct communication even in the face of disagreement.

If, instead of disagreeing and getting over yourself, you become silent and withhold, or become fake-nice and judgmental, or if you go for the throat and fight tooth and claw for hours without really resolving anything, or stop only when one person gives in, well then, you may want to take a look at your "Family Communication Virus."

The Master of the Obvious says:

You can't MAKE somebody understand or agree with you, and if you set out with that as your objective, you set yourself up for failure.

You can't change anybody, especially not your partner. Sure you can threaten, punish, and nag someone into compliance some of the time but that is NOT relating and what they do is not change. It's damage control. The cost to the relationship isn't worth your temporary sense of victory.

If either of you keep score, you're in big trouble, and will need to interrupt yourself as quickly as possible and get a grip. You have flaws; s/he has flaws. End of story.

You can't resolve the present by dragging up the past. If you have old unresolved resentments, deal with them and get over them. Don't use the past as "evidence" that you are right and your partner is wrong.

Explaining, justifying, and defending your "position" will not work. Talking about what actually happened, by revealing thoughts, emotions, and imagined meaning, rather than whose position is "right" will lead eventually to resolution, requests, and forgiveness.

A repeating fight that seems to be over clutter, or a forgotten birthday, or an unpaid bill, might really be a way to drive your partner away so you don't have to be responsible for ending a relationship or a lifestyle you do not want. Often these complaints are really about an unspoken desire for more appreciation, or an unspoken suspicion that your partner doesn't find you attractive any more, or the complaints are evidence you use to sell yourself the story that you aren't successful in keeping a relationship. So start there. Be honest with yourself about what is going on with *you*.

If you discover that you do not LIKE your partner (friend, spouse, sibling) even though you may love him/her, then consciously and deliberately revise the relationship rather than driving yourself (and the other person) nuts. Yes, this may mean a divorce or a break-up. Love alone is NOT the best reason to stay married. If love is not grounded in compatibility and friendship, you're setting yourself up for high drama.

The most simple, honest, and elegant way to communicate is to reveal what is going on for you, rather than default to blame, accusation, manipulation, wheedling, whining, or bullying. Yes, it will take practice. Practice on the fly. Interrupt yourself, mid-holler if necessary, and take a breath, or call a time out, or apologize, or redirect your thoughts and start over, until you are proficient in communicating WHILE you disagree. The more you practice separating the facts from the many imagined motives and meanings you add to an event, the better you will get at relating authentically. The happier you will be. The fewer things will trigger your irritation and the faster you will get over upsets.

When you learn how to stay in contact when you disagree, rather than go into "prove you wrong" mode, then you will be much more able to resolve and get over disagreements with your coworkers, boss, mother-in-law, or anyone else you may have a conflict with. You don't have to resolve every issue that comes along to be happy, you just have to get better at knowing when to pick your battles, based on what is important to you. Sometimes, ending an argument by agreeing to disagree is the best solution, and sometimes an argument is a set-up for a hidden agenda. Maybe the argument is a symptom of a much larger issue.

We Encourage People to Produce What We Filter For

Sheila and Eric: Living Into Limiting Beliefs

Sheila filters for men who are (like her dad) always trying to do things for her that she could do for herself. She labels the behavior condescending and controlling, maybe even dismissive. Since Sheila and her partner, Eric, moved in together, his tendency to take care of things for her has increased. He usually orders her meal when they go to a restaurant, he takes the car in to be serviced, he manages the money (even hers), he finds the best landscaper, picks the movies they go to, and he even chose the dress she wore to the office party. Sheila silently resents him, and sometimes withholds sex to get even. She feels guilty because, she rationalizes, he's just being "helpful." She wishes he'd treat her like an adult.

Let's rewind to the beginning of the relationship. Sheila and Eric each had separate apartments, bank accounts, and lives. She habitually asked him for advice about trying new foods when they ate out. When he asked her what movie she wanted to see, she'd usually say "I don't care." When Sheila moved in with him, she said that she thought that having one checking

217

account would be easier (though really she thought that combining funds was a way to force Eric to make more of a commitment). When Eric suggested that Sheila contact a landscaper or plumber to solve a problem, she put it off or "forgot," secretly thinking "men are supposed to do that." Eric started taking her car in for maintenance after he found out that she ruined her previous car by neglecting to change the oil.

In other words, unconsciously Sheila was acting like a child and she set Eric up to take on a parenting role. Although she told herself she was just asking for his input or his opinion, in reality she was training him to make decisions for her. Eric thought he was giving Sheila what she wanted—solving her problems and being a useful and attentive mate. All the while she judged and criticized him thinking, "He started out OK, but now he's just like all the rest of the guys I dated!" Meanwhile, Eric's having a similar thought. "Wow, she appeared to be independent and intelligent, but she's just a helpless ditz like all the other girls I dated! I guess that's just the way women are."

Both Sheila and Eric took the not-so-easy but familiar way out. They both get to be right about how the opposite sex is, yet each of them contributed to the training process and neither of them is satisfied. What could they have done differently with a bit more self-awareness?

Sheila might have:

- revealed that she usually attracts caretakers
- asked him if he usually attracts women who want to be taken care of
- requested that he check in with her if he started feeling resentment
- verbalized her own resentment, rather than hide it and pretend to feel OK
- recognized that she was co-creating a parent-child dynamic

- talked openly about how she would interrupt those old habits

Eric might have:

- refused to make decisions for her
- encouraged her to do things on her own
- tried new ways to convey love and affection
- revealed his pattern of care-taking and then resenting women

Had Sheila caught on to how she was training Eric (or had he caught on to how he was training her, too) then they both would have had the opportunity to create a healthier and more satisfying relationship.

When you reveal patterns that sabotage your satisfaction and consciously negotiate the behaviors, you can do a new and more pleasurable dance. Had Eric simply refused to make her decisions for her, that would have changed the dance too. However, Sheila may have then viewed him as pushy or neglectful or some other thing that made him wrong. Making the other person wrong or demanding that they change to make you less vulnerable to your own inner programming does not work. Revealing what you think, how you feel, and what you do, then negotiating the waters of your combined neuroses in the same boat, is preferable to the more common (and useless) strategy of blame, shame, and attack.

Above all else, you must remember that filters literally limit what you see, hear, accept, and believe. *In other words, it's good to get a second opinion before you believe your own conclusions in any area of life in which you are chronically unsatisfied.*

When the filter is filtering for something or filtering out something else, a person's favorable behaviors can be overlooked and the behaviors that trigger you may become all you can see. Conversely, if you have the filter of only seeing the "good" about a person, you may miss the red flags that are clearly visible to your friends.

When in doubt, ask your friends—the ones who won't lie to you, sugar coat things, or spare your feelings, and who do love you and would like to see you break whatever crappy habit is preventing you from getting what you want. Honestly, unless every friend you have is infected with the same filter (not likely) they will see through your unconscious training program in a flash.

Here's what it looks like when filters work in your favor.

Harry and Anna: Filters That Work

Anna's parents were both hotheaded immigrants who fought and loved out loud and got over their many differences and tough times, staying in love for more than 56 years before they each died of a heart attack within a month of each other. They were openly affectionate and they believed in "Never go to bed angry," which in their case meant a few late nights battling their way through their disagreements.

Harry's parents, while more reserved, both in their expression of affection and anger, also had a long marriage, even though Harry's Dad had spent several years in jail for embezzlement, during which time his mother had had an affair. His parents believed deeply in the power of forgiveness and in making amends, and though they spent nearly six months after his dad's release angry and hurt, they kept talking, kept crying, and did eventually forgive each other so thoroughly that, in their golden years, they referred to that tough time as their "wild and crazy days."

Harry and Anna had been married for 8 years when the trouble started. Anna had suspected something was deeply wrong and had been prodding Harry to tell her what was going on, asking why he was rarely home. She would follow him around the house accusing and interrogating and he would become silent, or get angry and lie. After a few months of this, Anna, sure that he was lying, convinced herself that he was having an affair. She started sleeping with her college sweetheart, who had moved back to town.

She was furious with Harry, and after just her third hot date, she came home hollering and told Harry she was fooling around and that he'd better decide pretty quickly what he wanted—the marriage or whatever bimbo he was seeing. Harry then told Anna that he was deeply in debt and had been gambling away their savings, which included a good part of Anna's inheritance. She was momentarily relieved, and then furious for a whole new reason. Harry was out of his mind with jealousy. They fought for nine hours straight. No kidding.

Then, exhausted, Harry said, "So, what're we gonna do?" and, Anna, equally out of steam, said "Let's go to sleep and figure it out in the morning." And they did.

Harry got some help with the gambling, Anna took over doing all the finances, and Anna arranged a lunch with "Biff" as Harry called the college ex, and they both sat down with him and explained that the affair was over.

It's not as if they didn't have any more fights about it. One or the other of them would get mad all over again and they'd be off to the races, but they both realized that not being honest about what was going on was the cause of all that pain, and they learned how to work out their differences with greater ease and efficiency over time. They forgave each other. They became closer, more honest, more intimate. They each came through it with a greater apprecia- tion for each other's fears and with greater trust in each other and their ability to work through conflict.

So in this case, the filters for relating that each of them "inherited" from their parents became the foundation for getting over hurt and anger and making their relationship stronger than it had been before.

HOW to Face Lifestyle Differences with a Potential Partner

I have worked with plenty of people who were miserable and felt guilty because, having achieved the American Dream formula of big income, big promotion, big house, big car, and "perfect" family, their achievements had become the source of deep unhappiness, and even suicidal thoughts, rather than inspiration and satisfaction. The one question they never asked themselves was: *Is the life I have the one I want, or the one I think I should have?* Start there. Ask yourself that question and answer it honestly, then use it to have a conversation with your partner now, before your dissatisfactions get large enough to ignite a serious conflict.

Here's an example. Say you desire a close-knit family, lots of vacation time spent fishing and camping, a modest home that's easy to maintain, no outstanding debts to speak of, a feeling of contribution to the world, and a wife that enjoys your company more than your paycheck. You meet someone who is charming, attractive, and has many of the qualities you want in a mate. If, underneath that initial appeal, that person is a workaholic who prefers living beyond their means, believes carrying debt is good for the economy, sees boarding school as the ultimate character-builder, and thinks staying in a hotel without room service is roughing it, you may find yourself sacrificing your satisfaction to accommodate her desires, because, after all, that's what "affluent" people do, and you should want to be affluent, right? That's what we're all supposed to want. Doing that will not only make you miserable, it will kill you. If it doesn't kill you physically, by way of a heart attack or stroke, then it will kill you figuratively by robbing you of the joy, the juice, and the pleasures of having the kind of life that gives you real happiness.

Frank's Story: Happiness is a Warm B-and-B

Frank, a high-profile lawyer, met the owner of a bed and breakfast inn and fell in love with her. He divorced his wife, quit his job, gave up both homes and the SUV, and married the innkeeper. He also fell in love with the life at the inn—the mountain view, the intimacy of cooking and sharing breakfast with the travelers, and the physical work and sense of community his new life entailed. He took his high-powered legal skills into the community and occasionally took on *pro bono* cases for landowners or individuals whose cases moved him. Frank's family was outraged, his ex-wife took him for every cent she could, and his lawyer buddies turned their backs on him with a lot of head shaking and tongue wagging.

A decade after I coached Frank to go forward with his dream, I ran into him at an airport and he told me he was still "profoundly happy," and that his ex-wife had married his former boss, who had since had a heart attack and was also up for trial on charges of fraud. Much to my surprise, Frank, who had once been a real "you're getting yours and I'll make sure of that" kind of guy, said, "I thought I would hate him, or feel good about his mess, but I feel sorry for David. We were once friends and I know he came from a long line of farmers and always longed for the open fields and a simpler life. He just wouldn't let himself quit."

"What, Frank — have you suddenly become the Buddha??" I asked.

"Hell no, I just feel really good about my life and my marriage, and can't help but wish that David, and even Maggie (the ex), would get a real life. A lot of people would be a lot happier if they did."

Wow. This is the kind of satisfaction that makes the world go ' round! And yes, what Frank did is a great example of how to turn your life into a genuine Holy Adventure. A quest. A way to be the hero of your own tale. These truly satisfying moments happen when we recognize that our friends, our families, our annoying neighbors and irritating co-workers could indeed surrender to their own dreams and, in so doing, change the community and, ultimately, the fabric of society. Occasionally in moments when the "Franks" remind us of the potent force of self-awareness, we feel giddy with visions of a planet in which we cooperate as a global family to solve our collective problems that seems close enough to touch. Heaven on earth. It truly starts with what you and I do today and every day right here and now in the simple choices of our daily lives.

HOW to Revise Your Relating Skills: A Review

Give up blame. Blame = powerlessness. The buck stops with you; otherwise, your life will unfold as if you are a victim of circumstance. Oh, and don't blame yourself either.

Replace "Why" with "HOW?" Words direct us towards or away from solutions Asking "Why?" and looking for "Because . . ." creates a dead end loop. We interpret events (guess) rather than observing, and we believe our imaginings as if they are facts. The reasoning mind spits out reasons.

Practice simple, clear, direct, and honest communication. Interrupt justifications, defenses, explanations, and manipulations, replacing those habits with *noticing and reporting the information that is the most honest.*

Reveal, respond, and request replaces reaction or at least follows soon thereafter. This will take practice. Be willing to screw up. It definitely will still turn out better than whatever you're doing now.

Use fewer words. Learn to take a breath and interrupt the usual automatic bullshit that comes out of your mouth. Check in with your body. Use your whole body as a "truth machine" to guide your communication. Investigate your filters, stories, and other reality blinders, and be honest about what you discover. Honesty is NOT spewing every thought and irritation that comes up, but an ongoing revelatory way of communicating multiple layers of truth as you discover them. It is transparency.

Correct your course as soon as you can. If you say "yes" when you mean "no," contact the person as soon as you realize you have agreed to something you don't want to do and reverse your decision. You can even practice saying "no" first. Then later, when you're alone and not feeling obligated, you can consider whether or not you want to say yes. This is great practice.

When in doubt, check it out. When you find yourself mind reading, interpreting, deleting information, and making generalizations and assumptions, stop and check on the validity of your thinking. Speak up, reveal your thoughts, make your requests, and let reality—not your mind—inform you.

Learn to be present. You must be *in* the moment to change how you feel and what you think in that moment. You must live in the present to direct the future the way you want it to go. That's why we recommend (ask, beg, plead, and demand) that you meditate and practice other forms of mindfulness. This is the secret of awakening and activating our bullshit detector, especially when we have been lying to ourselves. To be able to notice and interrupt your usual reactive mind, you first must be able to catch yourself in the act. This skill requires practice. T. Thorn Coyle's e-book, *Crafting a Daily Practice* is a great way to move into making meditation and self-observation a part of daily life. It's the "Couch-to-5K" training program for meditators.

Tell the truth. Not as a moral imperative, but as good common sense. There's less to remember later. People you want to be close to can only know you, and know what you want, and what you enjoy—and dislike—if you tell the truth. Mind reading is not a reliable option. Stop it.

Partner with your subconscious. Practice noticing your surroundings and the sensations in your body. Real life happens moment by moment and we miss much of this if we are checked out, living mostly in our thoughts.

Heaven on Earth. It is possible. It is within our grasp. It begins when we stop lying to ourselves and to others. The idea of truth-telling is not a moral imperative. It is about the singular and funda-mental key to creating a life that is satisfying. The honesty that will serve you and your community well requires telling the day-by-day truth about what you think, what you feel, what you want; and often includes revealing the mistakes you make, and the judgments you have. That's how we can get out of our own way, and get back to the moment, where we belong.

Authenticity and clarity transmit an invitation to others to be honest and at ease. We relax around people who are honest and at ease. Their words, manner of speech, emotions, and body language are congruent. Our bodies respond to that. The more transparent and relaxed you become, the more you have the kind of human-to-human contact that can open hearts, make friends, heal differences, produce empathy, initiate forgiveness, generate businesses, topple limiting patterns, change your life, and change the world. You can be a human BE-ing rather than an obsessive Doer.[1]

CHAPTER 13

Memes, Viruses, and Societal Filters (Oh My!)

"Don't ask yourself what the world needs—ask yourself what makes you come alive, and then go do it. Because what the world needs is people who have come alive."
—Harold Thurman Whitman

New filters and patterns may be generated no matter how old you are, so although many of the most irritating and potentially limiting filters are created at an early age, viral thoughts infect minds every day, and the brightest advertising and marketing people know exactly how repetition and emotion hook us. When TV commercials "work," it's not because logic prevails, but because the emotion that is repeatedly generated and associated with the product or service becomes the real item that is purchased.

A meme, according to our old stand-by, the Merriam-Webster dictionary, is "an idea, behavior, style, or usage that spreads from person to person within a culture." Some of those cultural tidbits live a long time. For example, I'd wager that even nonsmokers among you can finish the jingle, "Winstons taste good like . . ." and when you remember that, it comes with music playing in your brain, right?

Ideas operate in a society in a fashion similar to the way a true virus operates. Glenn Grant, on his website A Memetic Lexicon, notes that "[a]n idea can parasitically infect your mind and alter your behavior, causing you to want to tell your friends about the idea, thus exposing them to the idea-virus. Any idea which does this is called a 'meme.'. . . Typical memes include slogans, ideas, catch-phrases, melodies, icons, inventions and fashions. It may sound a bit sinister, this idea that people are hosts for mind-altering strings of symbols, but in fact this is what human culture is all about."

Many memes are useful, and some are silly and benign. Some viral ideas link together and are able to produce powerful awareness that leads to positive change and evolution of consciousness, or an unfortunate "slumber" that misdirects us from reality and from the truth.

It can be a short walk from a viral idea to an ideology—a doctrine or dogma that includes a set of beliefs that form a position and subsequent course of action. We have the good, the bad, and the ugly (there's another meme for ya) on exhibit in our history and in the present-day society. The sit-ins and protests that worked to bring about racial integration in the US resulted from an ideology that began with a viral idea, that all people are created equal. Then there's the viral idea that we have the right to kill those who do not share our beliefs, which has resulted in a host of atrocities and mayhem, from burning "witches" to flying airplanes into buildings to shooting physicians who provide legal abortions.

Morris Berman is a cultural critic who has made the wise distinction that "[a]n idea is something that you have, but an ideology is something that has you."

Sociologist and author Kingsley Dennis, who co-founded WorldShift International, says that the condition of our memes reveals our societal and species mind-set—and that it is imperative that ". . . we establish a healthy, positive, and forward thinking mind-set and perceptual paradigm."

There are already some newer memes catching hold. Honesty. Authenticity. Transparency. These ideas about ending secrets, revealing lies, and owning responsibility aren't new. What is new is the way they are being consciously and deliberately reinforced throughout a small but significant portion of society. Transparency in the boardroom, revelations of government secrets, and protections for whistleblowers are all a part of this shift. So are companies like NetFlix that reject the traditional work model for one that is a better fit for a technological age.

The ideas fueling these new memes, models, and ideologies contain most, if not all, of the ideas and practices you have read in this book. You can apply them to create more satisfaction in your own life, and in doing so you contribute to the creation of more satisfaction in our society and our culture. They are connected. WE are connected. The repeating thoughts we think matter more than we know.

If you haven't noticed, we are a world in flux, and large-scale changes are already in the works. Not the end-of-the-world, Hollywood doomsday scenario kind of change, but rather the change that comes from clear and open communication, access to information, and acknowledgement of our value as human beings.

Dennis's astute words make the point: "Our cultural development mirrors our perceptual capacities, and both influence each other. ...Evolution of species, society and individuals involves long periods of relative stability punctuated by windows of accelerated transition that create new paradigms of perception. Thus, our thoughts constitute a powerful language, one that will become increasingly more active."

So the thought we want to leave you with here, before we take a deeper look at the unconscious mind in all its glory, is this: It is time to change our personal and cultural stories. As we do, the myths and beliefs that shape our lives can then support a greater awareness of the true nature of our human being-ness. Our interrelated, interdependent, entangled lives and minds give us a tremendous power for magnificent positive revisions in our global community.

We humans are open systems. We pass on ideas, emotions, and ideologies both consciously and unconsciously all day, every day, having an impact not only our own lives, but on the moods, thoughts, and choices of those around us. In turn, those around us have an impact on us.

At first glance you may think that this power of **HOW** may only help you and those close to you. Yes, it will; but that's not where the story ends. If you have ever desired to change society, change the world, or if your scope is not that inclusive, maybe just upgrade the way your community at work or school or church operates, well here's the thing: The more you are willing to be honest, to challenge your assumptions, communicate with clarity, own responsibility for your happiness, cultivate forgiveness and live with transparency, the more your life and your happiness changes people, society, and the world thought by thought, action by action, all day, every day.

Part One Summary

The many conversations and practices in this section can be reduced to these basic concepts. If you review this summary regularly, it will help keep you awake and on track as a conscious creator of your life. In any area of life you wish to transform, you must evolve from unconscious incompetence (when you don't even think about how you keep getting what you don't want, you don't know what you don't know), to conscious incompetence (when you don't know how you're getting the result you don't want but you know you are the source) to conscious competence, (as you know and practice the new thoughts and behaviors but still have to work to overcome the old habits) then finally to unconscious competence–the point at which you unconsciously think, feel, and act in ways that bring you what you DO want.

To move through these stages with greater ease, here are the most important things that will rewire your brain and set up powerful life changing patterns:

- Own 100% responsibility for every outcome/experience you have.
- Find people who already have what you desire and befriend them.
- Meditate and exercise daily, sleep and eat to support a healthy body and mind.
- Be honest with yourself and others deliberately, even when you're afraid.
- Get over lingering anger, resentment, fear, or sadness quickly through self-expression.
- Read and have conversations that reinforce these positive, proactive ideas and beliefs.

- Generate powerful pleasant emotions and get off the pity train, remembering that reality follows thoughts and emotions. Spend time each day imagining the life you desire as if you already have it, and feel good, grateful, and confident.
- Practice kindness. Be kind to yourself and others consciously.
- Remember that feeling good is more important than looking good.
- Put happiness and satisfaction first, and success will follow.

PART TWO

Three Life Stories:
Clues, Patterns & Progress

CHAPTER 14

Raven's Story

Writing about my life is a way for me to share my journey from suffering to pleasure. It's about the setup of filters and patterns, how I used them and how they used me. This is about you, too, because we are all human, and all on a similar roller coaster called Life.

In the Beginning

I was born Robin Marie Robertson on February 24th 1955, at 2:20 p.m. in Yonkers, New York. My father, Robert, an alcoholic mortician, and my mother Anna, his silently depressed wife, lived with his parents George and Ann in a one bedroom fourth floor tenement walk up with me and my sister, Gail. She is nearly eight years older than I.

Dad's drinking, combined with Grandma's perpetual fault finding, contributed to the wear and tear on my mother, who worked countless hours at various dead-end jobs to add to the government check that my grandparents collected every month. Dad worked freelance as an embalmer, restorative artist, and funeral director. He drank between funerals, and both yelled and laughed with gusto.

Grandma was, to put it mildly, completely nuts. Don't get me wrong, she was a gutsy loudmouth survivor kind of a broad, who no doubt gave me her fair share of genetically enhanced sarcastic wit. And she could cook and bake Betty friggin' Crocker right under the table. She was unfortunately mean spirited, and loved to control and manipulate a wide circle of people by being Queen of Gossip Central. Fortunately, I was her favorite, and she never turned her evil wiles on me. Ruling the rabble was an art form, though, and God knows she took pride in her handiwork.

Sometime during the summer after I turned five, Grandma, who left the house once each month to cash the government check, quit going out of the house completely. (Except when urban renewal eventually forced us to move and tore down the neighborhood. Yes, the whole neighborhood).

Some of my earliest memories are the rich, thick, yeasty smells of bread dough and cool gray mornings and the slick warm feel of bacon fat as she let me knead it into the dough. After she'd mix the bread in a huge stockpot, she'd cover it then shove it under the blankets at the foot of the bed. Grandma was an early riser and I often shared her bed due to numerous illnesses that won me a reprieve from sleeping in the top bunk where my sister could torment me. I loved putting my feet against that cool metal pot in the early morning hours.

My grandparents had the one "real" bedroom while my parents slept on a fold-out couch in the living room and my sister and I had bunk beds that were crammed into a side pocket off the living room, opposite my father's big wooden dressing closet with all the wonderful, mysterious little secret drawers.

Inks and ribbons, jewelry and paper, drawings and hand painted ties were some of the treasures to be found in those drawers. Daddy wasn't just a run-of-the-mill embalmer. He was a brilliant restorative artist. He was often called in to restore faces other embalmers wouldn't touch. He had a reputation that allowed him to work on the rich and famous bodies as well as some military leaders.

His manner and wit served him well in most circles. He was respected and admired, unless of course he was three sheets to the wind and mad as hell. (Or worse, pissed after being sober for a few too many days.) He had local police and detective pals as drinking buddies. I can only imagine how many times they covered his ass when he'd been out drinking. They were returning the favor for him hiring them as pall bearers and paying them under the table. He often retold crime stories heard when taking them out for "coffee and" during the funeral service.

Daddy had quite the morbid sense of humor which earned him a stool at many a bar frequented by "important" people, though Daddy wasn't impressed by status. "They all shit, and they all die," is what he'd say about everybody from General McArthur to Bishop Sheen. And he meant it.

He also made engraved jewelry and hand-painted faces of the Madonna (and more than a few naked ladies) on silk ties, and on beautiful thick wide ribbons that were trimmed with pinking shears and used as bookmarks.

Dad loved music and was reported to be quite a drummer. He claimed to have known the famed Buddy Rich, a side benefit of getting restoration and other funeral jobs in Manhattan. In "The City", he met (and drank with) a number of famous people, including Jackie Gleason and Art Carney, who sent my mother a basket of flowers when I was born. There were a few bars in White Plains that he frequented, getting drunk with celebrities, and sitting in to play drums in whatever band happened to be playing. I inherited a keen sense of rhythm and an intolerance for bad musicians from daddy.

Daddy could be a mean drunk, but by the time I arrived on the scene, I'm told he'd mellowed some. The "mellowed" version of Dad punched a few holes in the walls, and ripped at least one phone off its moorings.

He usually fought with his mother, aka Grandma.

Once the yelling started it could go on for hours, sometimes days, stopping only when he passed out and starting again when he awoke. I remember that making Daddy happy was often the number one priority of the household, except when Grandma couldn't leave well enough alone and would get him going again after he'd slept it off.

I think that living with his parents made him feel inadequate and miserable, though he never said so, and in truth Grandpa wasn't getting enough to live on from the government pension. Daddy and Grandpa got along well. Like brothers. They clearly loved each other. Times were very tough for them for many years. We ended up in that tenement after the house they'd been living in went up in a blaze from an electrical fire.

Grandpa came back from World War I a morphine addict, but he quit cold turkey after realizing that the government was never going to help him quit. I remember Grandma saying that after Grandpa "got off the junk" as she put it, a lot of Daddy's fight went out of him. I don't know. They all were gone before I had the awareness to ask those kinds of questions. But, I guess watching your father go through morphine withdrawal and writhe on the floor will do that to a person.

My father was an only child, and he and Grandma were locked in some kind of eternal battle like that episode of Star Trek where the half white/half black man fought with the half black/half white man forever. Yep, my life was definitely some bizarre blend of Six Feet Under and The Adams Family with Twilight Zone music in the background.

I swear, the biggest fights were started by the dumbest things. Once war broke out over whether or not the potatoes for dinner should be mashed or cubed with butter and onions. Another time I remember Daddy punching a hole in the wall at the end of a battle with Grandma that started over which way the toilet paper was put on the holder. Honestogod. The war zone occasionally extended to include my mother, who only fought back in the last years of her life, but in the few years before my sister moved out, there were also regular shouting matches between my sister and my father.

Am I a "yeller," you may ask? Well, I started out silent and repressed through high school, graduated to self-expressed, then exploded into a full blown yeller after my early attempts at relationships generated the kind of misery I'd known in childhood. I yelled for about a decade, then dialed it back—which took a while, and plenty of effort—and now I yell only on very rare occasions. People who knew me as a kid wouldn't believe I ever yelled and people who knew me when I was a yeller wouldn't believe how calm and I am now.

All in all, my childhood resembled life in a gunpowder factory and my job was to keep the idiots I lived with from lighting matches. I got very, very good at reading subtle gestures and changes in tone of voice. Body language was truth when words were lies. I was sometimes able to deflect or disarm Daddy or Grandma by knowing what one of them wanted before they got cranky, and making sure they got it. Often it was a game of "distraction" in which I engaged one of them in a way that changed the emotional channel, at least in the short run.

Mostly as a kid I remember having a perpetual knot in my stomach that grew bigger, smaller, hotter, or tighter depending on the emotional weather. I was a goddamned excellent storm forecaster and to this day, my body is nearly 100% reliable when it comes to predicting other people's emotional weather—I have the ability to tell what is really going on in spite of the words people are saying.

Later my ability to "read people" came in very handy when in developing my life as a workshop facilitator, sales trainer, and as a coach. Unfortunately, it did me no good whatsoever in matters of love, since I filtered out the warning signals. Drat. Dammit. Sigh.

Grandpa was the sane one of our Addams Familyesque little troupe of nut jobs. He had a truly great attitude, and an earthy, grounded rock-solid demeanor and the right amount of laughs and hugs to keep me relatively sane. He talked to me, protected me, taught me, held me, and loved me. If not for Grandpa, I don't know how I could have survived my childhood with any possibility for sanity later on.

On those days when we escaped, I'd notice smells and colors and textures with heightened awareness. As soon as we headed towards home, though, my hands would get clammy, and the familiar tension, hot coal effect would start in my gut. It took me well into my 30s to hear shouting and not have my gut and asshole clench like a bear trap.

Grandpa was born just before the turn of the century and boasted about having been in every war there was starting with chasing Poncho Villa across Mexico. It's Grandpa—who came back from World War 1 after being missing in action for a year and a half with a collapsed lung from mustard gas, with a steel plate in his head resulting from a bullet that knocked his eye out, and with a powerful addiction to morphine—who gave me the finest lessons about life and human nature anyone could have given me. He was tenacious, generous, strong, humble, funny, and was clearly the authority in his own life. He had seen and survived some terrible things.

Mommy always worked and worked. I don't remember her being around much, and when she was home, she kept on working, cleaning, doing laundry by hand in the kitchen sink, and helping Grandma in the kitchen. I remember Mom being sad and distant. Today we'd have labeled her "depressed." I remember often thinking that she loved me but always wished she were somewhere else. My mother was the textbook model for self-sacrifice and repressed emotion. She was unreachable in her suffering, but slogged on seemingly tirelessly while her health irrevocably deteriorated.

I do remember Mom getting me ready for school in the morning sometimes, though I was an unwilling morning riser: slow, annoyed, and refusing to speak. Most often, her patience gave way and

Grandpa took over, sliding warm knee socks onto my fat little legs as I sat nearly comatose and staring into mid space. He'd tell me stories about children in other countries who weren't allowed to go to school, and places where girls were forbidden to learn how to read or receive any kind of education. He definitely knew how to motivate me. Even though I still loathed going, I did take pleasure from doing that which someone somewhere might actually try to stop me from doing. This theme has continued to play out in my life. *Sometimes it's been a very useful trait and then other times, deliberately doing what others say I can't or shouldn't do has been a way to avoid doing what I actually wanted to do. It took learning to get quiet and check my body to know what I wanted.*

Mostly I remember my mother working. I have lots of memories of my mother, on her days off, scrubbing at the washboard, hanging out steaming laundry, ironing and starching clothes, and "helping" my grandmother in the kitchen.

My Grandmother rarely missed an opportunity to point out the many ways in which my mother did not measure up. It was an awful and constant thing, her small sounds, eye rolling and sometimes flat out nasty remarks.

There was another set of relatives of course, but I never knew it until after my mother died and I met them at her funeral. I then discovered that Grandma, always in control of the "hood", had prevented me (and my sister) from ever meeting our other Grandmother, as well as an uncle and other relatives from "her" (my mother's) side of the family.

My mother was, not "allowed" to see her family, though later we found out that she had occasionally sneaked visits with her brother, Mike. Her family's poverty caused her to drop out of high school to work. She'd had rheumatic fever as a child, and wasn't expected to live very long. I do remember that she had varicose veins like road maps on her legs. And I remember that she had toenails that looked like talons, due to operations she'd had on her feet.

I don't know how my parents met or how long they courted. I have no idea how my father convinced my mother to deal with having his parents in the middle of their relationship. They were married by a Justice of the Peace. So, eventually, when my sister neared school age and they prepared to send her to the Catholic school (the public option was not an option in our neighborhood if one wanted to avoid knife fights in the schoolyard), they had to get married a second time. My sister remembers their second wedding. I remember the pictures of my mother, beautiful in her form fitted navy blue dress with white piping, smiling at the camera with my father standing behind her, holding her close.

I can't imagine being a newlywed, living with a mother-in-law who made no bones about her disapproval, and a morphine addicted father-in-law, forced into a four-room apartment with one bathroom for each floor of the building and a claw foot tub in the kitchen. That certainly wasn't what my mother had bargained for. My mother was the model victim. Silent, sad, hard working, self sacrificing, obedient, and broken hearted. She was buried on her 47th birthday.

Though I was confused and angry that last year of her life, I kept it to myself, not because I was supposed to be the Good Girl, but because I did not want to turn out "like my sister" who had moved out in an unprecedented display of rebellion not long after my mother's first heart attack. When nearly two years later my mother died before my sister made peace with my Dad, Gail was found "guilty" by my father and blamed for our mother's early demise.

YES I was a silent girl pretending to be "good" while inside myself I was free, wild, and had big dreams and plenty of anger. To be happy, eventually I had to set the "bad girl" free, make peace with her, and learn to be neither "bad" nor "good," but to be myself, own my mistakes and focus on what worked. To be honest, I was angry for a very long time, and used my anger to give myself permission to do what I wanted to do. All those years of silence wore on me, but I was determined that, unlike my mother, I would speak up and therefore survive.

I loved and feared my sister Gail. She was almost eight years old and had gotten used to being an only child by the time I came on the scene. My parents wanted to have a boy, got pregnant, and got me.

That's why, Instead of being Robert Mack Robertson, Jr., I was Robin Marie Robertson. Well, at least the initials were the same. I didn't have to be a rocket scientist to know that my gender was a major disappointment.

Consequently I made a decades-long error in judgment as my strong drive to be the sensitive, pretty female I was duked it out with the idea that to survive I had to be tough, suck it up, not ask for help, and think like a guy. I had a disdain for "girlie" activities, and suppressed sadness in favor of anger. I was miserable. Mercifully, I became a woman who befriends and understands men. For a while, feeling hurt and being sad was my "default" position any time I wasn't pissed off about something. As I faced that old hurt and grief and sadness, the anger slowly went away too. These days I am genuinely happy and at ease. And I admit that I am a sensitive and very feminine woman.

My sister acted out in a variety of direct and indirect ways. Of course, she said that if I told on her, my life would only get worse. She threatened to kill me. I believed her. On the bright side, she played lots of records on a tinny portable stereo and I fell further in love with music. I learned to sing and harmonize, (on key and quickly, to avoid my sister's wrath) a gift that to this day I appreciate her for.

Up On the Roof

Some of my very best childhood memories, the ones that were notable because I did NOT have knots in my stomach, were those of being up on the roof. Every day the weather allowed, I went up there to escape the tension below. My sister and I called it Tar Beach and brought up towels and iced tea so we could fry ourselves in the blistering sun. I especially liked being up there alone or with my Grandfather. For a nickel we'd get a cup of seed and I'd feed the pigeons. Sometimes we brought bread and lured a seagull to the roof. I even had a "pet" Praying Mantis for a whole summer. He was shaped like a clothespin and I fed him (or her, whatever) pieces of hot dog.

Most of all, I loved looking out over the buildings towards the Hudson River, watching the sun set into the Palisades and waiting for that magic moment when the lights of the George Washington Bridge came on. I played a game in which my wish would come true if I was looking at the bridge when the lights came on.

The roof was my safety, my refuge, and my sanity.

The roof was also great for watching fireworks, and for standing in torrential hot summer rain. It was a place for watching the homing pigeons fly in patterns, and for hearing the train. You could also set your watch by the mom who at five p.m. yelled "Haaaarrrrrrold" to call her son home for dinner. It was a place for smelling the mouthwatering smell of baking bread wafting from the neighborhood bakery, and for watching storms roll in from the bay. Sometimes the sky would get so dark that the streetlights would come on in the middle of the day. The sky would turn green and my grandmother would holler for me to get my ass downstairs.

On the roof I was in the clean (well, comparatively speaking) air, away from the tension and billowing blue funk of cigarette smoke below. I couldn't hear yelling, either, which was a bonus. My sister, being the fair skinned one, couldn't tolerate as much sun as I could, so things worked out perfectly. I could twirl around, talk out loud, recite poems, sing, and generally be myself and relax.

I still love heights, bridges, and watching the sun set over the water. It's certainly not coincidence that I live on Lake Erie and rarely miss an opportunity to watch the sun sink into the lake. I always feel at ease and spiritually alive at that time. The lake is my place of restoration, meditation, and refuge.

I had never, like other kids, ridden a bike or played at someone's house or been invited for dinner. I didn't know any kids. *I finally*

*learned to ride a bike when I was 38. No kidding; thirty-eight! I was 28
when I learned to drive a car, so what's it to ya?*

When I was sent to first grade at five years old I went into shock.
The only kids I'd ever seen up close were the much older kids, mostly boys, that hung out in the park where Grandpa took me to play.
I watched them run, play tag, and play ball. So when I was taken
to first grade I was completely terrified. I'd only been with adults.
Never went to anything that resembled kindergarten. No play dates.
Nada. I had no idea what was expected of me. I hated the smelly,
whiney, prissy chatty girls in my class. I felt completely betrayed by
my mother, who walked me into that first grade classroom.

I quickly learned to hide in plain view. Even though I was often still afraid, I felt powerful. Like Grandpa, you could gas me and
shoot me, but I'd still spit in your eye and escape in the end.

Those days on the roof still come back to me again and again,
triggered by the sweet smell of 3-in-1 oil that we used in the old metal
box fans, or in the sudden smell of hot tar in a parking lot under repair, or when I see pigeons dance their lazy figure eight in the sky, or
when I hear seagulls squawking, or the wind carries the smell of water to me. I'm transported in those moments to that roof, looking out
over the Hudson River, feeling the twilight breezes blow. My body
lets go. In those moments I feel young and warm and free. Right now
as I'm typing these words, I hear James Taylor singing "Up On The
Roof" as a car passes by in the street and all the hair on my arms is at
attention. Well, maybe my family is looking in on me.

A Snapshot Moment

It was late morning. The sun was shining and the sky was very blue
out the kitchen window. I was looking out the kitchen window into
the airshaft, vision blurred, counting bricks, trying not to cry. My
hands were fear-cold and I kept putting them in my armpits. My
gut was in a hard little burning knot. Daddy was at the small kitch-

en sink, shaving; punctuating his razor strokes with outbursts of profanity. His face was red. He was hung over, worse I think, still slightly drunk from the night before. My Grandmother was fighting with him, egging him on about godonlyknowswhat, driving him towards rage the way a skilled cowboy drives cattle into a valley. This would be his excuse to head for the liquor store after today's funeral service. "Oh, shut up! Shut up!" My Mother pleaded silently with her wild eyes, from the other end of the kitchen. I started to pace. My Grandmother grabbed me by the wrists, and pulled me over to my Father, slapping my ice-cold hands against his back. She was *using* me as guilt-bait, to stop the fight she had instigated. At first, I hated her for it and pulled away. But then, my Father settled down, and even occasionally glanced at me in the mirror. For a few moments the kitchen was entirely silent. This was a moment of peace. And contact of sorts. And relief flooded warmly through me the way sensation returns to your foot when it's fallen asleep. *I'd been Noticed and my fear noted. It was a novel experience and I got a head rush, my face and chest flooding with the heat of it.* It was embarrassing, too, like being suddenly pushed out from behind the curtains into a spotlight.

He dressed in the other room and came out in his suit, smiling a tight smile before he left to be the Funeral Director for a few hours. I knew then, that even if he returned at two p.m. with his pint of vodka, ready to pick up the fight where they'd left off, that I'd been seen—and I could be seen again. I learned that the cold hands, pale face, and racing heart did win a few precious moments of being noticed—my feelings considered, even.

That was very heady stuff. Mostly I rose on the seesaw of hoping to be seen and acknowledged and dropped feeling invisible and not worth noticing.

As I grew, this became a liability. While I sometimes used my fear and anxiety to acquire attention, far worse was the worthlessness I felt as an invisible being, only seen when needed to troubleshoot. A second pattern is how I turned into a sap for any person who gave me a little unsolicited kindness. A smile or kind word could reduce me to tears. A compliment and I'd obligate myself to lifelong friendship, gifts, or sexual favors that I hoped proved how very grateful I was to be acknowledged. I was certainly gullible and susceptible to manipulation; what was worse was that I knew what I was doing was pretty whacked, but my desperate need for contact and my hunger to be wanted overrode my common sense for a long time. Eventually, as I got better and better at taking care of myself and asking for what I wanted, the intensity faded. Sometimes I am still moved to tears by the kindness and generosity of others, but I no longer feel that I owe them my undying, unfailing gratitude until the end of time. I simply can say thank you, and move on, knowing that I am and have always been worthy of the kindness of others.

Itches and Twitches and Sisters, Oh My!

I don't think Gail ever forgave me for being born. I grew up quite clear that the reigning dictator was bigger, stronger, and meaner than I could ever hope to be. To say I was afraid of her doesn't nearly paint the picture. I felt a fear comparable to that of someone trapped in a burning house. My sister was the gasoline and the matches.

I was the quiet child, but my sister was seen as the troublemaker. Defiant. Angry. I remember my father saying, "If she were a boy, I'd knock the shit out of that kid." I often secretly wished he'd knock her on her ass for the things she did to me, but he never knew. No one did, I imagine.

I do remember my sister hitting me. Often. And pinching me so much, that the purple and green blossoms under my arms were as big as pansies, and as colorful. I avoided sleeveless shirts, even in the 90-degrees-plus sweltering heat of the top floor tenement super-heated from above by a hot tar roof. She would hit me with a steel bristled hairbrush until my upper arms were covered with pinpricks of blood.

Here's my all-time most frightening memory. My sister sitting on my chest, holding a pillow over my face, telling me she was going to suffocate me. I can't breathe, not as much from the pillow as from her entire weight, which was a considerable bulk over 200 pounds pressing against my chest. Eventually I'd do some kind of Jedi trick to quiet my panic and go limp. Then, eventually, she'd get off me. I don't know if she got bored or worried that I actually passed out. My mouth is dry even now as I write this and I'm feeling a little light headed. I absolutely believed her every time she threatened to kill me.

Since there were six of us crammed into three rooms I just can't figure out how nobody noticed what she did to me. She was some kind of stealth tormentor. The queen of cruel.

I was not like some Buddha that floated untouched by the insanity. My own craziness was like an infection that started as a little red itch that would seep deep into my bones, turning my body into a battlefield.

At some point between the shouting, the onset of my Grandfather's cancer, and my sister's torment, I developed symptoms. Puhlenty of them.

By four years old, my eyes were extremely sensitive to light, and without sunglasses I had eyes that looked like somebody cut two slits in my face with a razor. In addition to squinting, even on an overcast day, I developed a nervous eye-blinking, eye squeezing, eye-rubbing routine that lasted until I started meditating when I was 14.

I also sniffed and/or wheezed. Dust; Raid; smoke; cold, wet air; cats; dog hair; and mold all got me dripping or wheezing. Living in a roach-infested tenement where Raid was used as often, and with as much flair, as Glade Air Freshener probably had something to do with my problems. That and having three rooms crammed with six people, three of whom were chain smokers. (At least until my Grandfather was diagnosed with cancer and later my mother with heart disease, then only Daddy kept puffing away.)

That's the upper body report. Heading south, often I was either painfully constipated to the point where I bled when I finally squeezed out the first cement-like turd, or had such chronic diarrhea I could hardly keep from crapping myself. As if that wasn't unpleasant enough, by age 10 my bladder was real trigger-happy. Probably had something to do with how much coffee I was drinking by then.

So much for my insides, now for the external report. I was sensitive to the sun and broke out in hives in late spring or early summer. Big, red, itching hives. I can still feel the sensation of a cotton ball soaked in cool pink lotion being slathered on my arms. I hated that smell. I itched anyway. Fortunately, that only happened for about three weeks when the weather turned hot for the first time. After the initial breakout I could be in the sun for hours, tan splendidly, and never burn. That was the summer fun.

In mid-winter my feet itched so badly I'd rub them raw and bloody on the carpet. Now I'm sure it was some fungus or another blooming in the dark hell of my saddle shoes after sweating for a few months in the superheated classrooms.

At some point I can't clearly place, I started counting. I counted to keep the pent-up anger, fear, and frustration to a dull roar. My body had some weird life independent of me, my family was nuts, and I hated school. Counting soothed me, so I counted. Counted my steps. Counted beads. Counted buttons. Counted my breaths. Counting was reliable and predictable. My mind could go blank into the numbers, much the same way that watching your breath helps you to meditate. Lots of days I was just trying not to explode. At least that's how I felt. That if I just didn't keep a lid on myself somehow, I'd just short out like an old TV. My eyes blinked and twitched with a life of their own. I was, to put it mildly, a fucking weird kid.

Measles, mumps, and German measles were in the mix somewhere too. I missed an amazing amount of school but managed to always pass my end-term exams. And did I complain? Never. I was the quiet one. The stoic one. The Good Girl by Default. Thankfully, I got over being so goddamned poisonously good when I grew up.

I lived on blackberry brandy, copious amounts of paregoric (anhydrous morphine—made from opium. WARNING: May be habit forming), baby aspirin, and large doses of food. I was not only sick and neurotic as hell, I was fat. Fucked up. Drugged. Crazy and fat.

Not chunky, or pudgy. Goddamned fat. Size 11 first communion dress. Size 14 confirmation dress. Size 20 at eighth grade graduation, weighing in at 235 pounds. Needless to say, that single issue pressed against my possibility for happiness more than all the others combined. I could twitch, itch, piss every 15 minutes, and count every step I took and still be recognized as bright, creative, and witty. Once the fat took over I was a zero, a freak to be tormented or ignored by my peers. Nothing else separated me from the pack as much as my size. Even my sister, who was a heifer herself, tormented me. Told me no one would ever want me. Said at least she didn't "waddle." Told me boys would never look at me twice. By this point she was using speed and starving herself. She got down to a thinnish 180 pounds, bleached her hair blond and got a boyfriend that she hid from our parents.

Every Day a Little Death

I often felt that I was living one step ahead of death. Not mine. Everybody else's. I'd have dreams that there'd be a nuclear bomb, or an earthquake and everybody would be dead but me. I worried that my sister would die in a car wreck, or that my grandfather would die of a heart attack. I worried that Daddy would pop a vessel in the middle of an alcohol-soaked screaming fit. I worried that Grandma would keel over from sheer meanness. After Grandpa was diagnosed with throat cancer I had him buried every other day for a while.

I was 11 when Grandpa was diagnosed with cancer. He started getting radiation treatments. He looked bad. Then surgery and a permanent tracheotomy. He lived on. As it turned out, he outlived his daughter-in-law, his son, and his wife. Then just as Grandpa was starting to look a little healthier, the other shoe fell.

One evening after my mom got home from work, I walked with her to the grocery store to go shopping. The air at home was thick with tension. The air outside was sticky and humid. We walked in silence. When we got about a half block from the store, she slowed down. She handed me the shopping list. Motioned me to go in first. She was pale. That was very much unlike my mother with her olive complexion and rosy cheeks. There was a turnstile entrance. I went through and kept walking towards the carts. I looked over my shoulder and my mother wasn't next to me. When I turned around she was slumped in the turnstile, white as a sheet. I tried to help her through. She couldn't move. I couldn't lift her. I went to the customer service window and pushed ahead of the people in line and said something like. "My mother is sick. Something is wrong with my mother." The next memory I have is of the ambulance pulling away and my grandfather holding my hand. The next memory I have is days later, seeing my mother in the hospital. Knowing she'd had a heart attack.

It was close but, finally, my mother was home. No more working long hours and spending hours pin curling her hair. She sat around looking grim, cried a lot, gained about 25 pounds from the medicine and let her leg hair grow in thick and dark. Ugh.

Well, I just wasn't happy. I mean you'd think that after having my mother off working since forever, I'd have been happy to have her home. The problem was that I just felt more oppressed than usual. When my father would say, "Tell Mommy you love her" or "Bring your mother some ice cream and give her a hug," he might as well have asked me to sprout wings and fly to the moon. I went through the motions and felt guilty that I couldn't rally myself to the cause, but I simply had nothing to give. I was a wrung-out sponge.

During eighth grade, in between my grandfather's visits to Dr. Fodor, the Hungarian eye, ear, nose, and throat specialist who had all the charm and good looks of a cadaver, and my mother's visits to the heart doc, the third shoe fell. Grandma got weird. Ok, weirder than usual. She started drinking red Kool-Aid by the gallon, having dizzy spells, and looking drunk. My father realized right away what was going on and called the family doc. Not surprisingly, my grandmother had developed diabetes. Fortunately, diet (which she stuck to for about 45 seconds) plus pills quickly got her back on track. But God knows, we just hadn't needed another major death scare. My sister, who was working in a hospital, dropped by just long enough to give me mono.

So God knows, not to be left out, my throat swelled nearly shut, and I found myself in the hospital for three days getting my throat swabbed out by Dr. Cadaver himself. Mononucleosis. Finally, mercifully, I got to sleep for a few weeks. It was the best thing my sister ever gave me. Another benefit was that Dr. Deadman also informed my parents in no uncertain terms that my nonexistent dental care left me with a head full of rotting and broken teeth that had to come out. So for the first time in my life, I got regular doctor and dental care. I felt all warm and tingly about that. Honest. Eighth grade ended with quite a mental and emotional pile-up.

The fall rolled around and I started high school. High school gave me the opportunity to explore myself and my potential by interacting with some very intelligent people. At home though, things were continuing to go wonky but in new ways. Urban renewal was going to tear the neighborhood down and we were going to have to move. OK fine, the "hood" was a creepy unsafe place anyway.

But just as I got settled into thinking we were all at this new level of sick-but-stable, the unthinkable happened. My mother died.

I'd just turned 14 on February 24. My mother's birthday was March 6, just ten days after mine. On March 3 I woke early, noticed a light snow had fallen, and asked to stay home from school. I felt uneasy. My mother was sitting on the couch sewing underwear. My father took her pulse as he did each morning. This day, it was a little faster than usual. She took a pill. It was a new prescription. I was standing in the living room watching her sew. Grandma was in the kitchen. Grandpa was doing something at the window. Daddy was just off the living room getting dressed. Her head went back, her eyes rolled up. Her lips turned blue. I hollered, "Grandpa! Daddy!"

Daddy started rubbing her arm. Told me to rub the other arm. Grandpa was holding her head. My father was calling her name. "Anna . . . Anna" The room telescoped. I heard ringing in my ears. I was looking at the scene, this insane tableau, from a distance, thinking, "She's dead, you morons! Stop messing with her."

I stepped back. My father had called the ambulance. Grandpa and Daddy moved her flat on the floor. Daddy was pressing on her chest. Grandma took me by the hand and told me to get dressed. I put on a yellow moo-moo. The paramedics sounded like a thousand horses coming up the stairs. When they rushed past the kitchen, I tried to go in behind them.

I stayed in the kitchen with Grandma. The kitchen door to the hall was closed. The kitchen door was only ever closed before when I was little and Santa brought Christmas presents down the hall because we didn't have a chimney. Now the door was closed because the paramedics were taking my dead mother away.

This wasn't supposed to be happening. She was supposed to be on the mend, doing fine. I was distracted from praying by noise. Stretcher going down the hall, I thought. There she goes. I didn't get to say goodbye.

The kitchen door opened. One paramedic remained. He looked at me, then at my grandmother. He said, "I'm sorry. We did everything we could."

I welled up. The first tears started to fall. "Don't cry," he said.

I blinked them back.

I didn't cry for my mother again for 10 years. She was buried on March 6, 1969 on what would have been her 47th birthday.

So yes, my rebellious, abandoned, needy, insecure, guilty, frightened teen self has been a major player in my life. I have had to learn, sometimes painfully, how to pay attention to her, take care of myself, forgive myself, and hardest of all, I had to learn to stop waiting for someone else to take care of me. Yes, I was a responsible and intelligent survivor, but the cost was that I would, for years to come and in numerous relationships, sacrifice myself, what I wanted, my dreams, even my health for a crumb of attention, choosing people who were simply not capable of being there for me. Slowly though, as I learned to integrate that teenager, I was able to resurrect and keep alive the tremendous gifts she had. These gifts include, music, wonder, trust in the universe, poetry, seeing the best even in the worst of situations and people, tremendous sensitivity, and relentless drive.

More Good News

Because of (rather than in spite of) the powder-keg reality of my home life and the antisocial nature I had developed, I had a complex and strangely satisfying inner life. I learned to read and write at a very early age, and could occupy myself for hours writing stories and hearing poems form in my mind fully finished and perfect, much the way music comes to me today.

I watched and listened my way through childhood. I observed and recorded what went on in my own head, not like a journal, but more like a documentary. I also noticed others. Their body movements, how they talked and what odd sensations I had in my body when my special "radar" told me a person was lying. Much later, it occurred to me that in my silent observations and assessments during childhood, I'd become damn good at reading body language and I possessed a fine-tuned bullshit meter.

My sister, evil rat that she often was, did, with her records and singing, open up the world of music to me. I have a very good ear and an excellent ability to harmonize. Words and music bloomed in me like heather on the Scottish hills. I had found a place to be, a secret world of stories and dreams, poetry and rhythm, harmony and voice and in that world I lived most fully.

I have fond childhood memories about stories and music. My grandfather whistling intricate melodious tunes and dozens of bird-calls is one of my earliest musical memories. All of us sometimes sat around the living room and put Mitch Miller albums on the stereo and sang and sang. We shared our word sheets, or put Mitch on TV and followed the bouncing ball. Around Christmas we dug out the holiday Mitch albums, though Grandma didn't favor holiday songs, that "sanctimonious religious horseshit!"

Sometimes, on a Saturday night, we'd push the furniture against the walls, put on polka music and dance in the living room. Once or twice around the holidays, I remember that Annie Sokol from down the hall came over and danced too.

Another musical memory that comes back to me now is the time my mother taught me to sing "You Must Have Been a Beautiful Baby."

The next day in school I sang for my class and then my teacher had the principal call my sister down from her eighth grade class to hear me sing. She was red-faced and embarrassed to be watching me sing, since unbeknownst to me at the time, my sister had a reputation for being quite a good singer. After that, though, she did start letting me listen to her records with her to learn songs and harmonies.

When I was sick, which was at least 50% of the time, I'd sleep in Grandma's high bed and Grandpa would climb into the sweltering top bunk above my sister in the little alcove off the living room. Late at night, after everyone was in bed, sometimes Grandma would sing "Old MacDonald," "I've Been Workin' on the Railroad," "When Johnny Comes Marchin' Home," or some other war songs. Once in a while I could even get "Itsy Bitsy Spider" out of her even after I was, according to Grandma, "too old for kiddie tunes." Even though her voice was like a cross between an oilcan and sandpaper, I liked hearing her sing. In the dark, with just the sound of her voice and the warmth of her body next to mine, I couldn't remember how people could dislike her.

The stories she told made a big impression on me, too. She wasn't just the daytime version of Grandma, who was a mean-spirited, nasty-mouthed, order-giving, self-righteous, moralistic bitch on wheels. I saw the soft place in her heart in the dark. And the places that still hurt, that by the light of day, she covered over with the crusty scab of indifference.

Sometimes I'd wake up in the middle of the night and slowly sit up to lean on the window ledge and watch the black clouds scuttle across a thin Cheshire smile of a moon. If Grandma "smelled me thinking," and she woke up, I'd usually hear about one of her childhood adventures.

She told me about the time she and her friends got paid to round up a sack of frogs for the rectory. They didn't kill the frogs like they were supposed to and when Grandma got elected to take in the two pillowcases, she found the kitchen empty so she opened them up and let thirty frogs go free, on a spiritual adventure of sorts. The thought of a bunch of priests "Scared like little girls over a few frogs" still thrilled her after 40 years.

There were lots of stories about "the farm in P-A" where she grew up. I heard about chickens that ran around with their heads cut off, and about her cow, Daisy, that broke her leg crossing a stream and so was shot by her father while she looked on. I heard about snakes in the kitchen, and how her father, "the rotten alcoholic sonofabitch," would raise hell and beat the shit out of her mother. Drinking and beating was apparently the regular weekend routine until, at age 13, my grandmother ran her father off the farm with a shotgun screaming "If you come back, I'll kill you dead!" He took the hint, and from then on Grandma, despite having an older sister, Helen, pretty much raised her siblings while her mother worked the farm.

Grandpa and Daddy told stories too. Though I had a few sleepless nights over headless chickens and dead cows, I never could completely wrap my head around the stories the men told until I was much older and heard stories from returning Vietnam vets. They told war stories. They may have been patriotic, but they weren't warmongers. They weren't jingoes. They had plenty of bad things to say about war, the government, and the old men who sent young men to be killed. Their stories were so graphic that they took on a movie quality in my mind's eye. I think I just couldn't have lived with those stories in my head otherwise.

My grandfather told of seeing a German up close, eye-to-eye, and literally smelling his fear. They both froze, two terrified young men looking at each other, guns raised, and a moment of understanding passing between them as if a silent agreement had been made to let each other live. Then another American beheaded the German with a bayonet. My Grandfather said those blue eyes watched his as the head tumbled to the ground and he saw the lips move, mute words falling from a dead man: "Ach mein Gott." "Oh my God," it had said. I remember my Grandfather's eyes fill with tears when he told that story, and I simply could not fathom what sort of power, what set of beliefs, could make one young boy kill another like that.

My Dad had his own stories to tell. Once, one of my father's friends was blown nearly in half by a land mine, and all he could do as a medic was try to push back in the loops of sticky intestines until the priest came. He saw the priest running past and called out to him for last rites. The priest, interested in saving his own holy ass, kept on running. My father, promising his dying friend he'd bring the priest, ran after him, tackled him and with his service revolver to the priests' temple, informed him that he could die right there, or give last rites. When they returned to his friend's side, the boy was barely conscious and although last rites were given, Daddy told the priest he'd piss on his grave for letting that boy die without being able to hear the words.

Many years later, my father, who was acting as funeral director at the burial of a retired general, left the gravesite to relieve himself. Dad had had a few too many the night before and the pot of coffee he'd thrown down to shake off his hangover wanted out. In his frenzied need to piss, he'd found the nearest tall gravestone, hid behind it, and started to take a grand leak on the opposite grave. (At this point in the story I once actually saw gooseflesh pop up on his arms.) In mid-stream, he said, his eyes focused on the gravestone beyond his fountain of urine and he realized that he was literally pissing on the grave of "that useless rat-bastard priest." While my father never had much good to say for men (or women) of the cloth, I do believe that day restored his faith in his version of a just God.

That music and those stories were two beacons of comfort and real family that existed in my otherwise weird and turbulent childhood. They were the sail and rudder that got me out into the open sea and sustained me for many years thereafter.

The music and stories of my childhood are a lifeline that I used to haul myself up out of bleak and desperate times over and over as I grew up. I appreciate and value those times and my family for those gifts. I learned about the power of music, the magic of stories and personal myths and legends. I learned empathy, and that ALL people are good AND bad, kind AND mean, smart AND stupid. Through these experiences I learned the value of hearing and really listening to the stories people have to tell, and the power that transforms people when they do share their secrets, their pain, and their fears. I learned that we do the best we can and that all people are flawed and that doesn't mean we don't also have plenty of good in us.

I learned that a person can, through sheer force of will, beat death if he wants to, or like my mother, die if she wants to. I learned about the power and destruction of war, and the pain of addiction, and the misery that follows when a person cannot or will not step up and get over the past. I also learned that accepting people as they are is the only real definition of love. Most importantly, I learned, eventually, that our repeated thoughts and emotions—our mindset—determines our experiences, and that we are never victims of circumstance.

I learned how sometimes the magic happens and a kindness comes, like a whisper is bestowed from the gods. I have struggled through my filters, made lots of mistakes, and created suffering for myself, especially in relationships. I have also ended up pretty happy with two reasonably well-adjusted children and no soul-eating resentments left infecting my life. I love what I do and I'm good at it. I enjoy my own company. I have amazing, intelligent friends whom I trust and can count on. I write music and play in a band. I have learned to tell my stories, get over my history, take the very best from my past, and let the rest go into the ground where it belongs. I dream big, fierce, happy, new stories for myself, and for you. Life is good and the exciting journey continues as my awareness deepens and the Reality Train takes me to new exciting places. And yes, I am still uncovering threads of the past and finding shadows in the corners that sometimes haunt my life. But I know where to look and what to do about them now. That's all part of waking up.

"Everything is determined . . . by forces over which we have no control. It is determined for the insect as well as for the star. Human beings, vegetables, or cosmic dust—we all dance to a mysterious tune, intoned in the distance by an invisible piper."—Albert Einstein. Quoted in interview by G.S. Viereck , October 26,1929. Reprinted in *Glimpses of the Great*, 1930.

CHAPTER 15

Sherry's Story

On a superficial level, my upbringing was a whole lot more "normal" than Raven's: small town, parents with college degrees and good jobs, three kids, and a dog and the center-hall colonial with the big back yard. What lay under that surface was this: two people who adored their children and did their level best to overcome their own "issues" to raise us the best way they knew how. I am grateful for that, and I recognize that, despite their best efforts, the dysfunction bled through. It's no coincidence that I never wanted kids and that I avoided commitment and marriage until I was in my late 40s.

Where Raven is a storyteller, I tend to be a professor. No getting around that, so I'll do what I learned to do when writing lectures: I'll tell you what I'm gonna tell you, then I'll tell you, then I'll tell you what I just told you. That way you can skip the meat and just eat the bread if that's what you prefer.

I'll start with a summary of my filters and stories, in the form of a list of rules. Then I'll give you a narrative of how I acquired them, how I used them both to my advantage and to my disadvantage, and then I'll tell you how it all turned out.

The Rules I Learned (In No Particular Order)

Here is a quick summary of what I learned as a kid. I managed to unlearn some of this, and make good use of some of it, too. I talked about this a bit in the first part of this book, and more details will follow below.

- No one will ever explain things to you. You have to figure out everything by yourself, and you shouldn't ask questions.
- You have to do everything yourself, and you shouldn't ask for help.
- You especially shouldn't ask questions about people and why they do the things they do.
- It is important to have enough money and be financially secure.
- Avoid arguing and fighting at all costs.
- If you are in a relationship with someone and you have a fight, it means the relationship is over.
- You can't ask for anything you want directly.
- Hinting and manipulating are the way to get what you want.
- The worst thing you can do to your body is to "let yourself go" and get fat. Fat people are lazy and have no self-control.
- It is important to do work that is of service to others and to the community.
- All types of work have value and dignity.
- Being intelligent and knowledgeable and clever and funny is good and will be rewarded.
- It's ok to complain and kvetch and gossip about people in authority but don't take action.
- Be kind to people who are less fortunate than you are.
- It's a good thing you're smart, because you aren't very attractive.

- People will try to blame you for things you didn't do.

What follow are a few stories about how I learned all of this.

Me and My Family

I was born in 1956 in a small factory town of about 25,000 people in southern New Jersey. My hometown was "southern" in the geographic and the cultural sense. It was in the part of New Jersey that is south of the Mason-Dixon line, and the local culture was very closed-in, conservative, and racist. My father was "from" my hometown, meaning that his family (on his father's side) had lived there for several generations. My mother was born in a town that eventually became a suburb of Philadelphia, and was definitely not "from" my hometown (although she lived there for more than 50 years).

Dad was raised by an unhappy mother and a father who physically abused his wife and children. He was the youngest of three and the only boy. As a young teenager he got into trouble and was sent to military school on a music scholarship (he was a percussionist). He hated military school, but it was his entrée into the middle class. He was the first in his family to go to college, and after college and marriage to my mom and a couple of years in the Army (he was drafted during the Korean War but was stationed in the US), he returned to his home town to work as an accountant in one of the glass factories.

Both of Mom's parents had college degrees. Her father was a soil scientist with the US Department of Agriculture extension service, and her mother taught elementary school. She grew up on a farm with an older brother and a male cousin who lived close by, and she was an athlete in high school and college.

My parents met as undergraduates in college and married in 1952, immediately after graduation. My mom moved back in with her parents while my dad was posted to an Army base in Massachusetts. After my Dad got out of the Army they moved to his home town. While Mom was pregnant with me, Dad was transferred by the company to a different state. My mom stayed behind with her in-laws while my Dad took care of finding a house and moving their household. Mom never got into details about it, but I know this was a hard time for her. My paternal grandmother never liked her very much and could be pretty mean.

Mom was about three weeks overdue and had a long labor. Her doctor convinced her that because she was in the midst of moving, attempting to breastfeed would be "too inconvenient" (say what? Bottles and formula are convenient?), so she didn't breastfeed me. According to family lore, I cried pretty much nonstop for the first few weeks of my life, and ended up in the hospital for "failure to thrive"—I wasn't gaining weight. Mom felt like a failure and was pretty depressed by that time. It took an observant nurse to figure out the problem. I have a very small mouth, and I was choking on the normal-sized baby bottle nipples. Smaller nipples were all it took. I think it is pretty likely that that experience of constant hunger, followed by a week in the hospital on a glucose drip, were the start of my lifelong craving for sugar, and for my struggle to maintain a healthy weight. I am also proof that just because you don't have a big mouth, doesn't mean you can't BE a bigmouth.

Right after all of that, Mom and I moved to be with my Dad—in a new city where she had no family or friends. We lived there for a few years, long enough for my younger sister to be born there in 1958.

My mother's mother died when I was about two years old, at age 63 of a massive heart attack. She called me "Peaches" and adored me. My only memory of her is a body memory—she was a large woman with an expansive bosom, and I have a memory of the feeling of being held against her soft breasts and rocked.

My parents moved back to my Dad's hometown shortly after that, and my youngest sister was born in 1960, when I was four. I have a memory of my father calling my aunt to come take care of my sister and me one evening after dinner. I remember them bringing the baby home, and I remember sitting on the sofa in our living room, holding the new baby, propped up with pillows.

We lived in a small bungalow with a large yard, near a pond and a lot of woods. The only other kid my age in the neighborhood was a boy, so I played with a lot of "boy's toys" like trucks and little green army men. The neighborhood grew slowly as some of the woods were turned into houses and yards. We had neighborhood cookouts and I had more kids to play with.

I was a smart kid. Thanks to my being the oldest, and for a couple of years the only child, my Mom talked and read to me a lot and I had a pretty big vocabulary for a two-year old. By the time I was four I could read.

My birthday was in late September, and in 1961 there weren't any "pre-school" options (or, if there were, my parents couldn't afford them), so my Mom enrolled me in kindergarten before I turned five. My physical and emotional development weren't nearly as fast as my intellectual development, and I spent childhood and adolescence attempting to catch up to my classmates.

Kindergarten gave me my first memorable experience of discrimination on the basis of gender, when my kindergarten teacher refused to let me play with the trucks because they were for boys, and insisted I play dolls and house with the girls. With all the righteous indignation that a four-year-old can muster, I went home and told my mother that my teacher was "stupid" because obviously girls could play with trucks because I did it all the time at home! I was a fast learner, and it didn't take long for me to realize that, apparently everywhere except on my street, girls did not play with trucks and that I'd better play with the dolls or the other kids would think I was weird. So peer pressure won out in the end.

Most of my childhood was pretty much the small-town stereotype. We ran around in the woods, rode bikes and walked all over town, went on school field trips to the Big Cities (Philly, New York, Washington).

Both of my sisters were (and still are) petite and slim and blond and very cute, and being smart and clever and funny was how I got the praise and attention that made up for being the fat and (relatively) homely girl in the family. At the same time, I learned that being too smart or clever annoyed some adults, so I got good at figuring out what to reveal and what to conceal.

Bodies and Biology

When we were little, my parents let my sisters and me see them naked, and they let us run around naked without making a big fuss about it. We all burped and farted out loud at home (still do). My father subscribed to *Playboy* and copies were in the magazine rack with *Life* and *Look*, so my sisters and I read them, too. Despite the presence of *Playboy* in the living room, and a not-very-well-hidden stash of harder core material in a bedroom closet, my parents never talked to me directly about sex or sexuality. Once again, I learned everything I could about sex from those sources, and from the few books I could find in my local library and bookstores. When I was a teenager, my parents did make it clear that I was not to get pregnant until after college, and they also made it clear that they did not want to know what my boyfriends and I did or didn't do. Even though I was attracted to, and fell in love with, girls as well as boys from the time I went through puberty, as a teenager and young adult I conformed to the expectation that I was only to act on my attraction to boys.

So, I grew up with the message that the body isn't shameful but sex and sexuality are not to be talked about, and I had a pretty warped idea of what women were supposed to look like. In addition to the visual input from Playboy, eventually supplemented by that Bible of teen girlhood, *Seventeen*, I heard a lot of criticism of women who were fat—they were lazy, had no self control, just let themselves go.

I had my tonsils removed when I was in third grade. It was a terrifying experience from start to finish. I had a vague idea of what a hospital was, and I knew other kids who'd had their tonsils out, but no one took the time to explain things like call buttons or bedpans or anesthesia. I was so frightened the night before the surgery that I didn't sleep. I knew (because the very loud, very mean nurse told me so) that I wasn't supposed to get out of bed. But no one told me I could ask for a bedpan, and I had no idea such things existed. So when I could no longer take the pain in my bladder, I let loose in the bed. When this was discovered, all hell broke loose among the nurses, and I remember being dragged out of bed and scrubbed painfully hard with a very rough washcloth which the nurse repeatedly scraped over the large cold sore on my lower lip. I was pretty sure I was in deep trouble. After the surgery I woke up vomiting the blood I had swallowed, and at that point I was absolutely certain I was going to die. I didn't die, but after that surgery I did start to gain weight. I mention this because I know of other people my age (including my husband) who experienced the same thing—being a normal-sized kid, getting their tonsils out, and then getting fat.

From fourth grade until ninth grade, I was a fat kid. I knew I was fat, because relatives (on my Dad's side—more about them later) made sure to comment on my weight in front of me. By the time I was in sixth grade I was painfully ashamed of how I looked. By that time I had also learned that it wasn't ok to ask for help, and that adults weren't too bright so that you had to figure everything out for yourself (see tonsillectomy experience above). Despite that, I took the very difficult (for me) step of asking my mom for help. Well, I didn't ask her out loud. I wrote her a letter. She did talk to me, but all she—the farm girl who ate like a horse and didn't weigh more than 100 pounds for most of her adult life—could tell me was that it was just "baby fat" and I would probably lose it when I started getting my period.

By the time I was in eighth grade I still had that "baby fat" and was determined to lose weight. This time I didn't ask for help, I just started by reading a bunch of books about nutrition and exercise. I stopped eating sugary snacks and junk food, and by the start of ninth grade I was at a healthy weight. I was never good at sports, but I started teaching myself yoga (from books, of course; there being no yoga teachers in my home town). Thanks to a male friend who was on the track team I discovered "jogging," bought a pair of Adidas and fell in love with distance running. I started taking ballet classes when I was 16, just for the exercise and discipline, and I loved dancing, too. The downside of the ballet lessons was that spending time at a ballet studio led me to being a bit obsessive about food and my weight for a while (at my thinnest I weighed about 105 pounds, and I was five feet, three inches tall). After a friend who was also into ballet dropped to 85 pounds (and wanted to lose another 10) and contracted a severe bout of mononucleosis, I woke up to what I was doing and started eating a bit more normally again.

It is certainly no accident that I ended up studying biology in college, doing a Ph.D. in physiology, and then forged a career in health and research advocacy—I was primed by spending most of my adolescence learning about human biology and health. As a child, I got attention and praise and rewards from adults for being smart and precocious and knowing the right answers—a formula for success in school and college.

I've also become a bit more relaxed about my diet, weight, and my fitness. Although I'm not an athlete, I'm in pretty good shape. I've rediscovered the gentleness of yoga and I get around on a bicycle most of the time—which delights my inner tightwad when gasoline prices are $4 a gallon and up.

Money and Work

As I grew up, I believed, based on what I heard from my parents, that we never had enough money. My mom talked about not having money to buy things and needing to save money or not spend money. We never really lacked for anything as far as I could tell. We always got new clothes for school; had plenty of good, healthy food;

and we took summer vacations to the Jersey shore or to visit my parents' out-of-town friends. All that anxiety-talk about money made a definite impression on me, though. As an adult, I track my income and expenses very carefully, I have saved as much as I can for my retirement, and I know I can be tight with my money, sometimes unnecessarily. As I've gotten older and advanced in my career, my income rose to a level where I felt comfortable using my discretionary income to support causes I believe in. Aware of my own anxieties about money, I made a conscious decision to support people who sacrifice financial security to add beauty to the world as performers and musicians and artists. I could never stand to live on the financial edge the way they do.

Until my youngest sister started first grade, my Mom was at home with us. When I was 11, she started working part-time as a substitute teacher, then a few years later she took a full-time job teaching English at the local high school. She was a popular teacher and I don't remember being bothered that she taught at the school I attended. If anything, it helped at home because she was so familiar with the environment in which I was spending most of my time.

Throughout my childhood and adolescence, my Mom did all the cooking and housework and laundry herself, even after she started to work full-time. She never had a housekeeper, and she never asked my Dad or my sisters and me to help. What I took away from this was that you have to do everything yourself, and that you shouldn't ask anyone for help.

When I was in my forties I asked her about this, and she said she wanted us to be free to have fun, study hard, and participate in activities like orchestra and sports and the school paper. She also told me that she doesn't really remember much about her forties, because she was always so tired and had so little time to herself.

The anxiety about money and the beliefs that I couldn't count on anyone else to provide what I needed, and that I had to support myself were filters I held in place until I was in my late 40s. I was good at getting romantically attached to people who were irresponsible about money, or who were incapable (for whatever reason) of being a full, and fully reliable, partner. I kept myself in a place of low-level discontent for decades, and while I would stay in these relationships for years, I never wanted to marry these guys. I mean, who would?

My father worked in the accounting department at a local factory until I was 10. Then the company decided that to get a promotion, he would have to move to Texas. He left that job rather than leave his hometown and uproot his family. He was out of work for a few months, and then took a job as business manager for the brand new two-year community college that was about to open in our county. He stayed in that job, eventually becoming the college's first Dean of Administration, until he died. He was good at what he did and he worked hard. It was for the most part a nine-to-five job, and he was almost always home for dinner and went to school plays and concerts and my sisters' softball and field hockey games.

So, for most of my life, both of my parents worked in education, and they both enjoyed their work. I now realize that my Dad probably could have made a whole lot more money working in the private sector, but the opportunity to help build a community college from the ground up was the kind of thing he found appealing and really wanted to do.

I also remember admiring my Dad for his ability to talk to, and relate to, anyone—from the "junk man" who picked through our trash every week (my Dad knew his name and his kids' names) to the school janitor to local politicians and VIPs. When my mom went to work we became, of necessity, a two-car family, and my dad bought a late-50s model Ford that he drove for a few years until he could afford a slightly newer used car. He didn't trade that Ford in—he sold it to the local "junk man" for one dollar, and the junk man drove it for several more years. The story I took away from that is that all work has dignity, and that everyone deserves to be treated with respect and kindness. It was a powerful message and it has served me well.

Feuding and Fighting

My father fought with his family a lot, and there were a lot of grudges and feuding between him and his parents and siblings. Much of the fighting was indirect and done at a distance—one person would tell another person something, and they would pass it on to the third person, etc. There was little to no direct communication, and we would go to family gatherings for holidays and everyone would pretend all was fine and dandy. As a child I found it confusing to try to figure out and remember who was on what side of what argument, especially since I never knew what the arguments were about. As an adult, I stayed in touch with my father's sisters and mother, especially after he died, but I kept my distance and tried to stay out of the ongoing feuding and fighting. I had some interesting conversations with my father's mother and learned a bit about what was behind some of the fights, although I'm not sure she told me the whole truth. As she told it, there was petty crime, adultery, abuse, and acts of not-so-quiet desperation. Basically, life as it is in small-town blue-collar America.

I know my Dad was determined not to pass along his own father's abuses, and I don't remember him ever hitting any of us. Dad had a wonderful sense of humor, and he had a sharp tongue and a tendency to use sarcasm to express disapproval. I never saw or heard my parents fight or argue. About the closest they came to fighting in front of us was when my Dad would use sarcasm to put my Mom down or criticize her in front of us. I asked my Mom about this (Dad had died by this time), and she told me they really didn't fight, she just gave in and did whatever he wanted. Looking back, she wondered if it would have been better if she had stood up to him more often.

There was one thing that I wished they had fought about. When I was a senior in high school, I had my heart set on going to St. John's College, the "Great Books" college in Annapolis, Maryland. The application was a set of essays, and I spent hours and hours working on them. Then I got the fat envelope—I was accepted, and they wanted information so that they could determine my need for financial aid. My Dad decided (without trying) that he and my mother made too much money, and I would never qualify for financial aid, so he refused to fill out and return the forms. I was broken-hearted, and his decision added to a sense of alienation from my parents and my sisters, along with the conviction that I was nothing but a burden on my parents and the sooner I was out of the house and on my own, the better.

On the Outside Looking In

That sense of alienation started long before the St. John's College decision. I have memories from the time I was about eight years old of feeling left out, excluded, or somehow marginal in and to the family. I still don't exactly know how this started, but somehow I just felt different. Combine that with the "figure it all out for yourself" messages I kept getting, and then playing developmental catch-up from kindergarten through college and I guess it's no wonder I felt a bit "alien." When I talked to my mother about this, she had an interesting take on it. She said, "You were always so good, so well-behaved, and so self-reliant. I think we probably neglected you to some extent, and paid more attention to your sisters." I think she was probably right.

That feeling, a mostly unconscious sense of being on the "outside," became so familiar and comfortable that I worked pretty hard to hold it in place with my family, and replicated it over and over again—at school, in college, in graduate school, at work, in my intimate relationships, in my spiritual pursuits, pretty much everywhere. Whenever a group of people I liked and cared about tried to embrace me, include me, or celebrate me, I looked for and found evidence that I wasn't accepted, that I wasn't even wanted. Then I would find a way to run away. Sometimes literally—I would leave the room, leave the building, leave the group, always with a perfectly good reason for going, of course. Other times I would just behave in a way that drove people off. Either way, I got what I wanted, that familiar comfort of being on the outside again.

Trust and Betrayal

As a young teenager I was "driven" (that was the word I used at the time) to explore religion and spirituality. My parents were not churchgoers, although they had had us all baptized in the Methodist church in which they were both raised, probably to keep my Dad's family off their backs. (Interestingly, although Methodists baptize newborns, they held the baptism after my youngest sister was born and had us all "done" at once.) I attended Sunday school occasionally, mostly because I heard my cousins talking about it and was curious, but I found it pretty boring. When I was 15, I acquired a new best friend who attended the Presbyterian Church. They had just installed a new pastor who was young (early 30s), handsome, progressive, sometimes daringly irreverent, and generally a breath of fresh air in my very conservative hometown. I started going to church, Sunday school, and youth fellowship with her, and within a year I had joined the church. A rather unusual form of adolescent rebellion, I suppose, but it worked for me.

A year later, the pastor persuaded the church Session (the church's board of directors) to create a position of "youth deacon" and appoint me to it. Deacons in the Presbyterian Church are ordained, so at the age of 16 I was ordained in front of the congregation and given responsibilities for visiting the sick and housebound, taking up the collection, and serving communion. He and I became very close—he talked to me as an adult to an adult, discussing theology, spirituality, philosophy, the social upheaval of the 60s and early 70s, psychology. He gave me books to read. By the time I was a senior in high school, I was sure I wanted to be a Presbyterian minister. I also had a deep crush on him, which I did my best to hide because, after all, he was over 30, married, and had two kids for whom I babysat. No way would he be interested in me THAT WAY.

My time in the church also brought me one of the deepest and most enduring blessings in my life: my friendship with the woman who was then the youth fellowship advisor at the church. Although the pastor was an inspiration to me, she became the adult to whom I entrusted all the things I just couldn't tell my parents. Although I later learned that she was struggling with an unhappy marriage to an emotionally abusive boy-man, to me at the time she seemed knowledgeable and wise and "together." I trusted her. I am still close to her today, 40 years later.

Of course, in keeping with my comfort at being on the outside, I had to find a way to put myself on the outside of this church community that had embraced and nurtured me. I discovered Pentecostalism. I was "born again," baptized in the Spirit, spoke in tongues and prophesied. That lasted about a year and a half, through my senior year of high school and first few months of college. The problem was that I could never buy the "Bible is the literal and inerrant word of God" stuff. I loved what I now recognize as the ecstatic mysticism inherent in Pentecostal worship, but I couldn't stomach the theology. By the end of my first year of college I had given up on the church (and the idea of becoming a minister) entirely.

My "crisis of faith" was cemented when, after my first year of college, I went to visit the pastor, who had moved to another church by that time. Shortly after I arrived, we went for a walk in the evening after dinner. Standing in the dark, in front of his house, he hugged me—nothing unusual about that—and then I realized he had an erection and he wasn't trying to hide it. Then he kissed me. I distinctly remember the smell of alcohol on his breath. From that moment, realizing what he wanted, I felt myself slip away. That's the best way I can describe it. For the next few days, until we did eventually have sex, I felt as if I were living an inch or two outside my body, watching what was happening, having no choice or control over what would happen next. This went on for days. We had sex exactly once. After that, I seemed to "snap out of it." I imagine I was hurt and angry. What I really had wanted was to be able to trust him not to take advantage of my "crush," to stay my friend and just let me grow out of it. I also felt terribly guilty. I immediately wrote about what happened in my journal and then "accidentally" left it where his wife would find it—not too subtle, but definitely in keeping with my "never ask for help directly" pattern. She found it, they fought, and he barely spoke to me for the rest of my visit. As he drove me to the airport, he did make me promise not to tell anyone, and I kept that promise for more than 15 years. The first person I told this story to was my therapist.

Education, Formal and Informal

By the end of my first year of college I had given up on college, or at least the college I was in. The college I had attended wasn't a great fit, and I had lived through the humiliation of my first unrequited crush on a woman.

When I dropped out, I had all kinds of schemes—I was going to join a commune, become a lay midwife, anything but go home to New Jersey. My Mom convinced me to come home first, before I took off for anywhere else. So I got a job and stayed with my parents. At a party that summer I met a guy I knew from high school who had also dropped out of college and moved back into his parents' house. We started dating and I fell in love with him. He, like me, was smart, funny, widely read, and really good at keeping himself on the "outside."

He bought a 1966 Ford Econoline van, and we spent a year working, saving money, and fitting the van out as a camper while planning a trip across the US. My parents never believed that I would actually do it, and were astonished when we drove off in May of 1976.
We drove from New Jersey to the West Coast and back, had a great
time, and I hatched a plan. After we got back to New Jersey, I would
NOT move back in with my parents. I would declare myself eman-
cipated and go to St. John's with financial aid based on my own finances. Yeah, that would show them! And of course it would further
support my position as family outsider.

Well, that didn't happen. I did stay with my boyfriend when we
got back to NJ. He got a job, I enrolled at a state college, and we made
each other miserable for the next year. Rather than telling him I was
miserable, I presumed that he was miserable (and later learned that
yes, he was). Rather than actually having a conversation or two or a
dozen about our relationship and our misery, I decided I should
just give him what I thought he wanted (or what I thought he should
want)—some time on his own. The way I saw it, I was a burden on him
(yeah, that old virus again) and my leaving for a while would be better
for both of us. I came up with a clever and elaborate scheme for getting out of the relationship while doing something I wanted to do that
would have the approval of my family, friends, and academic advisor.
I applied to spend a year abroad and was accepted as an exchange student at a polytechnic (now a university) in England. I did not tell my
boyfriend about this plan until it was irrevocably in place. In my delusion that I somehow knew that this was what he wanted, I was befud-
dled that he was upset at my decision to leave for a year.

The Olde Countrye

I loved living in England, my coursework at the poly, and the friends
I made there. I completed a year of course work, sat the exams with
the other students, and was invited to come back to complete my

degree. Thanks to the pre-Thatcher levels of educational funding, it didn't cost my parents much more than sending me to college in the States, and I think they were relieved I wouldn't be going back to my boyfriend, so they agreed.

My penchant for figuring things out for myself worked pretty well in a lot of the situations I found myself in while travelling. I travelled all over the British Isles by train, ferry, hiking, and hitchhiking, staying in hostels, and occasionally with friends at their family homes. I quickly picked up British English: I went to the loo, washed my face with a flannel, and corrected my crossword mistakes with a rubber. I learned British slang, and developed a "mid-Atlantic" accent—not really British, but not American either.

The not-asking-questions pattern served me less well in my coursework, particularly in the laboratory. I would spend hours trying to figure out why some experiment wasn't working when I could have saved the time and effort just by asking a lecturer or a lab assistant for help. Despite that, my childhood habit of seeking rewards and praise by doing well academically continued to serve me well. In fact, part of what I loved about being at the poly was that, unlike my experience at college in the US, there was no stigma attached to being ambitious and working hard to excel in your courses. And being an outsider was pretty easy, given that I was the sole American in my classes. Although, as my friendships there deepened, I did have to find ways to perpetuate my outsider status. Overall, these were two great years and I am still friends with many of the people I knew at the poly.

The Halls of Academe

I decided to go back to the US for graduate school, in part because Margaret Thatcher was now in office, and funding for research was being cut dramatically, thus limiting the number of Ph.D. spaces in the UK. Once again, I asked no one for advice or counsel and simply applied to programs that I thought looked interesting in places that I'd like to live. I wasn't too modest about it, though, and applied to some of the top programs in the country. When I got my acceptance—based solely on my paper application and a telephone interview—I was amazed that it had been so easy. That's because, despite my successes and superb grades as an undergraduate, I was still convinced that most of the other students around me were smarter than I was and knew more than I did. I started graduate school with a bad case of "imposter syndrome"—convinced that my admission was a mistake and if I slipped up in any way I'd be done.

I also started graduate school with an extra burden of grief and fear and anger. A few weeks before my classes started, a close high school friend of mine was killed by her ex-boyfriend in a planned murder-suicide. She was beautiful, brilliant, and working on an MBA at Stanford at the time. I went to her funeral a few days before I moved from my hometown to start my PhD program. I pretty quickly got a reputation for being a man-hating bitch, because I worked very hard to keep all the men in my program (there were only three other women in it) at a safe distance.

I had a rough time my first few years in graduate school. The courses were hard, I was at a loss as to how to decide on a research project (and, of course, I never asked for help), I managed to alienate most of the other graduate students (no surprise there, either), and I even set up a way to work through my grief, fear, and anger. At the time, I would have told you my righteously indignant tale of being "stalked" by a man who was obsessed with me. And that was true—he was obsessed with me, and he did stalk me. The rest of the truth is that I behaved in ways that manipulated him in order to perpetuate the situation. As scared as I sometimes was, he also gave me a suitable target for that fear, and for my anger, not to mention a regular dose of excitement. After a couple of years (no exaggeration—the last time I heard from him was about six years after all of this started), I reached a point of exhaustion and realized that he wasn't likely to harm me physically, that I was the one perpetuating my own suffering, and it was time to let it go. I did a little ritual, imagined him as an annoying insect that occasionally would fly past my face, and gave up the need to react to him. It worked, and I got rid of a significant source of day-to-day stress.

I did find an advisor and a research project and managed to complete my dissertation and earn my degree. And in the meantime, there was a bright spot in the midst of all this gloom. I got involved in the newly resurrected graduate and professional student government at the university, and learned that I had a knack for organizing people and making change happen. We started with representatives from a dozen departments in the graduate school and a small amount of funding from the Dean's office, and by the time I left we had all of the professional schools signed on with the exception of the divinity school (answered to a Higher Authority, I guess). We went from sharing a cubicle with the chess club to having offices in the student center. By the time I left, I was as proud of that accomplishment as I was of my new Ph.D.

Work and Growth

While I was finishing my Ph.D., I was also busy looking for an escape route. I realized that while I was good at research, I didn't really like doing it. I disliked the tunnel vision that was required. I got into biology because I loved biology—all of it, from the ecosystem level down to what happens to molecules inside cells. I knew I wanted a career in science but not as a grant-supported academic researcher. I explored a lot of options, including working in the pharmaceutical industry. In this process I had several conversations with a director at a nearby nonprofit that did work on contraception and maternal and child health in developing countries. Since my research was on gonadal steroid hormones (testosterone, estrogen, etc.) he was working to create a job for me on his team. Then the organization's president and board made a strategic deci-

277

sion that, in hindsight, was both appropriate and successful. They shifted the focus from contraception to the then-emerging epidemic of HIV/AIDS, and my job opportunity evaporated. When I play "what-if" I imagine that had I gone to work there, I would have done yet another degree, this time in public health, and might still be working in that field.

Instead, I took a postdoctoral training fellowship in another laboratory, and spent the two years of that fellowship exploring myself, my strengths and weaknesses, what I liked and didn't like, and where I wanted to live. I wrote a "job description" for my ideal job, and turned that into a cover letter and resume combination that said "Here is what I want to do, here is what I know, here is what I've done so far; will you hire me to do what I want to do? I spent hours in the library (no internet back then) researching prospective employers. I sent out nearly 100 resumes, cold. And one day I got a phone call from someone saying "How did you know about this job we haven't advertised yet?" I got that job, and the organization moved me (and my then-boyfriend) to the Washington, DC area.

How did it never occur to me to apply this same highly effective process to finding a life partner? Well, I had this complicated story about love and romance and how it's all just supposed to happen like magic and you should never fight or disagree or actually talk about anything having to do with the relationship and it should all just be sunshine and light and glittery fairy poo. The flip side of that was my story that marriage was just a way to subjugate women and would mean that I could never, ever do or have what I wanted again because it would all be about what my partner wanted or needed and I would have to go along with that, blah, blah, blah. Learned that one at my mother's knee, I did. I was also averse to giving anyone else any measure of control over my financial situation. By that time I knew several women who had been through divorces that took them from comfortably middle-class to low-income in the space of a year or two. I was not going let the happen to me.

I have held a number of jobs throughout my career, and my family virus symptoms showed up in all of them. It looked something like this:

1. Make friends with the people at my level and below, but keep the boss at arm's length

2. When the boss does something I don't like, bitch and complain to other people but never take the complaint directly to the boss

3. If unhappy with the job (or even just parts of the job), say nothing to anyone at work, but quietly start looking for a job elsewhere

4. Upon accepting the offer for the next job, surprise the boss with the announcement that you are leaving.

5. Lather, rinse, repeat

Not all of my jobs ended quite that way. In an interesting reversal of steps three and four, I was once let go because " . . . it just isn't working out" even though I had just been given a sterling performance review, a raise, and a new program to run. Oh yeah, I met my match in that boss.

At my first couple of jobs I made more friends among the "support staff"—secretaries and administrative assistants and lab technicians—than with management (and I was, clearly, management—or on that career track, at least.). That's who I ate lunch with and gossiped with. My summer jobs had all been doing secretarial and administrative work, so it was easy to relate to them. This worked for me in that I never had a problem getting what I needed from them, and as I advanced in my career I made it a point to treat the support staff as fellow professionals who justifiably take pride in their work. I learned that from my Dad.

Where I got in my own way was in avoiding developing close relationships with other management staff. This was also in keeping with my "gotta figure it all out and do it all myself" story. I never sought out a mentor, was afraid to ask my boss when I wasn't sure what to do, and at the same time did a lot of complaining and gossiping behind my boss' back.

That pattern of indirect communication and manipulation (or attempted manipulation) of those in authority carried through all but one of my work situations. I was pretty good at choosing bosses and places to work that had cultures steeped in gossip, backbiting, indirect communication, and management by manipulation. I managed to succeed despite all that, but looking back I realize I could have made it so much easier on myself and those around me. How? Clear, simple, and direct communication would have been a good start. Noticing how my own behavior taught those around me how to behave and how to treat me, then being able to interrupt myself and choose something different would have been good.

I did succeed—I'm smart, I learn fast, I have a remarkable capacity for retaining and using information, and I'm not afraid of doing things that scare a lot of other people, like public speaking and media appearances. My career chugged along; with each new job came bigger responsibilities, a bigger staff, and a bigger salary.

And while all of this (and the relationship stuff I'll talk about shortly) was going on, I was working on myself. I continued my spiritual explorations, and through those contacts encountered Brad Blanton and Radical Honesty (the book and the practice), and through Brad I met Raven. More on that later, too

Gradually, I became less and less happy and comfortable working in a place that was run by gossip and innuendo. Then I took a job as the Big Boss—I became CEO of a small scientific society. I knew going in to the job that my predecessor had been exactly like my two previous bosses—passive-aggressive, indirect, and very fond of gossip. I was determined to change that, and I did. At my first staff meeting as CEO I established a no-tolerance policy for gossip, and I talked about much of what we have written in this book—specifically, the importance of simple, clear, and above all, direct communication; the importance of asking directly for what you want and need;

and the importance of realizing that this will take practice to change long-seated behaviors. It took about two years, but it worked. And the key is that it worked for me as much as it did for the rest of the staff. When I held that meeting, I described to them my ideal workplace—the kind of culture and atmosphere that I wanted to create for myself and that, as the Big Boss, I had the authority and power to create. I asked for their agreement with my desire, and for their cooperation and support in creating it, which they could (and did) give me by committing to changing their own behaviors.

I came, I asked clearly and directly, and I got what I asked for. I bid goodbye to a load of old stories that no longer served, and I created a lot of satisfaction for myself and for those who worked with me. That's the power of how.

"Don't Ask, Don't Yell"—It Don't Work

The story of my love life pretty much parallels the story of my career. My discomfort with asking directly for what I wanted, coupled with my conviction that one fight meant the end of the relationship—call it "Don't ask, don't yell"–was a pretty good formula for failure.

I appeared to be a serial monogamist from my first boyfriend at 14 until my late 30s. I say "appeared to be" because part of the fallout from my "Don't ask, don't yell" belief system was that I tended to cheat. If I weren't getting what I wanted or needed from my current flame, rather than ask for it and risk an argument I'd just look for it elsewhere. Often, "elsewhere" became the next relationship in the series.

I also had a penchant for getting involved with people who needed, or, rather, whom I believed needed, rescuing. My favorite flavor seemed to be "depressed but not excessively needy"–people who loved me in part because I cheered them up, but who were as reluctant or unable as I was to really commit themselves in a relationship. The side-benefit was that people who are depressed are usually easy to manipulate, so I could often get what I wanted from them without actually asking.

So my pattern was:

Meet someone who fit the profile—slightly depressed, not interested in full commitment, slightly but not too obviously needy

1. Immediately (or very nearly) have sex with them to establish a false sense of intimacy

2. Reach a point of dissatisfaction with them and the relationship

3. Flirt and/or have sex with someone else

4. Generate some drama with the current partner

5. Leave them for that person I just flirted and/or had sex with

6. Lather, rinse, repeat

Those family viruses infect everything, don't they? The drama I generated in step five was usually along the lines of "You don't really love/want/need/understand me. . ." But how could they? Under my strict policy of "Don't ask, don't yell" I never asked for what I wanted, never told them when they did something I didn't like, never expressed anger, and got defensive or self-righteous (or both) if they asked if something was up with me.

And Then It Was Now

So how did I get from there to here? A lot of work; a lot of support, help, and a few swift kicks in the ass from my friends, and a set of tools that, if you've read the rest of this book, you now have, too.

I mentioned my involvement with Radical Honesty earlier. I got interested in it when a friend, Clara Griffin, made some remarkable changes in her life, and did it with what seemed, from the outside anyway, strength and grace. I watched this unfold and thought "I would like some of that in my life." She had been working and studying with Brad Blanton, and encouraged me to read his book and do a workshop with him. I did one of his three-day introductions and then joined my friend's weekly practice group. I stayed with that group for more than 10 years, uncovering my stories and filters and the ways I was getting in my own way. Then I did a couple more of Brad's workshops and met Raven. When Raven and Clara began working together, I did their workshops, too. I got better at interrupting myself when I was heading off in a comfortable, familiar, but entirely wrong direction. I had honest conversations with my mom and my sisters, got lots of practice in clear, direct communication and asking for what I wanted, and my life began to change.

Where did all this get me? Here is little sketch of my life today:

I live in a beautiful 1920s-era bungalow in Washington, DC, with my husband, Larry Haller, who is my dance partner, consort, vegetable grower, favorite bartender, and best friend. We met when I did some intensive work with Raven to fix my picker, which I described earlier in the book. In fact, I totally blame Raven and Clara for the healthy, drama-free, honest relationship I have with Larry. Well, ok, Larry probably has something to do with it, too. When we met, I was smart enough to recognize that this guy did not fit my pattern of picking "fixer-uppers." Thanks to Raven's coaching, I was also brave and foolish enough to be honest with him from the start. The magic happened when he responded in kind. I told him the truth, he told me the truth.

Of course, our relationship is not all sunshine and roses and glittery fairy poo. We fight, we argue, we annoy the hell out of each other at times. And we get through it, and we carry on. I overturned my policy of "don't ask, don't yell" when we met, and I have no regrets about that.

I am self-employed, and this book is part of my plan for building a consulting and coaching business aimed at transforming the way we work. I work with highly motivated and creative people who understand that, when it comes to work, results are what matters, and the best results come from human beings who are relaxed, happy and healthy, and who gain satisfaction from their work.

I have close relationships with both of my sisters, whom I count among my best friends. I have a circle of friends with whom I spend time laughing, arguing, dancing, drumming, eating, drinking, and playing. We support each other, challenge each other, and work side-by-side to create the world we want to live in.

The End

So that's what I started with—a bunch of rules and stories and filters, some of which worked for a while and then tripped me up, some of which I'm still making use of, for good or for evil.

I've written here about some of the ways these showed up in my family, my work life, and my love life. I left out a lot of tales and examples that would have been more redundant than enlightening, and it is enough to say that I am still doing this work, this practice. Clear, simple, direct. Notice, interrupt, redirect. I will be doing it until the day I die.

I'm still uncovering the many ways in which I limit myself, trip myself up, stop myself, and otherwise get in my own way. I am doing what the 19th century esotericists called "The Great Work"—self-knowledge, self-determination, and the grace of self-possession.

So I lied. This isn't the end. It's the end of the beginning, maybe, but it isn't the end.

CHAPTER 16

Brad's Story

(Brad Blanton is a psychotherapist and author of Radical Honesty and many other books. For more of Brad's story, read his autobiography, *Some NEW Kind of Trailer Trash*.)

My father died when I was six years old. My brother was four. My sister was 12. My mother remarried when I was seven to a shell-shocked alcoholic wife beater and child abuser. My half brother was born when I was nine, and at the same time my sister left home to avoid being sexually molested by my stepfather.

I learned to survive in that context.

I did it by developing skills for dealing with my life circumstances, which required me to take care of my younger brothers because my mother and stepfather were often too drunk to do so. I learned to be wary, alert, and quick to respond to cues to predict mood and likely behavior changes in alcoholics, so I could keep them from killing each other or hurting one of the kids. I learned when to fight, run away, avoid, confront, demand, threaten, and control. I considered myself a smart kid and a hero and I couldn't afford to admit to being scared and feeling sorry for myself. I became sensitized to subtle cues about human behavior, and I wanted to try to help people who were hurting.

In effect I was designed by my life circumstances to be a helper who wants to keep those already hurt from being hurt more.

Sounds good, right? Like a yin/yang karmic universe balance being struck. Right?

A noble, just, and righteous reaction to a crappy set of circumstances.

But as noble as that may sound, following that automatic reaction can be just as poisonous as any other reactive life.

Here's what I mean.

I ended up wanting to help people, take care of them, teach them how to take care of themselves, and show off my perceptiveness. I resented people when they didn't appreciate me a lot, if they did not act on what I said they should do, and if they did not turn out the way I thought they should.

I purchased the allegiance of the people I helped, but I did it in an inexplicit way—by creating a vague sense of obligation to bind them to me. This, in turn, protected me from them, and got me praise. I became a manipulative, co-dependent, lying survivor. My life became organized around showing off, letting people in general know they had better not fuck with me and letting women know they could. As a psychologically reactive, homemade, individual humanoid, I ended up with a hand-built, home-built set of neurotic survival techniques, my carried-around-with-me-at-all-times way of getting-along-feeling-protected-and-surviving tool kit.

Then I discovered what transformation is. *I discovered I could transform my relationship to my automatic survival machine instead of being victimized by it, criticizing it, resisting it, or trying to "fix" it. I can choose to serve people of my own free will, and use it.* I discovered that transformation is really *using what used to use me.*

Montaigne said, "A person is not hurt so much by what happens, as by his opinion of what happens." As in the movie "Groundhog Day"— once the lead character finally surrendered to having one day happen over and over again without resisting it, it finally became a new day.

So I have now chosen to serve people as a design for my life, simply because it is a good choice given my design, which I am condemned to live with. I can now escape the oppression of the historical personality that automatically drives me, even though I cannot escape the personality itself.

Notice that I said "escape."

I can't make it go away, change, or fix it (in fact, there's nothing broken). The machine that tries to run me will probably always be there. But I can now escape the automatic control that my life-story has had over me. In other words, the original story I made of my life without any choice on my part, from the life, times, family, and culture I was born into and formed by, was not under my control. *What is under my control today is (1) how I choose to use that personality and history as a creative instrument and (2) what I use it to create.*

Rather than continue to react to the past that designed how I should live at about age seven or eight or nine, *I can transform my life by my own design, by choosing to do what I have been condemned to do.* I can design the projects of my life, using my developed skills in surviving to bring about the results I consciously plan to bring about. If I consider myself as this being in the present moment, and my history to be something possessed by my present-tense self, I can use my memory for ideas and images to co-design a future to live into with others in the present. I can use my personality and case history and reactivity to bring about my dreams for the future. Instead of trying to fix myself, or change my self, I can simply *use* my self to create the life I want—and to contribute to others the way I want.

One of the main ways I want to serve people is to present to them the possibility that we are *all* alike in the way I have just described— we can have either an *unconscious, reactive life* or a *conscious, creative life.*

Meet Your Other Mind

"The upshot of all this is that we live in a universe whose age we can't quite compute, surrounded by stars whose distances we don't altogether know, filled with matter we can't identify, operating in conformance with physical laws whose properties we don't truly understand.
– Bill Bryson, *A Short History of Nearly Everything*

Surface Mind and Deeper Mind

We have two minds that dance together, creating our experience of ourselves, of what surrounds us, and of anything we can imagine. This is the true and natural magic that orders our lives. As we explore the dance between these minds you will come to see that you are a citizen of two worlds. You have an opportunity to claim that dual citizenship and travel into the Unknown Country, where you will discover that dreams and images, daydreams and synchronicities have a profound impact on how we experience "real" events. In fact, the visionary qualities of the Other World offer us a powerful way to be more fully awake in our lives.

In this section, we will call these two minds Surface Mind and Deeper Mind. Deeper Mind also translates the energy around us into the sensory experience of matter and one aspect of Deeper Mind also takes care of unconscious processes like breathing and body temperature regulation.

Most of the time, Deeper Mind is invisible and unknown to Surface Mind, primarily because we have learned to ignore and downplay its messages. Deeper Mind does not use the linear, rational, logical language of Surface Mind. Deeper Mind speaks in a multilayered language comprising symbols and signs, dreams and daydreams, imagination and synchronistic "coincidences." When we were little and we understood the flow and interconnections between the surface and imaginal worlds, we were automatically tuned in to much of this symbol language.

You can remember how to decode many of the symbols the Deeper Mind uses to communicate. Sometimes however, we can only fully understand these messages when we're in the territory of the Deeper Mind. The things that happen in dreams for example, may make perfect sense and seem entirely normal when experienced within the dream, but when you wake up and try to describe or understand the dream, the meaning and the messages may seem confusing, or silly, or simply incomprehensible. The Deeper Mind reveals itself, and your Surface Mind may be left with a feeling, an impulse, or a course of action seemingly unrelated. You can still honor whatever you can recall just by jotting it down.

What if, in every experience you have, there are embedded symbols, signs, and encoded communications from Deeper Mind? What if the experiences we have are themselves symbols? Learning to interpret and flow with the signs and symbols of your experiences will give you a larger understanding of who you are and what you are capable of. This section will give you a taste of that awakened state, leading you to step outside the habitual trance that is your daily routine, and to engage with Life in a new and dynamic way.

Our Surface and Deeper Minds are partners. Together they give us the experience of a continuous unbroken reality, although science informs us that the reality we seem to experience is subjective, depending on each individual. We think the experiences we have are objective reality, while they are not objective in the least. We mistakenly believe we are experiencing "reality" as it truly is, moment by moment, when we are actually experiencing an interpretation of energy through our particular filters shortly after whatever happens actually happens. In other words, we are never actually experiencing anything right in the moment that it happens. That's fun to think about, isn't it?

We can describe the minds as having two distinctly different "operating systems" that dance together to seamlessly create our experiences in high definition, 3-D, surround-sound reality. Our Surface Mind, the tip of the iceberg, operates in a logical, linear, one-step-at-a-time, one-foot-after-another manner. Deeper Mind operates at extreme speed compared to Surface Mind. Deeper Mind, the much larger system of awareness that operates below the surface, juggles masses of bits of interconnected information far too quickly for your "everyday" mind (Surface Mind) to follow. Deeper Mind communicates information through symbols, images, feeling, sensory cues, and grasps the gestalt, the whole as well as the parts, of things.

Surface Mind is like a dancer moving gracefully in a single spotlight while Deeper Mind is a Cirque du Soleil troupe moving through time and space with precision and speed that staggers comprehension and leaves us breathless and teary-eyed with awe. When our two minds dance together well, Surface Mind is able to attend to tasks with ease and focus playfully with pleasure and excitement on whatever increases happiness. In turn, Surface Mind generates energy and emotion that informs the choreography of Deeper Mind's leaps, slides, and spins. When our two minds are dancing together, we are in touch with our Larger Self, the masterful and creative being that each of us embodies.

When we ignore and deny the dreams, symbols, synchronicity, and coincidences that bring us messages from Deeper Mind and attend only to what has happened and what seems possible to Surface Mind, we negate much of our ability to correctly diagnose issues and easily course-correct. The imaginative workings of Deeper Mind are what enable us to create the magic door through which beliefs and expectations become experience. To the degree that we remove ourselves from these causal realities understood through Deeper Mind we are, in essence, less alive. We are citizens of two worlds, and we need both to properly inform our lives.

"In each of us there is another, whom we do not know"
—Carl Jung

Deeper Mind also contains the master template that holds possibilities waiting to be activated. One function of the Deeper Mind is connectivity—think Google to the millionth power. Our Larger Self speaks to us, even if we fail to listen. We can be moving slowly toward an action or new idea for weeks, months, or decades but only when a tipping point is reached in the inner patterns of Deeper Mind can we access the information and act. This is when thought, emotion, and action align and become congruent. Road signs, often in the form of dreams, symbols, and synchronicities, show up to validate that congruence and invite us to take action.

This section of the book will help you communicate with and interpret information rising from your Deeper Mind. It will help you generate that tipping point through observing, listening, interpreting, and acting on the information you receive.

Translating information from Deeper Mind will require that you see yourself and the world around you with new eyes. You will have to learn to notice and then decode the symbols that arrive in your everyday life. The language of Deeper Mind includes dreams, symbols, seeming coincidence, gut feelings, sensations, images, emotions, synchronicity, patterns, repeating events, and coded events—all of which, like dreams, hold layers of meaning. To communicate back into Deeper Mind you can use art, images, music, sensation, rhythm, emotion, poetry, ritual, stories, myth, symbols, and symbolic acts. Transcendent experiences and moments of "Wow!" reach Deeper Mind.

Logic-defying mysteries and seeming miracles, as well as mind-bending synchronicities and potent dreams are the stuff of Deeper Mind. Anything that we do not understand looks like magic, and when it looks like magic we may just dismiss the experience as "not real" or "just a dream" or "only a coincidence" when really it is in our very best interest to be paying closer attention to these coded messages.

Deeper Mind is the place where we can "Google" a desired experience and find the road, the connections, that take us to the places and experiences beyond the familiar patterns. Deeper Mind exists in the perpetual present, heedless of any apparent separation between past, present, and future. Linear time is a product of our linear Surface Mind, and time experienced "out of sequence" to Deeper Mind is normal and useful.

"People like us, who believe in physics, know that the distinction between past, present, and future is only a stubbornly persistent illusion."— Albert Einstein

When we speak to our Larger Self using images and symbols, we can bypass layers of constraint imposed by beliefs, patterns, and filters. In this way, we give the Command Center within our Deeper Mind input that can transform experiences in astonishing ways. Magic? Perhaps. Wild and Potent? Definitely.

By this process we can defy the "rules" we live (and suffer) under and turn our lives around—for the better—in the twinkling of an eye. Entire patterns can be transformed through alignment with Deeper Mind. Or we can resist and ignore the daily memos, gaining a brick to the head and a stream of "bad luck." Even that, if we're paying attention, can show us where and how to change course.

This deeper ineffable layer of awareness— this Other Self—is the One who actually directs our lives and makes the majority of decisions that we think we make consciously. It is a sobering and humbling experience, at least until we forget again and return to the comfortable charade that our little ego-mind is making decisions and driving the Reality Train. Which it is not. And thank your lucky stars for that, because if we actually had to consciously think about the faster-than-thought reactions that save our sorry asses from oncoming cars, falling tree branches, and other life-threatening events, we'd be goners. Not to mention what would happen if we forgot to breathe.

Farther out beyond the miraculous way in which our bodies take direction from Deeper Mind, there is also another realm of connection and communication that streams between minds, events, and hidden realities. THIS is that place, that Unknown Country, in which sudden far-reaching life transformations can and do occur.

> *"The conscious mind is like a tiny stowaway on a transatlantic steamship, taking credit for the journey without acknowledging the massive engineering underfoot."*—David Eagleman, *Incognito: The Secret Lives of The Brain*

Yes, yes, I know. All those pages in Part One are full of mental redirection and communication tips, and NOW I'm telling you that your unconscious reigns supreme. Everything you learned in Part One is still useful. Those things get Surface Mind working on the things it does best so it can support, rather than interfere with, the information that rises from the Deeper Mind. Our Surface Mind functions with less confusion and second-guessing as we learn HOW to communicate with, and correctly interpret information from, Deeper Mind.

Because Surface Mind is s.l.o.w. compared to Deeper Mind, the best vehicle for this communication is the language of signs and symbols, which is rich with complex nuance and meanings. Surface Mind cannot accurately translate all the layers of meaning that are simultaneously known and understood by our Deeper Mind. We often have to "be with" the information and contemplate the symbols to reveal the layers of meaning contained within them.

In other words, information from the Deeper Mind is always experiential—not like facts that can be intellectually known but still ignored.[1]

The most complex tasks, like driving a car, often feel "simple" only because you have made it through the four stages of learning: unconscious incompetence, conscious incompetence, conscious competence, then finally unconscious competence. Once all the nuances of driving weave together and gain coherence, the action has its source in Deeper Mind and its faster-than-thought system of connections. Yes, I said faster-than-thought. It's a fact.

> "*In 1974 Nolan Ryan made it into the* Guinness Book of World Records *with his fastball clocked at 100.9 miles per hour.... Ryan's pitch crosses home plate in four-tenths of a second. Although the batter's eye can pick up the signals and make it through the brain's super highway just in time for the batter to swing... conscious awareness takes about a half a second longer than that. The ball travels too fast for the batter to be consciously aware of it!*"
> —David Eagleman, *Incognito: The Secret Lives of The Brain*

Get this idea firmly planted in your noodle: Deeper Mind is your best ally and faithfully tweaks, directs, and triggers your experiences to reproduce more of what you habitually focus your daily attention on. Yes, every repeated image, assessment, complaint, hope, longing, and wish that you consciously entertain is also a memo being passed on into your unconscious GPS, reinforcing or changing the direction of the Reality Train.

If you want to help drive the Train, *first you have to make friends with the Conductor.* While we can't stop our "reasoning" Surface Minds from assessing, judging, and assigning meaning, we *can* learn to notice and inhibit the process enough to allow new possibilities and experiences to surface. Meditation, yoga, and similar practices are tried and true ways to "inhibit the modifications of the [Surface] mind"[2] and connect with Deeper Self. These practices help us see into the gap between an experience and our interpretation of that experience, giving us an opportunity to stick our fingers in that gap and choose or create something different.

Imagine something new. Something you've never experienced but can imagine yourself having or doing. Feel awe and pleasure as a result of that new imagined outcome. Repeat this regularly and you can call that experience into your life. You can revel in a dream and heed its advice, envision or re-vision something, cut out images from a magazine that "feel" like the solution to a problem. All of these are viable ways to make something new happen. When we put our attention on something with emotion and repetition, the chemistry we make, the thoughts we have, and the actions we take modify the experience and our outcome. Change the channel. Flip the switch, and get the Train to go down a different track. Sometimes instantly. Such is the power of making friends with the Conductor of the Reality Train.

You may even generate seemingly "magical" results as you learn to notice and listen to the constant stream of information waiting in your subconscious to be mined. In fact, if you get good at this, your entire world may shift, revealing rivers of information that until now have been hidden in plain sight.

This information is not new and it is not woo-woo. There is science behind it, and I don't want to clutter up this section with lots of explanations and articles and other Surface Mind fodder. (We have a list of books in the bibliography that will do that.) So if your Surface Mind is prattling on and starting to get in the way, just take a breath and keep reading. Meanwhile, the best "proof" is in the thousands of experiences that people have had with this way of listening to and seeing experience. You'll get plenty of those reports to appease your curiosity. Blow away the mind foam, and follow along.

To begin, all you need is your curiosity, and that sense of wonder and awe you likely had in childhood. You will use those to look with new eyes across your daily experience for the emergence of emotions and images, dreams, symbols, and drives that rise seemingly unbidden, like fish breaking the surface of awareness leaving ripples in their wake.

"I have no special talents. I am only passionately curious."—Albert Einstein

As you free your imagination you will open deeper layers of possibility, and learn to read and trust the information coming to you from these deeper places. You will gain confidence knowing that life is an interactive event, building on complex and delicious relationships within the Unknown Country in which 90% of your dual citizenship resides. You will begin to shift from feeling that life is a job to realizing that life is more like a four-dimensional interactive game. The more joyfully and energetically you play, the more fun life can be.

Your daily experiences will shift and open to reveal a stream of information, like clues written on a wall, or hidden in a drawer, that will guide you. You will come to recognize that you are being guided in a vital and interestingly symbolic way. Your awareness of deeper connections between people, things, events, and experiences will become more obvious. You will develop a level of trust in your gut feelings, your intuition and instinct that can profoundly enhance your life and produce results with greater speed and clarity. I am reminding you that the world as you think it is, is really a filtered version of reality set to the tune of your beliefs and expectations.

All of the practices in this section involve some awareness of liminal states, the state of mind in which dreaming, imagining, and deeply focused play open the gateway between one country and the Other.

Reverie; creative acts such as singing, dancing, drumming, theater, even coloring with crayons; anything in which you can get lost in the process can open this space within us. Ritual, whether personal or religious, produces a liminal state, as does dreaming, guided imagery, myth, story telling, and even acts such as gazing into the night sky.

The threshold places, the spaces between, have always been sacred, and for good reason. It is on mountaintops, at crossroads, under the Milky Way, on the banks of rivers and oceans, at dawn or at dusk, and at the changing of the seasons that we are historically more likely to experience the World behind the world.

Begin to ask, "What else is here that I'm not seeing (hearing, feeling)?" Ah yes, that's the right question. Here, in the liminal places, you can have glimpses of the true nature of the complexity of the natural world and the magnificent nature of the being that you are.

Now, together we will enter the creative world where dreams blend into waking life and provide shortcuts for the Reality Train to take you where you long to be.

The First Way: Re-Telling Your Tale

Everyone is familiar with some version of the Fairy Tale. There are now many modern day Fairy Tales—called books and movies—that follow the traditional pattern. Once Upon a Time, a hero or heroine embarks on a difficult journey; experiences intervention or help from an unexpected or magical ally; goes through the trial, initiation, or challenge; and, with help, experiences a shift in Awareness, completes the challenge, returns victorious and forever changed, and brings back something to the ordinary world that changes the world (or the community around the Hero) for the better.

There are also stories in which the would-be hero or heroine refuses the call, or ignores the ally, or becomes seduced by the dark side, and ends up a wreck, incapable of rising from the murky shallows to save the day, or his or her own ass for that matter. These stories are ones we are most familiar with. They show up as the stories we tell each other in the form of gossip, and as the Victim Stories we tell about ourselves, endlessly reinforcing the unhappy ending. What if the hero never gets the girl, the heroine never saves the world, the kiss that rouses from unconsciousness is never given? Do you want your story to end like that??? Hell no! Well then, here's one way to get your own story back on track.

Rewrite Your Story with a Happy Ending

You can inform your subconscious that it's time to find (or become conscious of) an ally, accept the challenge to live your life fully, be the hero of your own tale, and have a happy NOW that is also the source of the happy ending and happily ever after you're looking for.

HOW to Write a Brief Fairy Tale

- Pick an overall theme or a challenge in your life that repeats.
- Use animals or fairy tale creatures as your characters.
- Start the story in a way that includes you and describes the issue symbolically.
- Have the middle of the story include an ally or magical intervention of some kind.
- Next describe how the problem/issue is resolved once and for all.
- Finally, celebrate your success and tell how the tale will end. (It doesn't matter if external Reality has not caught up to the new story. After all, this is a set of directions you are giving, in code, to that part of you that creates your experiences. Just do your part and write the story.)

- After, be willing to ACT on the story in whatever way feels right, and pay attention to your dreams, for they are a good source of info from Deeper Mind.

Here's an example: You read a bit about my life in Part Two. Well, here's a distilled version that speaks directly to my subconscious in its own language, deals with a specific issue, and creates a clear destination for that Reality Train.

Joseph Campbell said "Healing is what happens when we move beyond suffering into myth."[3] Here's how to do it.

My Fairy Tale

Once upon a time in a magical kingdom there lived a family of Trolls under a bridge. The Trolls were loud and gruff and scary-looking, but they were also kind and wise and sweet at heart. Trolls are also beings of great Light, who are known for their ruthless honesty and hard work keeping the bridges between the Worlds in good repair and well-guarded.

The littlest troll was more sensitive than most. The loud and scary manner of the Troll family, and the reactions of those who feared and judged all Trolls weighed heavily on her. The little Troll also had a great Light that shined brightly, but she did not wish to wear the coarse cloak that all young Trolls wore to hide their light. So the Troll family, in an attempt to help her, wove a magic invisible Troll-cloak around her to keep her light hidden and prevent people from taking advantage of her sensitive nature until she grew up.

Alas, the Troll family was called into service in another Kingdom, one from which they would not return, and forgetting the cloak they had woven 'round their child, they left, assuming that since she was growing up, she would soon become a Troll Queen in her own right, guard the Bridge between the worlds, and have a full and happy life.

Unfortunately, from then on, far and long into adulthood, the invisible cloak hid so much of her light that she was not recognized (and indeed did not even recognize herself) as a Troll Queen, even though her magic was potent and her skills were strong. She became accustomed to making do, settling, and accepting less than her true skills destined her to have. Eventually the invisibility magic of the secret cloak began to wear thin, and she became aware of the dense Troll cloak that was hiding much of her light. She now knew why she dreamed great dreams and worked magic for others but could not free enough light to help herself and to become Guardian of the Underworld Bridge.

She had no idea how to remove it. But that night, she dreamed a grand dream of living under a magnificent bridge, married to a handsome Troll, and helping many beings with her Light.

The next day as she walked through the rolling hills by the lake, a graceful vulture was circling overhead, and smelled the delicious scent of that old rotted magic cloak. "Friend Troll," she called, "Why do you wear that rotting Child's Troll Cloak?"

"It was made by magic" she replied, "and I don't know how to remove it."

"But I can eat magic!" Lady Vulture replied, "I eat all old decaying things that have lost their usefulness and need to pass into another realm."

"Please then, have my cloak!"

The Vulture signaled her friends and they swooped down, covering the Troll with their massive wings, pulling and tearing at the magic cloak, stripping it away, allowing more and more Light to pour out. The Soon-to-be Troll Queen lay helpless, frightened, and in pain as her identity was stripped away with that old confining magic—the magic that had once been used to protect her, which had become a prison.

Then they were done, and the Vultures flew high into the sky, calling down their gratitude for such a delicious meal, and also, they were happy to be of service by freeing the trapped Troll Queen.

And it came to pass that the Troll Queen became accustomed to her light and learned to be confident and be seen for who and what she was. As soon as her light was freed, she found the Bridge that was her True Home, and with great joy, she tended that crossing place, helping beings who sought her aid, all the while shining her light brilliantly without fear.

By and By, a handsome and kind Troll saw her Light and traveled from another realm to ask for her hand in marriage. Even though it had taken many years and many tears to remove the old cloak, what was and is always true is that it's never too late to have a happy ending. And so it was with the Troll Queen, as she lived happily ever after.

A Client's Fairy Tale

This woman had an accident every time she traveled for pleasure, and sometimes even on work-related trips. Some of these accidents were fairly serious and required casts, hospital visits, and substantial recovery time. Here is the re-vision of the pattern she used to create a new way that allowed her to play and enjoy life without injury.

The Princess and the Potion

A princess lived in a huge castle with the King and Queen and many servants. There were no other children in the castle, but the Princess did not let that discourage her from playing. She loved to run and slide on the palace floors and play with great abandon.

The moat was her personal swimming pool. The lone dragon looked forward to the Princess' swims and would accompany and protect her. The Princess would skip everywhere. She was constantly making up games and singing as she flitted about the castle. The King and Queen were worried because they did not think that the Princess' behavior was becoming of a member of the royal family. They wanted her to learn the history, tradition, and rules for assuming power. The Princess was not interested and she closed the books and skipped out.

The King consulted a friend who had magical ability. Some considered him to be a wizard. The Wizard concocted a potion to discourage the Princess from playing, so she would concentrate on her studies. The Princess would have milk and cookies before bed, and one night he slipped the potion into the milk.

The next morning, the Princess felt different, but she could not say how. She started skipping to the breakfast table when she twisted her ankle and fell. She picked herself up, enjoyed a hearty breakfast, and went outside into the sunshine and walked into the forest. She started to sing with the birds, and suddenly her throat felt scratchy, and she started to cough. She decided to cross a stream and jumped from one stepping stone to the next, but she slipped and fell into the stream. Afterward, she climbed to her favorite spot in a big old oak tree to look out over the forest. Climbing down, she skinned her knee.

Bruised and confused, the little Princess went back to the palace and rested on her bed. She didn't know what to do. She grabbed a book and decided to read, and she enjoyed the quiet and the story. She joined her parents for dinner, and went back to her bedroom to finish reading the book before she fell asleep. The next day was very much the same. The Princess tried swimming in the moat, but she nearly drowned when her foot got tangled in some weeds. Fortunately, her friend, the dragon, was there to help her break free. After more scrapes and bruises, the Princess returned to the castle and read another book.

This continued for weeks. The King and Queen noticed that the Princess had become quiet and sad. She rarely spoke and always had her nose in a book. The King approached the Wizard, who created another potion to counteract the first. Again, that night, he poured it into a glass of milk.

The next morning, the Princess felt lighter and happier than she had in a long time. She wanted to skip, but she was not sure whether she should dare. She skipped a couple steps and then, a couple of more. Then she tried jumping and running, and she felt as if she could fly. The Princess was thrilled, and she dived into the moat to swim with the dragon, who had missed her terribly.

After a day filled with the fun and excitement of play, the Princess returned to the castle to read, exhausted from her adventures. The King and Queen were pleased to see the Princess study, but they were more delighted to see her happy and confident. They realized that these are the qualities most important for living a royal life.

Another Way to Write Your Future Here Now

Write a series of letters as if you're writing to a friend or family member. And I DO mean WRITE—with a pen on paper—not type.

- For three consecutive days, write a different letter about the same subject.
- Describe in present tense a solution or experience as if it has just taken place or is taking place right now.
- Make sure the note has detail and emotional intensity.
- Pay close attention to your dreams, which may actively inform the process.
- Feel and convey your pleasure and satisfaction as if it actually is your present experience.

- After writing each letter, read it back aloud, then close your eyes and feel the energy of those happy, grateful, relieved thoughts and emotions wash over you.
- Next, ask the question *"What steps did I take to get this to happen?"* and quickly jot down whatever comes to mind, even if it doesn't make sense. *Don't try to make it make sense. Just write.*
- Now, *take whatever actions* you have uncovered in the process. Allow the experience to unfold.

Here is an example. And remember, you can write to solve a problem, to brave-up to face something, to overcome a challenge, or to create something new. Just follow the instructions.

Dear Bobby,

I don't know what I'd been waiting for, but after all this time I finally walked into the office, sat down, and told the boss exactly what I'd been thinking and feeling about this place and this job. I didn't have much fear about it once I started talking, and I felt confident and clean to be telling the truth—finally! Even though he listened pretty well, and even offered me a different position, I turned him down and gave notice! That felt fantastic! And Bob—the best part is this—the very next day, I got a call from a client testing the waters to see if I might be interested in a job at his firm. I never expected that, and I would love an opportunity to work there. So, all in all, I feel great and I'm doing well. I hope things are good with you, too!

Your Amigo,
Chet

Dear Dad,

I know you were really happy when I got my job and that you think it's a great opportunity. Well, I'm writing to let you know that it was never a good fit for me and I have given notice. I talked to my boss and I feel great about our conversation, and my decision not to stay. Dad, I feel so happy to be free to find a career that fits me! I'm done trying to live up to your expectations and I'm going to do what makes me happy! I hope you're happy for me, and if you're not, I'm not going to make that my problem. Dad, I'm excited about the opportunities coming my way and I'm proud of myself even if you disagree with me. I already have an interview lined up and I am looking forward to telling you all about it.

Love,

Chet

Hi Alice!

Today I went for the second interview at a company I've been interested in for a long time, and they want me! I quit that job I've been complaining about (I bet you're glad!), and right away got an offer to interview with this company. This is such a good opportunity! One of my clients has been raving about his job for two years and I researched them six months ago. They treat their people well, the pay is good, and I have already met with a few other people who have worked there for years. I feel great about all that's going on! Let's go celebrate! What are you doing this coming Saturday? Wanna get together for lunch?

Chet

Chet met with his father, revealed the whole story about trying to live up to his father's expectations, had a bit of a row with him, got over it, forgave his father, and got two job offers seemingly out of the blue (neither by the company mentioned in his letters). He felt that the offers were a sign to talk to his boss, so Chet had the talk, quit his job, interviewed with the companies—and then decided to go out on his own. With his father's financial and emotional support, he started his own business, and a year later his company got a contract with—you guessed it—that company he had mentioned in his letters.

Maybe you want to get married, or make more money, or forgive somebody. Maybe you want better health, or a bigger house, or to get over your ex, or reconcile with your mother. We want you to get it in your bones, that you absolutely can get your Reality Train to take you there. This isn't about "wishing up" a million dollars or never having a care in the world, or having the perfect mate or the perfect body overnight. *This is about waking up, partnering with the tremendous Force that coordinates your life, finding your allies, accepting the call, and leaning into the curve as the train takes the Hero in a new direction.* Your action and continued participation is still required, though in a very different way.

Rewriting History: Another Kind of Fairy Tale

This is a powerful way to revise your relationship to the past, as you amend and insert new useful pleasurable stories and emotions where they will take root and grow new patterns and expectations. Some people leave a tough childhood behind and become drug addicts and perpetual victims, while others become entrepreneurs, healers, and successfully happy individuals. The difference is not in their backgrounds, but in how they reframe the past and use it creatively, rather than be defined by it.

Write about the parent, or the ex-, that you have an issue with, *as if he or she had been completely different*, having given you the legacy (support, help, guidance, understanding, kindness) that made you the successful, well-adjusted person you are (or wish you were) today. Yes, it may be a Fairy Tale, but it is also a series of messages able to start generating the patterns you DO want affecting your decisions, experiences, self-worth and opportunities. Write it with gusto, then ask yourself the question: How would I look, act, and feel if this *were* my past? Invite any old versions of yourself that may be hanging out in the misery of the past to come join you in the experience of the New Version, and ask what you can do for yourself that will make you happier. Then, your job is: look like, think like, and act like a product of the New Past. **Not to pretend, but to integrate what you learn into your life deliberately, becoming a new version of yourself.** Allow yourself to be and feel renewed, competent, and powerful. Because you are.

Additional Creative Ways to Transform Patterns Through Writing

- Write a poem or rewrite a famous poem with a twist on the words that evokes emotion and provides a solution, happy twist of fate, a healing, or a resolution to a difficulty.
- Write a poem of thankfulness and gratitude, pouring images and emotion out that will reinforce the good you do have and do appreciate.
- Write a song that releases some old energy and brings in something wild, new, and positive. You get extra mojo for this since music carries information through to the deepest layers of awareness with the vibrations and tones.
- Try your hand at a short story about a version of yourself that lives in a parallel reality and has figured out something you have been trying to figure out. Go ask that you HOW it got worked out. Interview him/her. You may be surprised by the way the story, much like a dream, takes on a life of its own.
- Write a paragraph about your parents AS IF they are/were exactly the way you wanted them to be, allowing yourself to become fully invested in the fantasy, smiling and feeling the warmth and support, remembering the good advice and kindness they bestowed on you, and include saying how your talents and good decisions have created a life you love.
- Write a vision statement about something you passionately desire, as if you already have it, using language and images that evoke emotion and fill you with warmth and gratitude.

309

- Create a series of New Permissions that you will write and say consistently until the permissions become driven down into Deeper Mind and you develop the unconscious competence to act on those permissions. Check the notes at the end of this section for a starter list of permissions you can choose from and add to.[4]

For yet another fun, interesting, and visual way to play with words that trigger images and emotions, try this tool for creating a word cloud: http://www.wordle.net/create

The Second Way: Images and Imagery

Visual Ways to Play and Communicate with Your Decision-Making, Pattern-Building, Reality Train-Driving Mind

When we rehearse a speech in our mind's eye, or imagine a meeting with a lover, or daydream of a vacation we are planning, we are both practicing that experience and telling Deeper Mind in images and emotions where we want the Reality Train to go. The repeated images and the strong emotions that they evoke create a pattern of universal attraction, allowing coherence to occur between your thoughts and similar patterns. In other words what we call "coincidence" isn't coincidence at all. The flow of events and experiences in our lives moves faster towards us when an alignment influences the tides.

One of the most powerful imagery techniques you can use is also one of the most simple, and the most familiar. Pick something that you strongly desire. Imagine yourself having or experiencing whatever it is in detail, allowing all of your senses to engage as you daydream, fully aware of the way this experience ripples out through your life. Stay out there three to five minutes. When you come back feeling good, allow the idea that you already have what you desire to settle into the background of your mind. Repeat this practice three or four times every day, and as actions, impulses, and intuitions arise, act, honor, and follow them. This is a perfect formula for creating.

Guided imagery is one way to practice something internally in a way that absolutely affects the outcome. One common way to use this skill is by mental rehearsing. Athletes know this and use imagery both intuitively and deliberately.

Golfer Jack Nicklaus used mental imagery for every shot. In describing how he imagines his performance, he wrote: "I never hit a shot even in practice without having a sharp in-focus picture of it in my head. It's like a color movie. First, I 'see' the ball where I want it to finish, nice and white and sitting up high on the bright green grass. Then the scene quickly changes, and I 'see' the ball going there: its path, trajectory, and shape, even its behavior on landing. Then there's a sort of fade-out, and the next scene shows me making the kind of swing that will turn the previous images into reality and only at the end of this short private Hollywood spectacular do I select a club and step up to the ball." (from Brian Mackenzie, "Mental Imagery")

Physical preparation for any sport is important. However, being mentally prepared and mentally tough is just as important, if not more important. In the sport of basketball, mental imagery plays an important role, and often separates the great players from the average players. With the "line" being so small as to whether an athlete makes it to the next level or not, mental abilities can be a major contributing factor for the few that do make the transition. Michael Jordan once said, "I visualized where I wanted to be, what kind of player I wanted to become. I knew exactly where I wanted to go, and I focused on getting there." To read a perspective such as this from a legend like Michael Jordan is a testament to the importance of mental imagery for success in basketball or any sport. (from Albert Buckles, "Mental Imagery in Basketball")

You have certainly heard that "practice makes perfect," but that's not entirely true. Only PERFECT practice makes perfect. Vividly imagining what you desire as if you already have it opens your awareness to opportunity and coincidence that lead you towards that experience. Whatever you want, wants you. If your mind is still, it can find you.

Mental imagery, also called guided imagery, guided visualization, or pathworking, has been used to improve health with great success. Imagery is used to reduce blood pressure, speed healing, fight infection, select treatments, and reduce side effects.

Whatever you desire, imagery can build the tracks for the Reality Train to follow.

The Poster Project: Show and Tell for the Deeper Mind

That a picture is "worth a thousand words" is more than true. Images and emotions are inseparable, because images become associated with the state of mind we experienced as those images were seen. Pictures of your favorite playground are far more than pictures; they are gateways to memories and, more importantly, to the unconscious associations of how you felt/feel and thought/think and what life was like during the summers you spent on that playground. Your entire body responds, and you may feel light and free for a time, inspired to do something playful or to take your own kids to the playground, or in a few days you may have a "sudden" urge to call your Uncle Joe or Aunt Ann, unaware that the urge is another response to looking at those pictures.

Every year I create a new poster that contains images about what I want to experience and what's important to me now and in the coming year. I go through magazines and clip images that may or may not make "logical sense" but do make emotional and symbolic sense. When I'm done, I make a list, in words, called "stuff and experiences I am having this year." I make the list very long, very thorough, and then put it away until the following fall, when I pull it out, check off all the stuff and experiences that I got, and look at what's still on the list. I arrange "areas" on the poster such as "Health and Fitness," "Love and Romance," "Money and Career," "Vacation and Fun"—you get the idea.

I look at the poster on and off throughout the year, putting it away for a few weeks at a time when I "stop seeing" it, then bringing it back out to see it with fresh eyes. I'm always open to getting hints and clues about what I can do, and whatever might be in the way—a cow on the tracks, so to speak. Sometimes I create a second poster during the year just about one specific thing that I may feel "stuck" around. Often the insights about how I'm getting myself stuck will come suddenly as I'm in the shower, or in a dream, or during meditation. I know that when I get a memo like this, I'd better listen and act. Otherwise, I might get a brick to the head to get my attention. And I'm telling you, what gets brought to my attention isn't always pretty. Sometimes I call a friend or a coach and ask for some assistance, or write about it, then take whatever action needs to be taken. The Poster Project works!

It's been a tried and true method of conjuring up the right mix of daydreaming, insight, action, and coincidence throughout the years for many people who have taken workshops I co-led with my good pal Clara Griffin. I have heard dozens of success stories, as participants came back year after year to join the fun and start the year off with a real plan instead of "resolutions."

You can do this alone, or with a friend, or have a poster party and invite a group over for a night of Life Planning fun and games. However you play with this idea, it will open doors for you and help you discover what you desire to find you with greater ease.

After you create the poster, do these four steps:

1. Gaze at the images often, feeling the emotions wash over you as if you are having the experiences that those pictures represent.

313

2. Notice and act on any thoughts, dreams, opportunities, seeming coincidences and of course, you'll want to talk about what you're cooking up with others.

3. Say "thank you" and take a moment to bask in the warm glow of gratitude and satisfaction each and every time something happens that takes you closer to being/having/doing something the poster contains.

4. Pay attention to insights that reveal things about yourself that are keeping that cow standing on the tracks—and take action to resolve them.

Sherry's Poster Project Story

I, too, use this technique to communicate my dreams and desires to my Deeper Mind. One year I used a really big piece of poster board and covered the entire surface with pictures and a few key words. I had some left over, so I glued those to a smaller piece of board and then glued that to the big board. I finished, set it aside, looked at it occasionally, and went about my life. Within a couple of months, my life seemed out of control. Several work projects went from idea to action with amazing speed, my travel plans piled up, a house renovation project finally started, and on and on. I was so busy I barely had time to catch my breath. When the year was over, I pulled out my poster and got my brick to the head enlightenment. I, quite literally, hadn't given myself any space. Lesson learned. My poster for the following year? Lots of white space, gaps between the pictures, plenty of breathing room. Life proceeded, and at a much more relaxed pace.

A Different Version of the Poster Project

If magazines and glue sticks are just not your thing, that's OK, but I will tell you that the more hands on, the better the results. You can do something similar on your computer, and create a file with images and words, colors, and shapes that will work. You can make a series of pages, each one a category.

Try selecting five from these categories, or invent titles of your own:

Health & Fitness, Money & Income, Pleasure & Travel, Friends & Family, Love & Romance, (New) Career, Love & Marriage, Letting Go of the Past, My New Car, Spiritual Connections, Slim Healthy Me, Upgrading My Life, New Stuff, Contribution & Service, Friends & Allies, Creating Community, My Lovely Home, Reinventing Myself, My Life as an Author (or astronaut, restaurant owner, singer—whatever your dream is).

OK, you get the picture. (Ha ha ha!) Make each one a separate page, with a heading, and fill the page with meaningful pictures and images. Be sure you print it or place a link on your desktop, because you will want to follow the four steps above that will keep the lines of communication open between your conscious awareness and the great Deeper Mind below the event horizon.

Daydreaming

Daydreams are maps. Daydreams are how you can bring your desires into reality. Regularly spend time vividly imagining yourself having adventures, getting the great job, marrying your beloved, going to Paris, coming into money, or whatever else your heart desires. Revel in the excitement and emotions of those daydreams, follow the flow through conversations, read magazines, and plan ways to put yourself into those situations. Spend time with people who have the experiences you desire. All of this will communicate clearly to Deeper Mind where you want the Reality Train to go.

Take your time, and feel good about daydreaming every day. Allow yourself time to vividly imagine having and experiencing your desires, and leave room for ideas, directions, and signs to guide you into those experiences.

I once read a story in a book (the title of which escapes me) that illustrated this process very well. There was a woman, Teresa, who desperately needed to find a job. She'd been out of work for months, had used up her savings, and had no family to ask for help. She loved books, and spent lots of her time reading. In fact, going to the bookstore was the one treat she allowed herself to have. She imagined herself getting a job with books. She daydreamed about it, imagining that she could earn a salary and get to read all the books she wanted. She applied to libraries and bookstores. She dreamed about books at night, and felt compelled to keep reading the newest biographies and she followed a few of the romance authors. She found a book on a park bench. She found a book on the bus. She overheard a guy in the grocery store say he was about to publish a book. Theresa dreamed about a bookstore, a comfy chair and a beautiful tiffany-shaded light. She knew that store. It was in another neighborhood. With the very last of her money, instead of printing copies of her resume, as her friends had suggested, she went to the bookstore with the beautiful light. While she was poring over the new books, Carla, the owner, was deep in conversation with a man at the front counter. He owned a local newspaper and was looking for someone to write book reviews right away, because the columnist that usually handled books was in the hospital having a baby a month early. Carla waved Theresa over and introduced them. Theresa got her dream job.

Here is a solid example of the effect that our choice of interpretation of events has on our reality.

Viktor Frankl was a Jewish psychiatrist who spent three years during World War II living under unspeakable circumstances in several of the most notorious Nazi concentration camps. While imprisoned, Frankl realized he had one single freedom left: He had the power to determine his response to the horror unfolding around him. And so he chose to imagine. He imagined his wife and the prospect of seeing her again. He imagined himself teaching students after the war about the lessons he had learned. Frankl survived and went on to chronicle his experiences and the wisdom he had drawn from them. "A human being is a deciding being," he wrote in his 1946 book, *Man's Search for Meaning,* which sold more than 10 million copies. "Between stimulus and response there is a space. In that space is our power to choose our response. In our response lies our growth and our freedom."—Amand Enayati, *The Power Of Perceptions: Imagining The Reality You Want*

When we drive along a familiar route, we see signs, buildings, trees, a certain slope of the land, and we know that we are close to home, near the gym, or at the restaurant. When we begin an inner journey that takes us into new territory, there are also signs and landscape cues and symbols to let us know if we are headed in the right direction or lost in the woods. They arrive in our experience as synchronicity, symbol and dreams. We may ignore, downplay, miss, or misinterpret them, but when we learn to recognize them, our lives expand.

The Third Way: Symbols, Synchronicity, Rituals, and Dreams

Row, row, row your boat,
Gently down the stream,
Merrily, merrily, merrily, merrily,
Life is but a dream.

The more you use your imagination to reinforce good feelings and positive expectations, the easier it is to have more successes and resolve issues with greater ease and grace. **When you know that there is a powerful Ally communicating with you through symbols,** *images, and emotions, you don't feel like a victim, you learn how to listen, and you take action rather than trusting only your so-called rational mind.* Opening the gateway of communication with the deeper layers of your awareness gives you access to allies and road signs that otherwise you are likely to ignore.

Symbols and Superstitions

Everybody has symbols, personal superstitions, and signs that are interwoven through their lives. What are yours? Do you turn just in time to see a rainbow when you are worried? Does a bird in your house warn you to prepare for bad news? Does a white feather on the ground tell you that everything will be ok? Do you cancel your trip if Aunt Ann tells you she dreamed of you in a car wreck? Do you see hearts in clouds or leaves or a splotch of coffee when you doubt your sweetie? What speaks to you? Something surely does. You may not be listening, but the world around you is always giving you a "status update" about where you are headed. Whatever you look for also looks for you. This is the nature of things. This is the process that goes on behind the curtain whether you believe it or not. Some people find meaning when they see a certain animal, say a black dog for protection, or a red-tailed hawk for good luck, or a vulture reminding them to "let go." Some families have very specific symbols and create reliable markers for events that are taught and passed down through generations. What are yours?

Take a minute and jot down recurring themes, symbols, superstitions, animals, special archetypes that you relate to and maybe secretly rely on in times of trouble. Do you wish upon a star? Hang a crystal from your rearview mirror? Do you dream of or see certain people or animals and then know something with certainty? Just pay attention to this idea: "Experiences are Symbols that tell me how I'm really doing, where I'm headed, which direction is best, what trouble is coming, and what can be avoided." Oh yes. All of that.

I know someone who works very hard and pushes herself to extremes until her personal messenger arrives to remind her that she's got to take a break and play: she is visited by squirrels. She doesn't live in the country. She was raised in the country, where her mother, a single mom with five kids, taught her that when the squirrels showed up it was time to play and rest, storing up energy. Now a city girl with a high profile job, she once got in her car and found a squirrel on the passenger seat munching on an energy bar. One morning she woke to a squirrel rummaging on her dresser, and had a squirrel fall (who has ever seen a squirrel fall??) on her lunch table while having a business meeting outside at a sidewalk bistro one afternoon. Those are just a few of her squirrel stories.

I remember the stories from a neighbor who found dimes even in the most unusual of places when she especially missed her husband, who had died suddenly in an accident. She found dimes inside a newspaper, at the bottom of a coffee bought at a drive through, in a library book, and even stuck with gum on the back of a park bench.

I know a former client who made or refused business deals (worth millions) based on whether or not he got the right sign from the universe. He was well-known for his nearly magical and uncanny business acumen. What people didn't know was that he waited for a sign from pigeons. If he got the sign, he signed and if not, not. For him, it was 100% reliable. Once he was in a meeting on the 23rd floor of a building, negotiating with the CEO of a huge company that really wanted the deal. The CEO wanted him to sign right then and there—something this guy never ever did without a pigeon report. Just as he got up and walked towards the window to take a break from the meeting and grab a coffee, a pigeon smashed into the glass and plummeted 23 floors to the pavement. He did not sign, and oh yeah, that business went down the drain when the CEO was arrested for fraud later that year.

This is not coincidence. This is communication. When we enter the woods, there is always a hand that can show us the way back home.

My Personal Symbol Systems

When I was a young girl, my prized possessions were kept in a cigar box. I had colorful wild animals, farm animals, a lion tamer, a cowboy, a few ballerinas that I'd saved from birthday cakes, three pink plastic flowers with violet jewel centers, a seashell, six tiny pink plastic babies, and the inside of an old clock, which was my "tickey toy." I could lay out a scene and shrink down to "fit" into the miniature worlds I created under the old battered card table that Grandpa would set up in the living room for me to play under. With an old sheet or blanket tossed over it, I could have my own "room" and play undisturbed by my sister. Eventually, most of my treasures vanished, but a few—my black horse, the seashell, and my tickey toy, are still are in my possession.

I was in my late 20s when the first plastic figure arrived. I'd been feeling especially lonely. I was living in Denver, far from my friends, several of whom had recently died. Early one morning I had a dream about a green stuffed monkey hanging by one arm from my kids' bunk beds. I wondered where it had come from, and then "remembered" in the dream that it was a gift from a deceased friend. I woke surprised, not realizing that the dream WAS a dream until I woke. I took time remembering every detail of the green monkey. The dream feeling and images lingered in my awareness vividly. Then I walked to the grocery store with my girls, the little one in a backpack and the other by the hand. When we passed the vending machines, my older daughter asked for a coin to get a prize. Two plastic containers dropped down instead of one, so she gave me the second one, saying this prize was for me. In hers was a super ball. Mine held a green plastic monkey with one arm raised over its head. I smiled and squeezed my eyes shut against the tears that threatened to fall. That was the beginning.

From then on, meaningful plastic figures have appeared, as if out of nowhere. Once I was lying in the grass and when I got up, something, which turned out to be a small blue astronaut, dug into my palm. The next day I went to visit a friend for the weekend and met a real astronaut who had also been invited for the weekend. Once, on a day that my kids, Falcon and Pandora (nicknamed Panda), were with their dad and I was feeling blue, a small bear and a tiny bird were on my seat at the local coffee shop. Recently, a few days after I'd helped my grown daughter pick out a dog from a shelter, I found a beautiful small plastic dog, "Lady," standing right by the driver's side door in my parking spot, as if waiting for me. I also have a tiny clay magic lamp, an elephant, a swan, and a goose. They show up in my car, on the ground, in my laundry, in the grass, under my palm in the sand, in my mailbox. I mean, really, how many small plastic figures have YOU discovered in your mailbox, right?

Though each has a story, the relevance here is this intricate system of communication. What does it take for me to be in the right place on the right day for their unlikely and meaningful delivery? This symbol system has meaning and evokes a sense of magic, connection, and protection.

What speaks to you? What symbols in your life are markers that give you direction, or remind you that you are on the right track, or warn you to go another way, or remind you that you are protected? I'd like to hear your stories. Please feel free to go to my web site (www.stresswizardcoaching.com) and tell me about the ways you are given hints and clues in the language of symbols.

Sherry's Animal Signs

Messages come to me in the form of animals. Encounters with spiders tell me it is time to tend my web of connections, to make phone calls, or send emails, or visit with friends and family. Seeing a fox while out on a run is a sign that something is being kept secret that needs to be revealed, or something is unspoken that needs to be said. Sometimes they appear in dreams. Shortly before I met my husband, I had a vivid dream in which my mother dropped a fox carcass into a bucket of acid and I watched it dissolve—a powerful message that it was time to drop pretenses in order to have what I wanted.

Synchronicity

Strings of events can align in unlikely ways as our thoughts and emotions resonate out and are mirrored back to us, becoming road signs. Whatever you have your attention on also attends to you. Synchronicity isn't "just coincidence," it's a way that we interact with the archetypes—the complex patterns that intermingle with all human consciousness, creating the foundation for myths, religions, and heroic stories throughout all time.

Carl Jung wrote extensively about the experience of synchronicity:

A young woman I was treating had, at a critical moment, a dream in which she was given a golden scarab. While she was telling me this dream I sat with my back to the closed window. Suddenly I heard a noise behind me, like a gentle tapping. I turned round and saw a flying insect knocking against the window-pane from outside. I opened the window and caught the creature in the air as it flew in. It was the nearest analogy to a golden scarab that one finds in our latitudes, a scarabaeid beetle, the common rose-chafer (Cetonia aurata), which, contrary to its usual habits, had evidently felt an urge to get into a dark room at this particular moment.

The scarab is a classic example of a rebirth symbol. The ancient Egyptian Book of What Is in the Netherworld describes how the dead sun-god changes himself at the tenth station into Khepri, the scarab, and then, at the twelfth station, mounts the barge which carries the rejuvenated sun-god into the morning sky. – Carl Jung, *The Structure and Dynamics of the Psyche: The Collected Works of Carl Jung, Volume 8*

Here are a few examples from my own experience:

Once, when I went to visit a friend in upstate New York, I was amazed to discover that the author of a book I'd just purchased at the airport was also a guest for the weekend. He was smart, funny, and a joy to talk with about everything from the nature of reality to the best way to make coffee and our strategies for playing Risk. We connected, and that made reading and sharing his book much more interesting. Life got busy and my friend was going to move from his home, and a little more than a year had passed since that visit.

I had a dream about meeting the author, Michael, in a cosmic library that held the records of everyone's life contracts. The next evening I taught an Adult Education class in a high school and during the break, I wandered into an empty area near some vending machines and sat at one of the round tables. There was a single section of the New York Times on the table. I live in Ohio, so that's not a common find in a high school vending area. It was folded to display a column and picture. Michael's picture. Shocked, I picked up the paper and discovered that it was his obituary. He had died the day before I met him in the dream library.

Just yesterday I was sitting in a restaurant, reading a book, engrossed in a section about the appearance of certain birds as messengers in myths. The book was talking about the two ravens, Thought and Memory, who perch on the god Odin's shoulders and soar over the land, keeping watch. I had the thought that I've seen lots of crows and ravens but never just two flying together. Just then, my daughter Falcon came in the restaurant to join me. I looked out the window as she scooted in her seat and right there before me were two crows flying side by side.

Last week, after working on a section of this book, I headed to the gym, all the while thinking of the idea of the Reality Train and the Conductor. The street I usually go down to get to the freeway was closed due to construction, so I followed the detour and when I popped out on the next street I came up to railroad tracks just as the gate was coming down. Mine was the only car there. The slow moving train came into view, and the conductor waved to me. I laughed out loud. Wow. OK, I'll keep that analogy, thanks.

And here's one example from Sherry: Recently, I repeatedly encountered images of the elephant-headed Hindu God, Ganesha, who among other things is the Remover of Obstacles. Ganesha statues, Ganesha on t-shirts, books about Ganesha, He suddenly seemed to be everywhere. And the capstone? In 2012, my birthday was on the same day as Ganesha's birthday. While telling my yoga teacher about these encounters, the thought popped up, "I'm not sure I want all the obstacles removed, because then what will happen? Where will I be?" No matter, the obstacles are falling away. Ganesha is being insistent, and now his sister Saraswati, Goddess of knowledge, sciences, music, and art, has joined him, starting with the arrival of a statue loaned to me by a dear friend who said, "Here, I thought you might need her for a while." Yes, I believe I do.

Synchronicities are markers that remind us that we are connected in complex and intimate ways that reach far beyond the "logic" of conscious awareness. Maybe you think of someone you haven't heard from in a year and the phone rings or you get an email the same day. Wish I had a dime for every time I picked up my phone a second or two before it rang in my hand. Again, this usually happens while my Surface Mind is busy and I'm free to "get the memo." Even the Weather Channel has a show on right now called "Twist of Fate" that features real stories of heroic rescues made by people who were in the right place at the right time. It often contains a number of synchronistic events.

Robert Moss, in his book *The Three "Only" Things: Tapping the Power of Dreams, Coincidence, and Imagination,* writes about the way strong emotions fuel and multiply seeming coincidence—especially love, fear, times when we are making a leap of faith, and transitional times such as the events surrounding birth and death. He writes; "Strings of coincidence can strengthen us in our determination to follow our deepest intuitions even when they run counter to conventional wisdom... and on the other hand, negative synchronicities and counter currents tend to multiply when we are resisting change."

Moss also recounts a time when he and a friend, deep in conversation, walked all day and became completely lost in a forest in England. He said out loud, "I wish a guide would just appear out of nowhere and show us the way. Wouldn't that be fabulous?" His friend laughed, "like a crow," since they had not seen a single person in the woods all day, and they had covered at least fifteen miles worth of trails. Within a few minutes, however, a runner appeared, waved to them and asked if they were lost. Not wanting to break stride the runner said he'd leave them markers, and disappeared down the trail. They found an arrow formed with sticks at the next fork in the trail, and another, and another, leading them for two miles back to the main road.

Ah yes, many interesting benefits become available as you make friends with the Conductor of the Reality Train.

Divination Cards

Every culture has a form of divination, usually several, that can be used to bridge the communication gap between Surface Mind and Deeper Mind. Tarot cards, Angel Cards, and other kinds of decks (Oracle Cards, Book of Doors, and others) can serve as a valuable ally in reaching beyond Surface Mind to the deeper patterns of life. There are thousands of decks available, making it easy to find a set of images that speak to, and for, you. For our purposes, just ignore the "book meanings" of the cards. Instead, let the meanings arise in a personal way. Use the images on the cards as you would the images in dreams or daydreams, as triggers or pointers or doorways to the Other World. Here are some ways Sherry and I use the cards as a hotline to Deeper Mind.

A Daily Message

As part of your morning routine, shuffle your deck. Then, keeping the cards face down, pull one out. You may notice a card that seems to draw or attract your attention or your touch—that's the one to choose. Look at the image on the card. What part of the image immediately catches your eye? What feelings or connections does it have? What does it have to say to you, what does it point to? Jot all that down. What do you notice next? Keep this up until you feel done, as if the card has told you all it has to tell. Don't expect to always "get" the message right away, and come back to it once or twice during the day to see what else has popped up.

Card Dreaming

Shuffle your deck and, keeping the cards face down, pull one out. Spend a few minutes just noticing the images on the card, without trying to make sense of them. Close your eyes, take a breath, and bring the images from the card into your mind's eye. Now see yourself in the image—enter in whatever way seems right. Walk around, notice what you see, hear, smell, taste, touch. If there are other people around, talk to them, ask questions, or see if they have questions for you. Explore this world until you feel done exploring, then slowly bring yourself back into the room where you are sitting and open your eyes. Jot down your impressions and experiences.

Send A Message

You can use the cards to send a message to Deeper Mind—think of it as an intercom connection to the Conductor. When you want to point Deeper Mind in a particular direction or focus, turn the cards face up and flip through them quickly until you find one (or more) of them that convey the message you want to send. Gazing at the images, use them to tell yourself a story about what you want and where you want to go. Your story may be happy or sad, funny or poignant, whatever occurs as needed to convey your destination to the Conductor of your Reality Train.

These are a few of the ways to use tarot and other cards, and there are plenty of books and websites full of other techniques and ideas. So find a deck whose images call to you and set up your own hotline to Deeper Mind.

Rituals

We have all kinds of rituals in our lives. There are informal rituals, like a before-bed routine that helps you wind down and quiet your mind, or an after-work ritual that may include a shower, a drink, and the TV—always in that order. There are rituals for holidays that include seating arrangements, food, colors, candles, and songs. There are even rituals (called superstitions) that sports players engage in, that may include socks or a medal or some other talisman that is worn or touched. Your family may have rituals that have been passed down and called "traditions" for various holidays. We have rituals and symbols for protection, health, birthdays, safe travel, and even for the successful sale of a house! (Yes, I DO know people who have buried a statue of a saint upside down in the yard to sell a house!) There are rituals being played out all around us all day long.

When you deliberately use a ritual to imprint the pattern of your desired experience onto your decision-making Genius, you step into the story and participate consciously. The result can be a powerful shift in awareness and the transformation of an entire pattern in the blink of an eye. That awakening can, like a lightning bolt, illuminate and rewire us instantly. It happens more often than you may think.

Such is the power of rituals and dreams. Both take us straight into that liminal place beyond our usual expectations—the inner space, that cauldron of the larger mind in which something new, edgy, special, and sacred can occur. This is the place in which reality is cooked up, decisions are made, and minds resonate, aligning everything from "chance" meetings to heroic measures.

Throughout history rituals have been, and continue to be, used both consciously and unconsciously in our everyday lives. Religious rituals contain symbols, objects, scents, oils, movements, instruments, elements, containers, words, and music to convey complex and often ancient ideas, themes, and stories. Religious rituals are used to keep alive our awareness of the way the spiritual (or energetic, if you prefer) realm underlies and imbues ordinary linear experience.

If you don't believe in a "spiritual" realm, that's fine. The idea still works. Just think of it in terms of Energy—the realm of undefined energy out of which everything is composed. Yes. You and me and the plant, the tree, the book, and the toilet paper—all energy vibrating together in a happy little bandwidth that makes what we call matter available to be experienced through the instrument of our brain which receives and translates energy into images, sounds, and sensations. It's pure magic no matter how you cut the cake. By the way, energy beyond our spectrum of experience and whatever forms of matter and life it contains that we cannot see, hear, and feel is just as real, even though we are unaware of it.

Ritual invites us to peer into the always-open door between the world as we know it and the world behind the world—the places that our busy Surface Minds often hide from us in our attempts to maintain an illusion of control. Both dreaming and ritual can bring about insight, ecstatic states, healing, comfort, inspiration, connection with others, and union with numinous powers.

This sensory world is a reflection of the liminal world, and our awareness, once trained, can recognize things from the liminal world that have been hidden in plain sight all our lives. *We can learn to recognize the experiences of our lives as living symbols, and discover their deeper meaning.* Cultures from around the world and across time, including our own, have created and used rituals for all the transitions we experience throughout our lives, including birth, marriage, and death. Rituals enable us to interact more deeply with forces of life and death that we do not, and perhaps cannot, consciously ever fully understand.

Knowing this, and recognizing the potency of ritual, you can create your own simple rituals. Your rituals will call on your own rich inner symbol system to break free from old patterns, create new ones, invite inspiration, improve health, and just about anything else you can think of. Rituals work because they are an ancient, time-tested way of getting sacred congruency to occur—that alignment of vision and emotion through which connections are made, complex patterns instantly form, and roads that were invisible lead us out of the woods.

Ritual engages all parts of our awareness. When we think, act, feel, and move congruently we can use layers of symbol and meaning as the engine of transformation. Theater is a form of ritual, and the addition of music, drumming, and poetry adds to the potency of the symbolism and meaning. The most ancient forms of theater found in Egypt and Greece were spectacular ritual events that lasted for days. Those rituals used drama, poetry, music, and visual art to enable participants to transcend day-to-day experience and fully experience the stories of the Gods and the myths of great Heroes.

Rituals don't have to be complex or elaborate. Any time we align our thoughts and emotions powerfully, we shape experience. Here are a few simple rituals you can use to create a gateway to new thoughts, patterns, and behaviors.

How to Create Simple Rituals

Create a sacred space. That is to say, a space designated as your quiet space in which your intentions can align with your thoughts and emotions. This can be as simple as sitting in a special chair, drawing a circle around yourself (even an imagined circle), placing a few rocks or a candle on a little table, or putting on a special article of clothing. The more you repeat whatever special-space-creating practice you choose, the faster and deeper you will be able to quiet your mind and bring your intention, your thoughts, and your feelings into congruence.

Now, in your sacred space, if you wish, say a prayer, call allies to assist you, or simply imagine your space filled with golden light.

Here are four sample rituals to get your own creative juices flowing. Use these, adapt them to your style, or invent your own.

Ritual For Making New Connections

Pour yourself a glass of tea, juice, or some other beverage. Hold it up and really see it fully. Think about all the connections with ground, sun, people, travel that it took to be in your hands right now. Connections. Hundreds of them. Feel and imagine all those connections. Slowly and deliberately drink it down, feeling yourself drawn to the right people, places, and connections. Say thank you and exit your sacred space with respect.

Ritual For Having More Ease

Create a short list of permissions for yourself. *I give myself permission to rest when I'm tired, meditate every day, take the comments of others lightly, have more fun every day.* Get a small item that represents each permission, a fun symbol you can relate to. Put the items in a little bag one by one, as you speak and breathe the corresponding permission into it three times. Now carry them with you, or keep them on your desk where you can reach in every day, draw one out, and see what permission speaks to you at that moment.

Ritual For Letting Go

Draw the "story" of what you want to let go of (a fight, an ex, an old job) on a piece of paper, and don't worry about it if you can't draw. Use circles and squiggles; it doesn't matter, as long as you get the feeling of the story down on the paper in a way that's meaningful for you. When it's all there, and you feel some relief that it's out of you and on the paper, fold it up small, then burn or bury (as you prefer) the paper, and say, "I let this go and this lets me go," or whatever else feels right to say.

Buy a candle in a color or scent that has meaning to you as it relates to whatever you want the ritual to awaken in you and in your life. Hold the candle and imagine that it is filled with energy, bursting with untapped resources and connections, then say in a few words what that energy will do, clearly and simply. For example, a great new job, healing, confidence and clarity. Then daydream, meditate, or use music to enter into a calm state of reverie in which you see and feel that result. When you return, light the candle and put it someplace where it can burn safely and undisturbed until it goes out. While it's burning, pay special attention to clues, markers, dreams, and synchronicities in your environment. Take any actions you can to support the process, engaging your emotions positively.

A Big Story of The Power of Ritual

Marshall's story was told to me by a therapist, whose own life had been drastically turned around after a program inspired her to start incorporating shamanic ritual and creative writing practices into her work with others.

Marshall's mother, a heroin addict, abandoned him at two years of age. He was taken in by his aunt—his mother's sister, an alcoholic who had been repeatedly sexually abused by her father. At age 14 he ran away, and stayed with the family of a high school friend. He lived with them for four years and stayed close as "part of the family." His aunt never came looking for him. At age 19 he entered therapy for paralyzing anxiety, drug use, and low self-esteem. The therapist first had Marshall rewrite his history, creating a loving mother and a safe home, taking himself back over and over into a "new" past, using imagery to recreate his past as if his current "family" had always been his family. Within three months, he started to look different, to think differently, and to act with much greater self-confidence. At Christmas that year, he created a short ritual that he shared at the dinner table, in which he adopted them as his official family, *from birth*. He then asked his adopted "parents" and siblings to tell him stories about himself as a child, especially how they'd found him as a baby and took him in. They did. They created a new myth, all the while celebrating this now "official" mutual adoption. Marshall told the therapist how they'd all cried as they created and added to the story of taking him in, and that he actually somehow *felt* as if the child he once was had been found and saved. The therapist told me that she'd *never* seen "regular therapy" transform a person so thoroughly, and certainly not in three months. But he was ready. Marshall was the hero, had been through the trial, and had found his allies and his way home. He stopped using drugs, got a job, and went to college to be an engineer, graduating near the top of his class.

Dreams

Have you ever experienced a dream that made perfect sense—until you woke up? Then the "language" of the dream vanished, and the meaning along with it. Throughout history, dreams and visions have played, and continue to play, an important role in attaining knowledge not readily available in the waking state, in solving complex problems, and in healing. Pay attention to your dreams. Write them down. Be with them and share them with others.

Stay away from books on dream interpretation or other dream analysis information. I will repeat that: don't let anyone or any book tell you what *your* dream images mean. Those images can be literal, or visits from others, or purely symbolic, but in *your* symbol system. Yes, there are archetypes and other overarching cultural symbols, and it would be to your advantage to read some about that. You may want to look up names, words, symbols, and animals that appear in your dreams for their importance in indigenous cultures, rather than what the dream-meaning books say about them.

Most importantly, when you get in touch with the dream as communication, learn to ask the question, "If this dream wanted me to take an action, what might it be?" Then take action. Here is an example that will help you get a feel for how to explore your dreams.

I had two clients who, at about the same time, were each experiencing a similar family crisis and drama that revolved around their elderly mothers. Both clients (who do not know each other and live in different states) had several vivid dreams about a bicycle followed by interesting encounters with bicycles turning up in odd places. Each of them felt that the bicycle incidents were somehow related to their crisis but neither knew how or why. I asked each of them, "Tell me what you think and how you feel when you remember the dreams and the bicycle incident."

Client A : Oh I remember my first bike, it was wonderful to get away from the house and ride all day! I felt free and happy on that bike. I love bicycling!

Me: What action or actions do you think you are being invited to take?

After a brief pause, A said: "I feel sad. She gave me that first bike and I realize I have been focusing on all the mistakes she (her mother) made, all the things she's done that I don't like and that I haven't acknowledged how much value she's contributed to my life. And I also think I want to go get myself a bike and ride rather than riding the bike at the gym. I think that would really help clear my head. Wow, and I also think I have been *waiting for her to give me permission to 'be free'* but only I can stop repeating the old crappy family dramas."

She did those things and bought a bike, which she now rides often. She also discovered that while riding, she often has ideas and insights about how to stop getting caught up in the family dramas.

Client B reported: Oh well, first I thought of the Wicked Witch riding her bike in the tornado .. haha .. but ya know as a kid I hated being told by my dad to go outside and ride my bike. That always meant mom was shitfaced and trouble was coming. I'd ride around the neighborhood with knots in my stomach wondering if it was safe to go home. Sometimes I'd ride until dark, when I saw the light in the bedroom go out and I knew she was asleep. It was awful.

Me: OK, what action or actions do you think you are being invited to take?

Silence. Then: "Holy shit! A riderless bicycle just shot out of my neighbors' driveway and hit my trashcan. I kid you not! You know, I don't know why in the hell I'm still pretending she's not a drunk! I'm gonna call her doctors and tell them how much booze she's putting away every night. I mean, Christ! If she wants to keep drinking, that's her issue, but I'm sooooo done! My father hid that crap his whole life, but he's gone and I'm not filling in! Oh, here comes Jack after the bicycle. How totally weird. Sorry, what did you just ask me?"

Me: Umm, I asked what action or actions you think the dream is inviting you to take. (We both laughed)

Client B: OK, well I guess I got that message. I'm getting "off that old bike," going in that house and telling the truth to my mother, my sisters, and the damn doctor!

Yep. We speak to ourselves all the time, delivering clues and hints that can help us restore or create more balance and ease in our lives. Listening requires that we slow down the "reasoning" (often bullshitting) Surface Mind enough to first notice and then decode the symbols usefully. This is an individual matter and we can't rely on "dream interpretation" to get us there. Especially since meaningful images and symbols also present themselves when we're wide awake.

Curiosity, imagination, creativity, free-wheeling unconstrained thought, art, dreams, music, and movement are all players in developing this communication.

I encourage you to do some more reading about the powerful forces that are woven through dreams, rituals, symbols, and synchronicity. If you want to learn to communicate with the archetypes that weave the world behind the world, I suggest that you read and study the works listed in the bibliography, especially the works of Robert Moss, a world renowned author who specializes in the art of Active Dreaming.

Without cultivating a relationship with our larger Deeper Self and the wonders and mysteries that can be accessed only through those imaginal realms, we remain stuck in the jail of the Surface Mind. As Brad Blanton puts it:

We all tend to get lost in the swamp of our evaluative minds trying to make decisions and figure out how to behave and what to do next while constantly considering what we imagine others might imagine about us as a result of any action we anticipate taking. This concern about controlling the opinions of others and keeping control of ourselves kills more people than any form of environmental stress. (from *Radical Honesty*)

You are hereby invited to reclaim the wonder and playfulness of childhood, to use your imagination constructively and deliberately, and allow the guides and allies, symbols, and road signs to become visible in your life. Gifts and wonders await you.

A twenty-minute meditation, in an ocean of discord, mistrust, irritation, busyness, and frustration will be an oasis, yes, but it may not be enough to turn the tide on the pulsing, relentless outpouring of energy that the rest of your day is made of.

Listen and look deeply, following the trail of breadcrumbs, or the flight of a bird, or the path of a dream that may heal some part of your life. Allow your relationship with the Conductor of the Reality Train to deepen and revise how your thoughts and emotions exude energy. Breathe. A helping hand is always close by to point your way out of the woods.

Notes

[1]The words "conscious," "unconscious" and "subconscious," have many meanings and are used many different ways. In this book, when we say "conscious" we mean the thought activity generated by the logical, rational, fully aware part of your mind. (We also refer to the conscious as Surface Mind.)

The "subconscious," also referred to by researchers as the "adaptive unconscious," is where our filters operate. This is the part of the brain that automatically processes internal and external sensory input and decides what will become conscious and what will remain below the level of conscious awareness. We're going to show you how you can bring some of your subconscious awareness to the surface and become aware of what you are thinking, feeling and doing in new and more useful ways.

By "unconscious" we mean the activities of the mind that operate outside of conscious awareness and that, unlike the subconscious activity of filters, can only be identified indirectly. (We also refer to the subconscious and unconscious together as Deeper Mind. We will say more about how to work with the unconscious in Part Three.)

An excellent book that explains in much greater detail how the various parts of the brain work to create these experiences of the mind is *The Accidental Mind* by David J. Linden.

[2]Evidence for neuroplasticity – the ability of the brain to change its structure and function – emerged in the 1960's with some surprising discoveries. Contrary to the common belief that the brain stops growing and changing in childhood and can only decline with age, researchers found that the very structure of the brain changes

in response to injury, or to acquiring new skills and abilities, such as learning a musical instrument. The discovery of brain chemicals that encourage nerves to grow and others that control cell death helped explain how brain circuits can change throughout our lives. The discovery of neuroplasticity fostered new approaches to treating brain injury, mental illness, autism, and learning disorders. For more details, including fascinating case studies see *The Brain that Changes Itself* by Norman Doidge. Neuroscientist Jill Bolte Taylor's account of her own severe stroke and full recovery, *My Stroke of Insight*, is a powerful testimony to the power of neuroplasticity.

CHAPTER TWO

[1]In his book *Blink: The Power of Thinking Without Thinking*, Malcom Gladwell describes research studies conducted by Norman R.F. Maier in which participants were asked to find four solutions to a problem. Two ropes hung from the ceiling, far enough apart so that the end of one could not be reached if you were holding on to the other. The room contained furniture and other objects. Participants were given the task of tying the ends of the two ropes together. Most participants found the first three solutions pretty quickly: use an implement such as a long pole to pull one rope toward the other until they are close enough to tie together; tie the end of one rope to a piece of furniture placed as closely to the other rope as possible, then go get the other rope and stretch it over to the anchored rope; or lengthen one rope by tying an extension cord to it. A few people figured out the fourth solution: start one rope swinging back and forth, then move to the other rope, wait for the first rope to swing into reach, grab it and tie the two together. If the participant did not come up with this solution, Maier would walk across the room and "accidentally" brush against one of the ropes, setting it swinging. When he did that, most of the participants realized the fourth solution and completed the task. When asked how they came up with

the fourth solution, all but one of the participants gave explanations that did not include noticing that he had brushed against the rope. They had all seen it happen and had used the information unconsciously, but they hadn't consciously noticed it.

CHAPTER THREE

[1]What we experience as reality is not generated by a "logical" process. Advances in our understanding of how the brain works tell us that what seems to our conscious selves to be logical, rational thought is, most of the time, the product of reflexive emotional reactions established by previous experiences, which are then rapidly "explained" by our conscious mind so that they seem to be based in logic and conscious choice. Neuroscientists estimate that more 90% of our so-called choices are a product of this subconscious processing.

[2]In addition to whatever happened in your past, you are submersed in a culture that simultaneously celebrates certain pleasures (but only for those who are wealthy enough or beautiful enough or famous enough to deserve them), while it denies the importance of pleasure as a part of being human. This might be a good place to notice if you have a background belief sabotaging your ability to accept more pleasure in life. Begin by banishing the term, and even the notion, of a "guilty pleasures." Pleasure is pleasure, and as long as no one is harmed in the process, there is no need to feel guilty for enjoying it. Yet many (maybe most) people believe that pleasure must be "earned" or that pleasure must of necessity be expensive, immoral or dangerous. If you have any of those ideas bouncing around your noggin, start interrupting those killjoys right now!

CHAPTER FOUR

[1]We aren't the only ones rummaging around in the attic for unconscious beliefs and biases. If you'd like to more thoroughly explore

your own biases, check out these tools from the world of social psychology:

http://www.understandingprejudice.org/iat/

http://www.tolerance.org/activity/test-yourself-hidden-bias

CHAPTER SIX

[1]A recent study showed that the experience of sharing an emotional moment with other people isn't just behavioral. It literally alters brain function. Using sophisticated imaging methods, researchers showed that brain activity in people who were watching movies together became synchronized, so that the same parts of the brain were active at the same time. This kind of synchronization had been previously found in speaker-listener pairs, but this time it was seen in groups. The synchronization occurred in areas of the brain that register the relative pleasantness or unpleasantness of a situation, and areas that indicate the level of arousal (calmness or activation).

CHAPTER ELEVEN

[1]Warren Jones, professor of psychology at the University of Tennessee, is the author of several key studies of the effects of forgiveness on health and well-being. His research has found that forgiveness, both as an aspect of personality and as an act or emotion, is associated with better outcomes in five areas: physical symptoms, medications used, quality of sleep, fatigue, and complaints and symptoms that have no medical explanation. Being able to forgive contributed to mental and spiritual well-being and improved conflict management. Other studies have produced similar results. More about the research on forgiveness is available at http://stress.about.com/od/relationships/a/forgiveness.htm

CHAPTER TWELVE

[1]HOW to BE More in the Moment: Balance Between Doing and Being

Start by just noticing things. The sensations in your body. Your breath. Your quick background automatic thoughts. Your emotions, judgments, fears.

Take good care of the basics: food, sleep, touch, breathe.

Meditate, exercise, play and have fun. Schedule it if necessary.

Become a good observer of the meaning you attach to thoughts and experiences.

Recognize where in your own life you have repeated unwanted experiences.

Get your friends to help you identify how you get in your own way.

Make your communication with others simple, clear, and direct.

Interrupt and redirect yourself deliberately and out loud with simple, direct language, revealing what is going on and requesting what you want.

Repeat the new thought or action until it becomes automatic.

Practice to makes the new neural pathway permanent. Practice makes permanent.

Be more honest with yourself and other and choose authenticity over Image.

Hang out with people who already have what you say you want.

Chill. Talk less. Listen more. Be.

PART THREE

[1]There is no formal agreement on how fast Deeper Mind processes. Researchers at the University of Pennsylvania School of Medicine estimate that the human retina alone transmits visual input at roughly 10 million bits per second, at minimum. Another study suggests that Deeper Mind can process about 400 billion bits of

information per second and the impulses travel at a speed of up to 100,000 mph! Compare this to Surface Mind, which processes only about 2,000 bits of information per second and its impulses travel at 100-150 mph. We have 50 trillion cells in our body performing trillions of processes, so an enormous processing power is required. Another take: only about 0.01% of all the brain's activity is experienced consciously. (K. Koch, et al., How much the eye tells the brain, 2006)

[2]from Pantajali's Yoga Sutras, translated by Samskrita Bharati. Found at http://www.samskritabharatiusa.org/docs/shlokaspardha/dallas/ss_yogasutra_2012.pdf

[3]Quoted in Robert Moss, *The Three "Only" Things: Tapping the Power of Dreams, Coincidence, and Imagination.*

[4]***New Permissions***
I give myself permission to
Celebrate myself
Treat myself with kindness
Say YES to life
Say NO to stress
Ask for what I want
Let go of frustration
Express my joy
Please myself today
Surprise a friend
See the beauty in myself
Find beauty all around me
Experience pleasure each day
Be strong and determined
Do what my heart desires
Take a stand
Take time to enjoy the silence
Take a moment to feel grateful

Tell people what I like about them
Share myself honestly
Be the person I long to be
Rest when I'm tired
Play more
Play bigger in Life
Take risks and chances
Create fun excitement
Dream Big Dreams
Be my own happily ever after
Let go of the past
Enjoy the moment
Accept help when I need it
Welcome kindness
Stop and enjoy the Silence
Feel wonder and awe
Look up and get lost in the sky
Recharge in Nature
Lie in the grass
Count the stars
Be my own friend
Reclaim simplicity
Allow my thoughts to be still
Feel and express my emotions
Allow myself to be happy
Get out of my own way
Be the source of my own joy
Set myself free
Reward myself . . . just because
Acknowledge my successes
Celebrate my talents
Be silly with my friends
Do an unexpected kindness

Forgive myself for every mistake

Laugh more

Dance in the rain

Watch the clouds

Trade fear for courage

Express myself honestly

Be honest with myself

Feel competent and powerful

Make my desires known

Make time to play

Be relaxed and at ease

Change direction and go new places

Find my true friends and allies

Live where my heart takes me

Love freely

Feel confident and self-assured

Make good decisions

Embrace new possibilities

Do what I love

Make all the money I desire

Feel at home wherever I am

Bibliography

Part One

Berman, Morris. *Coming to Our Senses: Body and Spirit in the Hidden History of the West.* Seattle Writers Guild, 1998.

Brafman, Ori, and Rom Brafman. *Sway: The Irresistible Pull of Irrational Behavior.* Broadway Books, 2009.

Cuddy, Amy. "Your Body Language Shapes Who You Are." http://www.ted.com/talks/amy_cuddy_your_body_language_shapes_who_you_are.html

De Becker, Gavin. *The Gift of Fear: Survival Signals That Protect Us From Violence.* New York: Delta, 1999.

Doidge, Norman. *The Brain That Changes Itself: Stories of Personal Triumph From the Frontiers of Brain Science.* Penguin, 2007.

Eagleman, David M. *Incognito: The Secret Lives of the Brain.* Vintage Books, 2012.

Ekman, Paul. *Telling Lies: Clues to Deceit in the Marketplace, Politics, and Marriage.* 3rd ed. W. W. Norton & Company, 2009.

Easterbrook, Gregg. "Forgiveness is Good for Your Health." http://www.beliefnet.com/Health/2002/03/Forgiveness-Is-Good-For-Your-Health.aspx (accessed May 22, 2012).

Gladwell, Malcom. *Blink.* 13th ed. Little, 2005.

Grant, Glenn. "A Memetic Lexicon Version 3.2." http://deoxy.org/memelex.htm (accessed February 28, 2013).

Hecke, Madeleine L. Van. *Blind Spots: Why Smart People Do Dumb Things.* Prometheus Books, 2007.

"Implicit Association Test." http://www.understandingprejudice.org/iat/ (accessed May 22, 2012).

Lawler, K.A., J.W. Younger, R.L. Piferi, R.L. Jobe, K.A. Edmondson, and W.H. Jones. "The Unique Effects of Forgiveness on Health:

An Exploration of Pathways." *Journal of Behavioral Medicine* 28, no. 2 (2005): 157-167.

Linden, David J. *The Accidental Mind: How Brain Evolution Has Given Us Love, Memory, Dreams, and God.* Belknap Press of Harvard University Press, 2008.

Merriam-Webster. *Merriam-Webster's Collegiate Dictionary, 11th Edition.* 11th ed. Merriam-Webster, Inc., 2008.

Northcutt, Wendy. *The Darwin Awards Countdown to Extinction.* Reprint ed. Plume, 2011.

Nummenmaa, L, E Glerean, M Viinikainen, IP Jaaskelainen, R Hari, and M Sams. "Emotions Promote Social Interaction By Synchronizing Brain Activity Across Individuals." *Proc Natl Acad Sci U S A* 109, no. 24 (2012): 9599-95604

Ornish, Dean. *Love and Survival: 8 Pathways to Intimacy and Health.* William Morrow Paperbacks, 1999.

Ressler, Cali, and Jody Thompson. *Why Work Sucks and How to Fix it: The Results-Only Revolution.* Portfolio Trade, 2010.

Scott, Elizabeth. "The Benefits of Forgiveness." http://stress.about.com/od/relationships/a/forgiveness.htm (accessed May 22, 2012).

Siegel, Ronald D., Michael H. Urdang, and Douglas R. Johnson. *Back Sense: A Revolutionary Approach to Halting the Cycle of Chronic Back Pain.* Three Rivers Press, 2002.

Taylor, Jill Bolte. *My Stroke of Insight: A Brain Scientist's Personal Journey.* Viking Adult, 2007.

"Test Yourself for Hidden Bias." http://www.tolerance.org/activity/test-yourself-hidden-bias (accessed May 22, 2012).

Vedantam, Shankar. *The Hidden Brain: How Our Unconscious Minds Elect Presidents, Control Markets, Wage Wars, and Save Our Lives.* Spiegel & Grau, 2010.

Weingarten, Gene. *The Fiddler in the Subway: The Story of the World-Class Violinist Who Played for Handouts. And Other Virtuoso Performances By America's Foremost Feature Writer.* Simon & Schuster, 2010.

Part Two

Blanton, Brad. *Some New Kind of Trailer Trash*. Sparrowhawk Press, 2011.

Part Three

Bharati, Samskrita. "Pantajali's Yoga Sutras." http://www.samskritab-haratiusa.org/docs/shlokaspardha/dallas/ss_yogasutra_2012.pdf (accessed September 28, 2012).

Blanton, Dr. Brad. *Radical Honesty: How to Transform Your Life By Telling the Truth*. The New Revised Edition. Sparrowhawk, 2005.

Bryson, Bill. *A Short History of Nearly Everything: Special Illustrated Edition*. Broadway, 2010.

Buckles, Albert. "Mental Imagery in Basketball." http://thesport-digest.com/archive/article/mental-imagery-basketball (accessed October 1, 2012).

Dennis, Kingsley L. *New Consciousness for a New World: How to Thrive in Transitional Times and Participate in the Coming Spiritual Renaissance*. Inner Traditions, 2011.

Enayati, Amanda. "The Power of Perceptions: Imagining the Reality You Want." http://www.cnn.com/2012/04/11/health/enayati-power-perceptions-imagination/index.html (accessed October 1, 2012).

Fehmi, Les, and Jim Robbins. *The Open-Focus Brain: Harnessing the Power of Attention to Heal Mind and Body (Book & CD)*. Trumpeter, 2008.

Jung, C. G. *The Structure and Dynamics of the Psyche (Collected Works of C.G. Jung, Volume 8)*. 2nd ed. Princeton University Press, 1970.

Koch, K, J McLean, R Segev, MA Freed, MJ 2nd Berry, V Balasubramanian, and P Sterling. "How Much the Eye Tells the Brain." *Curr Biol* 16, no. 14 (2006): 1428-1434.

Mackenzie, Brian. "Mental Imagery." waccessed October 1, 2012).

Moss, Robert. *The Three "Only" Things: Tapping the Power of Dreams, Coincidence, and Imagination.* New World Library, 2009.

_____. *The Secret History of Dreaming.* 1St Edition ed. New World Library, 2010.

_____. *Active Dreaming: Journeying Beyond Self-Limitation to a Life of Wild Freedom.* New World Library, 2011.

_____. *Dreaming the Soul Back Home: Shamanic Dreaming for Healing and Becoming Whole.* New World Library, 2012.

Additional Recommended Reading

Achor, Shawn. *The Happiness Advantage: The Seven Principles of Positive Psychology That Fuel Success and Performance At Work.* Crown Business, 2010.

Brezsny, Rob. *Pronoia is the Antidote for Paranoia, Revised and Expanded: How the Whole World is Conspiring to Shower You With Blessings.* North Atlantic Books, 2009.

Buchanan, Lyn. *The Seventh Sense: The Secrets of Remote Viewing as Told By a "Psychic Spy" for the U.S. Military.* Gallery Books, 2003.

Burton, Robert. *On Being Certain: Believing You Are Right Even When You're Not.* St. Martin's Griffin, 2009.

Coyle, T. Thorn. "Crafting a Daily Practice." (e-book) Sunna Press 2012.

Haidt, Jonathan. *The Righteous Mind: Why Good People Are Divided By Politics and Religion.* Pantheon, 2012.

Ingerman, Sandra, and Hank Wesselman. *Awakening to the Spirit World: The Shamanic Path of Direct Revelation.* Sounds True, Inc., 2010.

Kahneman, Daniel. *Thinking, Fast and Slow.* Farrar, Straus and Giroux, 2011.

Lewis, T., F. Amini, and R. Lannon. *A General Theory of Love.* Vintage, 2001.

McEneaney, Bonnie. *Messages: Signs, Visits, and Premonitions From Loved Ones Lost on 9/11*. Reprint ed. William Morrow Paperbacks, 2011.

Talbot, Michael. *The Holographic Universe: The Revolutionary Theory of Reality*. Harper Perennial, 2011.

Tavris, Carol, and Elliot Aronson. *Mistakes Were Made (But Not By Me): Why We Justify Foolish Beliefs, Bad Decisions, and Hurtful Acts*. Houghton Mifflin Harcourt, 2007.

3738751R00196

Printed in Great Britain
by Amazon.co.uk, Ltd.,
Marston Gate.